Medieval E.

New Casebooks
Collections of all new critical essays

CHILDREN'S LITERATURE

MELVIN BURGESS
Edited by Alison Waller

ROBERT CORMIER
Edited by Adrienne E. Gavin

ROALD DAHL
Edited by Ann Alston & Catherine Butler

C. S. LEWIS: *THE CHRONICLES OF NARNIA*
Edited by Michelle Ann Abate & Lance Weldy

JACQUELINE WILSON
Edited by Lucy Pearson

PHILIP PULLMAN: *HIS DARK MATERIALS*
Edited by Catherine Butler & Tommy Halsdorf

J. K. ROWLING: *HARRY POTTER*
Edited by Cynthia J. Hallett & Peggy J. Huey

J. R. R. TOLKIEN: *THE HOBBIT & THE LORD OF THE RINGS*
Edited by Peter Hunt

DAVID ALMOND
Edited by Rosemary Ross Johnston

NOVELS AND PROSE

JOHN FOWLES
Edited by James Acheson

POETRY

TED HUGHES
Edited by Terry Gifford

Further titles are in preparation

For a full list of published titles in the past format of the New Casebooks series, visit the series page at www.palgrave.com

New Casebooks Series

Series Standing Order ISBN 978–0–333–71702–8 hardcover
Series Standing Order ISBN 978–0–333–69345–2 paperback
(*outside North America only*)

You can receive future titles in this series as they are published by placing a standing order. Please contact your bookseller or, in the case of difficulty, write to us at the address below with your name and address, the title of the series and the ISBN quoted above.

Customer Services Department, Macmillan Distribution Ltd, Houndmills, Basingstoke, Hampshire, RG21 6XS, UK

Medieval English Literature

Edited by

BEATRICE FANNON

First published 2016 by
PALGRAVE

Palgrave in the UK is an imprint of Macmillan Publishers Limited,
registered in England, company number 785998, of 4 Crinan Street,
London, N1 9XW.

Palgrave Macmillan in the US is a division of St Martin's Press LLC,
175 Fifth Avenue, New York, NY 10010.

Palgrave is a global imprint of the above companies and is represented
throughout the world.

Palgrave® and Macmillan® are registered trademarks in the United States,
the United Kingdom, Europe and other countries.

ISBN 978–1–137–46959–5 hardback

ISBN 978–1–137–46958–8 paperback

This book is printed on paper suitable for recycling and made from fully
managed and sustained forest sources. Logging, pulping and manufacturing
processes are expected to conform to the environmental regulations of the
country of origin.

A catalogue record for this book is available from the British Library.

A catalog record for this book is available from the Library of Congress.

Printed in China

Contents

Series Editor's Preface

Welcome to the latest series of New Casebooks.

Each volume now presents brand new essays specially written for university and other students. Like the original series, the new-look New Casebooks embrace a range of recent critical approaches to the debates and issues that characterize the current discussion of literature.

Each editor has been asked to commission a sequence of original essays which will introduce the reader to the innovative critical approaches to the text or texts being discussed in the collection. The intention is to illuminate the rich interchange between critical theory and critical practice that today underpins so much writing about literature.

Editors have also been asked to supply an introduction to each volume that sets the scene for the essays that follow, together with a list of further reading which will enable readers to follow up issues raised by the essays in the collection.

The purpose of this new-look series, then, is to provide students with fresh thinking about key texts and writers while encouraging them to extend their own ideas and responses to the texts they are studying.

Martin Coyle

Notes on Contributors

Valerie Allen is a Professor in the Department of English at the John Jay College of Criminal Justice in New York. She specializes in medieval culture and literature, and continental philosophy. She is currently editing an anthology of essays with Ruth Evans entitled *Roadworks: Medieval England, Medieval Roads* (Manchester University Press). Her publications include *On Farting: Language and Laughter in the Middle Ages* (Palgrave Macmillan, 2007), *The Age of Chaucer* (Cambridge University Press, 2004), and (ed. with Ares Axiotis) *Chaucer: New Casebooks* (Palgrave Macmillan, 1997).

Catherine Batt is Senior Lecturer in Medieval Literature at Leeds University. She has published on a range of medieval literature, from twelfth-century Anglo-Norman saints' lives to Middle English romance, and the work of the Gawain-poet, Thomas Hoccleve, and Caxton. Her published works include *Malory's Morte Darthur: Remaking Arthurian Tradition* (2002) and she is currently completing a translation of Henry, Duke of Lancaster's mid-fourteenth-century devotional treatise, *Le Livre de Seyntz Medicines* (*The Book of Holy Medicines*).

Lewis Beer is Senior Teaching Fellow at the University of Warwick. His research focuses on authors such as Boethius, Jean de Meun, Guillaume de Machaut, Geoffrey Chaucer, John Gower, John Lydgate and Shakespeare. His research interests include medieval allegory, love poetry and didacticism. His publications include 'Polarised Debates, Ambivalent Judgements: *Confessio Amantis* and the *Jugement Behaigne*', in *Machaut's Legacy: The Judgement Poetry Tradition in Late Medieval Literature*, ed. R. Barton Palmer and Burt Kimmelman (University Press of Florida, Forthcoming), 'The Tactful Genius: Abiding the End in the *Confessio Amantis*' (*Studies in Philology*, 2015), and 'Desire in a Good Mood: the Ambivalence of Hope in Machaut's *Remede de Fortune*' (Nottingham Medieval Studies, 2014). He is currently writing a monograph on the narrative poetry of Guillaume de Machaut.

Martin Coyle is a Professor in the School of English, Communications and Philosophy at Cardiff University. His research interests include textual editing and the textual histories of Shakespeare's plays as well as other aspects of Shakespeare. He is General Editor of the

New Casebooks Series and the Critical Issues Series. His publications include (with John Peck) *Write It Right: A Handbook for Students* (Palgrave Macmillan, 2005), (with John Peck) *A Brief History of English Literature* (Palgrave Macmillan, 2002), (ed.) *Shakespeare: 'Richard II', Essays, Articles, Reviews* (Palgrave Macmillan, 1998), (with John Peck) *The Student's Guide to Writing: Grammar, Punctuation and Spelling* (Palgrave Macmillan, 1999), (ed.) *'The Merchant of Venice'* by William Shakespeare (Palgrave Macmillan, 1998), (ed.) *Niccolo Machiavelli's 'The Prince': New Interdisciplinary Essays* (Manchester University Press, 1995), (ed.) *'Hamlet'* by William Shakespeare (Palgrave Macmillan, 1992) and (with John Peck) *How to Study a Shakespeare Play* (Palgrave Macmillan, 1985).

Roger Ellis lectured in English Literature in the School of English, Communications and Philosophy at Cardiff University for thirty-six years. He retired in 2003, although he continues to publish as an independent scholar and has affiliations with Sheffield University. He has published widely in medieval literature, including (ed. with Dee Dyas and Valerie Edden) *Approaching Medieval English Anchoritic and Mystical Texts* (D. S. Brewer, 2005), (ed.) Thomas Hoccleve, 'My Compleinte' and Other Poems (Liverpool University Press, 2001), (ed. with Ruth Evans) *The Medieval Translator*, Vol. 4 (Exeter University Press and Medieval and Renaissance Texts Series, 1994), (ed.) *Medieval Translator,* Vol. 2 (Westfield Publications in Medieval Studies, 1991) and *Patterns of Religious Narrative in The Canterbury Tales* (Crook Helm, 1986).

Ruth Evans is the Dorothy McBride Orthwein Professor in the Department for English at Saint Louis University. She is also Executive Director of the New Chaucer Society. Her research interests are in the period 1300–1580, with a particular focus on gender, sexuality and the body, and memory. She also has strong interests in feminist theory and criticism, the history of the book, translation theory and manuscript studies. She is currently writing a monograph entitled *Chaucer and the Fictions of Memory*, and co-editing a volume of essays with Valerie Allen entitled *Roadworks: Medieval England, Medieval Roads* (Manchester University Press). Her publications include (ed.) *A Cultural History of Sexuality in the Middle Ages*, (Berg, 2011), (ed. with Sarah Salih and Anke Bernau) Medieval Virginities (University of Wales Press, 2003), (ed. with Jocelyn Wogan-Browne, Nicholas Watson and Andrew Taylor) *The Idea of the Vernacular: An Anthology of Middle English Literary Theory, 1280–1530* (Exeter University Press,

1999), (ed. with Lesley Johnson) *Feminist Readings in Middle English Literature: The Wife of Bath and All Her Sect* (Routledge, 1994), and (ed. with Roger Ellis) *The Medieval Translator*, Vol. 4 (Exeter University Press and Medieval and Renaissance Texts Series, 1994).

Beatrice Fannon completed her doctorate at Cardiff University in 2012. Although primarily a Spenserian, her research interests extend to patristic literature and Christian theology, and medieval literature as well as Renaissance literature and the Reformation.

Sheila Fisher is Professor of English at Trinity College, Hartford, Connecticut. She is a medievalist who specializes in Chaucer, late fourteenth-century English literature and medieval women writers. She has published on Chaucer, the Gawain-poet and medieval romance. Her publications include *The Selected Canterbury Tales: A New Verse Translation* (W.W. Norton and Company, 2011), (ed. with J. E. Halley) *Seeking the Woman in Late Medieval and Renaissance Writings: Essays in Feminist Contextual Criticism* (University of Tennessee Press, 1989), and *Chaucer's Poetic Alchemy: A Study of Value and Its Transformation in The Canterbury Tales* (Garland Publishing, 1988).

Rob Gossedge is Lecturer in English Literature at Cardiff University, where he specializes in the literature and cultural afterlife of the Middle Ages. He has published numerous articles on Chaucer, Arthurian myth, outlaw legends, the twentieth-century Catholic revival and Welsh fiction in English. His edited collection of essays, *New Elizabethans,* is to be published by I.B. Taurus in 2015.

John Hines is a Professor in the School of History, Archaeology and Religion at Cardiff University. He is a specialist in archaeology, literature and the languages of medieval northern Europe and has published widely on Anglo-Saxon and medieval Literature and medieval archaeology. He continues to publish articles on Old and Middle English, and Old Norse literature and runic inscriptions. His publications include (ed. with Alex Bayliss) *Anglo-Saxon Graves and Grave Goods of the 6th and 7th Centuries A.D.: A Chronological Framework* (Society for Medieval Archaeology, 2013), *Voices in the Past: English Literature and Archaeology* (D. S. Brewer, 2004), *A New Corpus of Anglo-Saxon Great Square-Headed Brooches* (Society of Antiquaries of London, 1997), *The Fabliau in English* (Longman, 1993), and *The Scandinavian Character of Anglican England in the pre-Viking period* (British Archaeological Reports, 1984).

Stephen Knight is Honorary Research Professor of English Literature in the School of Culture and Communication at the University of Melbourne, Australia. He has published in many areas of medieval literature including Chaucer, Arthurian literature and the Robin Hood tradition, as well as other areas of literature, such as Welsh fiction and crime fiction. His publications include *Robin Hood: A Mythic Biography* (Cornell University Press, 2003), *Robin Hood: A Complete Study of the English Outlaw* (Blackwell, 1994), *Geoffrey Chaucer* (Blackwell, 1986), *Arthurian Literature and Society* (Macmillan, 1983), *The Poetry of the Canterbury Tales* (Angus and Robertson, 1973), and *Rymyng Craftily* (Angus and Robertson, 1972).

Helen Phillips is Professor (retired) in the School of English, Communications and Philosophy at Cardiff University. Her interests include Chaucer, Robin Hood studies, dream poetry, romance, nineteenth-century medievalism, and the political and cultural implications of late medieval writings and their afterlife. Her publications include (ed.) *Chaucer and Religion* (D.S. Brewer, 2010), (ed. with Nick Havely) *Chaucer's Dream Poetry* (Longman-Pearson, 1997), (ed.) *Bandit Territories: British Outlaws and their Traditions (Cardiff, 2008),* (ed.) *Robin Hood: Medieval and Post Medieval* (Four Courts Press, 2005), and *Introduction to the Canterbury Tales: Fiction, Reading, Context* (Macmillan/Palgrave, 2000).

Raluca Radulescu is Reader in the School of English at Bangor University. Her research interests include Arthurian and non-Arthurian romance, medieval chronicles, political culture and gentry studies, and, more recently, the cultural importance of the medieval miscellany as a repository of literary and non-literary texts, and medieval identity as expressed in visual representations. Her publications include *Romance and its Contexts in Fifteenth-Century England: Politics, Piety and Penitence* (D. S. Brewer, 2013), (ed. with Cory James Rushton) *Companion to Medieval Popular Romance* (D. S. Brewer, 2009), (ed. with Edward Donald Kennedy) *Broken Lines: Genealogical Literature in Medieval Britain and France* (Brepols, 2008), (ed. with K. S. Whetter) *Re-viewing the Morte Darthur: Texts and Contexts, Characters and Themes* (D. S. Brewer, 2005), (ed. with Alison Truelove), *Gentry Culture in Late Medieval England* (Manchester University Press, 2005), and *The Gentry Context for Malory's Morte Darthur* (D. S. Brewer, 2003).

Gillian Rudd is Senior Lecturer at the University of Liverpool with teaching and research interests in medieval literature, women's writing of the nineteenth and twentieth centuries, and children's literature. Her publications on medieval literature include *Greenery: Ecocritical Readings of Late Medieval English Texts* (Manchester University Press, 2007), *The Complete Critical Guide to Geoffrey Chaucer* (Routledge, 2001), and *Managing Language in Piers Plowman* (D. S. Brewer, 1994).

Chronology

1066	Death of Edward the Confessor (b. 1004); Harold (b. 1022, d. 1066) accedes to the throne; Harold defeats Harold Hardrada (King of Norway) at Stamford Bridge but is defeated at the Battle of Hastings; William of Normandy (William the Conqueror, b. 1025, d. 1087) crowned on Christmas Day 1066
1070	Lanfranc (b. early 11th century in Padua, d. 1089) becomes Archbishop of Canterbury
1086	Doomsday Book (the first comprehensive survey of the people and property of England)
1087	Death of William I; William II (Rufus, b. 1056, d. 1100) accedes
1096	First Crusade (1096–9) (proclaimed by Pope Urban II in 1095) led by Raymond of Toulouse, Robert of Normandy and Godfrey of Bouillon
1099	Crusaders capture Jerusalem (15 July); Godfrey of Bouillon made *princeps* (prince) of Jerusalem, the *Advocatus Sancti Sepulchri* (Advocate of the Holy Sepulchre)
1100	Henry I (Beauclerc, b. 1068, d. 1135) accedes after the assassination of William Rufus on 2 August in the New Forest
1135	Death of Henry I; Stephen of Blois (b. 1096, d. 1154), the son of Adela (Henry's older sister) accedes. A struggle with Henry's daughter Matilda ensues
1138	Geoffrey of Monmouth, *Historia Regum Britanniae* (History of the Kings of Britain)
1147	Second Crusade (1147–9) announced by Pope Eugene III (1145) and led by Louis VII of France (Eleanor of Aquitaine's first husband) and Conrad III of Germany, who was also the Holy Roman Emperor (reigned 1138–52)
1154	Death of Stephen; Henry II (b. 1133, d. 1189), the son of Matilda, accedes
1154	Wace, *Roman de Brut* (*The Romance of Brutus*, a history of Britain); end of the *Peterborough Chronicle,* the last branch of the *Anglo-Saxon Chronicle*

1160–90   Chrétien de Troyes' French Arthurian verse romances; Marie de France, *Lais*

1161   Thomas à Becket (b. c. 1118/20) becomes the Archbishop of Canterbury

1170   Thomas à Becket is murdered in Canterbury Cathedral on 29 December by four knights: Reginald FitzUrse, Hugh de Morville, William de Tracy and Richard le Breton

1173   Becket canonized by Pope Alexander III; Eleanor of Aquitaine and her sons revolt against Henry II; Eleanor is imprisoned

1187   Saracens recapture Jerusalem

1189   Death of Henry II; Eleanor is released; Richard I (Coeur de Lion, b. 1157, d. 1199) accedes

1189   Third Crusade (1189–92) proclaimed by Pope Gregory VIII (1188) and led by Henry II of England (and later Richard I after Henry's death), Frederick Barbarossa and Philippe II of France (reigned 1180–1223) against Saladin

1191   Crusaders capture Acre and Jaffa

1199   Death of Richard I in Limousin, France; John (b. 1167, d. 1216) accedes

c. 1200   Anon, *The Owl and the Nightingale*; Lazamon, *Brut* (a history of Britain)

1202   Fourth Crusade (1202–4) proclaimed by Pope Innocent III (became an attack on Byzantium) and led by Thibaut of Champagne and Baldwin of Flanders

1204   Crusaders sack Constantinople; Baldwin of Flanders becomes the first Latin Emperor of Constantinople; English crown loses Normandy; death of Eleanor of Aquitaine

1208   Albigensian Crusade called by Pope Innocent III against the Cathars in South of France

1208–14   England is placed under a papal interdict because John refuses to accept the Pope's appointment of Stephen Langton as Archbishop of Canterbury

1215   Magna Carta signed by King John and his barons at Runnymede on 15 June; Founding of the universities of Paris and Oxford; Fourth Lateran Council

1216   Death of John; Henry III (b. 1206, d.1272) accedes at the age of 10 years (William Marshall acts as regent)

1217	Fifth Crusade (1217–21) called by Pope Innocent III (later ratified by Pope Honorius III) to recover Jerusalem. The main force, however, was directed against Egypt; Damietta was taken but was later given up in 1221
c. 1220	Anon, *Ancrene Riwle* (a devotional manual)
1221–4	Dominican and Franciscan friars arrive in England
1222	Sixth Crusade (1222–9) in which the Emperor Frederick II obtained Nazareth, Bethlehem and Jerusalem by negotiation
1244	Egyptians capture Jerusalem from Christians
1248–54	Seventh Crusade organised and led by Louis IX of France (Saint Louis); Louis captured in 1250 at Mansura and remains in captivity in Syria for four years
1264	Pope Urban institutes the celebration of the Feast of Corpus Christi in his Bull *Transiturus* (8 September); the Pope's death (2 October) inhibits the adoption of the feast
1265	Birth of Dante Alighieri (May) in Florence
1270	Eighth and Last Crusade (1270–2) led by St Louis, Charles of Anjou and Prince Edward of England; St Louis dies in 1270 at Tunis
1272	Death of Henry III; Edward I (b. 1239, d. 1307) accedes
c. 1275	Guillaume de Lorris, *Roman de la Rose* (The Romance of the Rose, an allegory of love)
1290	Edward I expels Jews from England
1291	Saracens recapture Acre (end of the Crusades)
1292	Death of Pope Nicholas IV (4 April)
1294	Peter of Morrone elected Pope Celestine V (5 July); Pope Celestine V resigns (13 December), an unprecedented event; Pope Boniface VIII elected (24 December)
1295	Pope Boniface VIII crowned 23 January
1303	Death of Pope Boniface VIII (12 October); election of Pope Benedict XI (22 October; crowned 27 October)
1304	Birth of Petrarch (20 July); death of Pope Benedict XI (7 July)
1305	Execution of William Wallace; Pope Clement V (b. 1264, d.1314) elected; Clement is crowned at Lyon, and settles in the South of France because of unrest in Rome
1307	Death of Edward I; Edward II accedes

1307?	Dante Aligheri, *Divina Commedia* (The Divine Comedy)
1309	Pope Clement V takes residence in the Dominican Priory in Avignon, though not with the intention of staying
1311	Pope Clement V orders the universal celebration of the Feast of Corpus Christi at the General Council of Vienne
1313	Birth of Giovanni Boccaccio
1314	Battle of Bannockburn (Robert the Bruce defeats the English); death of Pope Clement V (6 April)
1315–22	Great Cattle Plague and agrarian crisis
1316	Election of Jacques Duèse, a former Bishop of Avignon, as Pope John XXII; he takes up residence at the Bishop's Palace (his former residence as Bishop of Avignon)
1320	German monk Bertholdus credited with the invention of gunpowder
1321	Death of Dante at Ravenna
1327	Edward II deposed and murdered at Berkeley Castle, Gloucester; Edward III (b. 1312, d. 1377) accedes aged 15; he is the first King to speak English as his chosen language
1330	Edward III reaches his majority and has Roger Mortimer (his regent) executed
c. 1330	Birth of William Langland; birth of John Gower
1334	Death of Pope John XXII (4 December); Jacques Fournier elected Pope Benedict XII
1336	Benedict XII begins the reconstruction of the Bishop's Palace at Avignon, which he turns into a Papal Palace
1337	Edward declares himself King of France following attack on French territories, thus beginning the Hundred Years War between England and France (ends 1451)
c. 1340	Birth of Walter Hilton
1342	Birth of Julian of Norwich; death of Pope Benedict XII (25 April); Pope Clement VI elected (7 May; crowned 19 May)
c. 1344	Birth of Geoffrey Chaucer; founding of the Order of the Garter
1346	Battle of Crécy (French defeated by the English); English defeat the Scottish at Neville's Cross
1347	Edward III takes Calais after a year's siege; first recorded use of cannons by the English

1348	The Black Death in England (in total the plague wiped out one-third of the population in Europe from 1347–51)
1349	Giovanni Boccaccio, *The Decameron* (1349–51)
1350	Pope Clement VI proclaims a Jubilee Year (pilgrimage to Rome)
1352	Death of Pope Clement VI (6 December); election of Pope Innocent VI (18 December; crowned 30 December)
1356	English victory at the battle of Poitiers where the Black Prince captures King John the Good of France; Turks take Gallipoli and thus settle in Europe
1360	Treaty of Brétigny (25 May), later ratified at Calais (24 October), in which Edward relinquishes his claim to the French throne, Normandy, Anjou and Maine, but gains Aquitaine, Poitou, Ponthieu, Guînes and Calais
1361–2	Bubonic Plague returns to England
1362	English replaces French as the language of the law courts and Parliament
1367	Pope Urban V attempts to return the papacy to Rome, entering the city on 16 October and taking up residence in the Vatican as the Lateran Palace was uninhabitable. This is where the popes have lived ever since. The papal court thus becomes split into two administrative centres, Avignon and Rome. William Langland, *Piers Plowman* (A text)
1368	Charles V of France decides to hear an appeal made by the Count of Armagnac against the Black Prince as Duke of Aquitaine
1369	Charles V of France pronounces the forfeiture of Aquitaine as a result of the 1368 appeal (30 November); Geoffrey Chaucer, *The Book of the Duchess*
1369–70	Two mounted English expeditions ravage France
1370	Pope Urban V forced to return to France in order to attempt to re-establish peace between England and France to ensure the stability of Western Christendom, rather than pursue diplomatic relations with Eastern Christendom, in which he had hitherto been engaged; death of Pope Urban V (19 December); election of Pope Gregory XI
c. 1373	Julian of Norwich, *Sixteen Revelations of Divine Love* (short text)

1373	Birth of Margery Kempe
1374	Death of Petrarch (19 July)
c. 1375	Anon, *Sir Gawain and the Green Knight, Patience, Pearl and Cleanness*; Anon, *Cloud of Unknowing*
1375	Death of Boccaccio (21 December)
1376	Earliest reference to the York cycle of mystery plays
1376	Death of Edward the Black Prince (the son of Edward III, heir to the throne and the father of Richard II); Pope Gregory XI (1329–78) leaves Avignon with the intention of returning the papacy to Rome (13 September)
1377	Gregory XI arrives in Rome on 13 January; death of Edward III; Richard II (b. 1366) accedes aged 11 years (John of Gaunt acts as regent); c. 1377 William Langland, *Piers Plowman* (B text)
1378	Pope Gregory XI dies on 27 March at the Vatican and Urban VI is elected pope. Urban quickly shows himself to be coarse, rude and tactless, causing thirteen French cardinals to leave for Anagni and declare his election null and void. At the encouragement of the French King, Charles V, they elect a new Avignon Pope, Clement VII (b. 1342, d. 1394), crowned 1 November 1378, thus bringing about the Great Papal Schism, or the great Schism of the West, in which there were two rival Popes
c. 1380	English translation of the Bible (the early version of the Wycliffe Bible; the later version was completed in 1390s); Geoffrey Chaucer, *The Parliament of Fowls*
1381	Peasants' Revolt led by Wat Tyler
1382	Blackfriars Council led by Archbishop William Courtenay finds heretical and erroneous propositions in Wycliffe's writings; earthquake in Kent, also felt in London
1384	Death of Wycliffe (b. c. 1320) (he suffered a stroke while saying Mass on 28 December, the Feast of the Holy Innocents, and died at the end of the year)
c. 1385	Geoffrey Chaucer, *Troilus and Criseyde*; Chaucer, *Legend of Good Women*
c. 1385	William Langland, *Piers Plowman* (C text)
c. 1387	Chaucer begins *Canterbury Tales*
1389	Richard reaches his majority; a great pestilence begins in England, which seems to have spread from the south,

	causing great mortality and persisting in some areas until Michaelmas (29 September) 1393
1390	John Gower, *Confessio Amantis* (The Confession of a Lover)
c. 1390	Death of Langland; Walter Hilton's *Ladder of Perfection*
1393	Julian of Norwich, *Sixteen Revelations of Divine Love* (long text)
1396	Death of Walter Hilton
1399	Death of John of Gaunt; Richard II deposed; Henry IV (Bolingbroke, b. 1366) accedes. Beginning of the House of Lancaster
1400	Richard II murdered at Pontefract Castle, West Yorkshire; death of Chaucer
c. 1400	Only surviving manuscript of the four alliterative poems *Sir Gawain, Pearl, Cleanness* and *Patience*
1401	The statute *De Heretico Comburendo* passed by the English Parliament, enabling the punishment of heretics by burning at the stake
1406	Plague kills more than 30,000 people in London
1408	Death of Gower
1409	Council of Pisa, an unrecognized ecumenical council, deposes Pope Gregory XII and the Anti-pope Benedict XIII and elects the Anti-pope Alexander V. There are thus three popes from 1409 to 1415 (the Anti-pope John XXIII replaces the Anti-pope Alexander V, who dies in 1410)
1410	Owen Glendower rebels against England
1411–2	Thomas Hoccleve, *The Regiment of Princes*
1412	Birth of Joan of Arc
1413	Death of Henry IV; Henry V (b. 1397, d. 1422) accedes
1414	Founding of St Andrews University
1414–18	Council of Constance ends the Great Papal Schism by deposing Anti-pope John XXIII (1415) and Anti-pope Benedict XIII (1417); Pope Gregory XII resigns in 1415
1415	Henry V revives claim to the French throne; 25 October Battle of Agincourt (French defeated); 4 May Wycliffe declared a heretic by the Council of Constance
1417	Pope Martin V elected 11 November and crowned 21 November

1420	Treaty of Troyes establishes that Henry V and his heirs will inherit the French throne on the death of Charles VI
1422	Henry V dies of dysentery at the Chateau de Vincennes, France (31 August); Henry VI (b. 1421, d. 1471) accedes aged 9 months; John, Duke of Bedford appointed regent, but Humphrey, Duke of Gloucester assumes this role while Bedford on campaign in France; earliest reference to the Chester cycle of mystery plays
1425	Anon, *Castle of Perseverance*
1425–50	Compilation of the N-Town Plays
1426	Death of Hoccleve
1428	Wycliffe's remains exhumed, burned and the ashes scattered in the River Swift
1429	Joan of Arc raises Siege of Orleans; death of Julian of Norwich
1430	Joan of Arc condemned by bishop of Beauvais for witchcraft and heresy and burned at the stake at Rouen, Normandy (30 May)
1431–8	John Lydgate, *The Fall of Princes*
1432–8	Margery Kempe, *Book of Margery Kempe*
1436	Henry VI reaches his majority
1439	Johann Gutenberg invents printing with moveable type
1440	Eton College founded by Henry VI
1449	Death of Lydgate
1450	First English Arthurian prose romances (*Merlin*); Towneley Cycle (1450–1500)
1451	End of Hundred Years War
1453	Battle of Castilion; loss of last English territory in France; fall of Constantinople to the Turks
1455	Wars of the Roses begin; Johann Gutenberg prints his Bible
1461	Henry VI deposed; Edward IV (House of York, b. 1442, d. 1483) accedes; Battle of Towton, the most devastating battle fought on English soil (29 March); Anon, Croxton *Play of the Sacrament*
1470	Edward IV deposed and Henry VI restored to the throne
c. 1470	Thomas Malory, *Le Morte Darthur*

1471	Henry VI deposed and murdered in the Tower of London while at his prayers; Edward IV regains the throne; death of Sir Thomas Malory; plague in England kills 10–15 per cent of the population
1472	The performance date of the Chester Plays moves from Corpus Christi to Whitsun
1473–4	William Caxton, *Recuyell of the Historyes of Troye* (a history of Troy and the first book printed in English)
1477	Caxton prints *The Dictes or Sayengis of the Philosophres* (the first dated book printed in England)
1478	Caxton's edition of Chaucer's *Canterbury Tales* published
1479–80	Plague in London and other areas of England
1483	Death of Edward IV; Edward V (b. 1470, d.1483) accedes aged 12/13; Parliament declares Edward IV's marriage invalid and Edward V illegitimate; 23 June Edward and his brother are murdered; Richard III (b. 1452, d. 1485) accedes
1485	Caxton's edition of Malory's *Morte Darthur* published; Battle of Bosworth; Richard III killed in battle; Henry VII (b. 1457, d. 1509) accedes. End of the Wars of the Roses and the beginning of the Tudor dynasty (traditional date of the end of the Middle Ages)
c. 1490	Date of manuscript of Towneley (Wakefield) mystery plays
1492	Christopher Columbus sets sail to the Americas (17 April)
c. 1500	Date of manuscript of N-Town mystery plays
1502	Prince Arthur (eldest son of Henry VII) dies (2 April) five months after his marriage to Catherine of Aragon (b. 1485, d. 1536)
1503	Treaty signed between Henry VII and Catherine of Aragon's parents, Ferdinand II of Aragon and Isabella I of Castile, for the marriage of the future Henry VIII to Catherine of Aragon; Pope Julius II grants a dispensation (December) for the marriage (Henry and Catherine were in a forbidden degree of affinity) on the understanding that there had been no consummation of the marriage of Arthur and Catherine
1509	Death of Henry VII (21 April); Henry VIII (b. 1491, d. 1547) accedes; Henry marries Catherine of Aragon (11 June)

c. 1510	Earliest print fragment of *Everyman*
1513	Battle of Flodden (9 September) during which James IV of Scotland (Henry VIII's brother-in-law, the grandfather of Mary Queen of Scots, and the great-grandfather of James VI of Scotland/James I of England) is killed
1516	Sir Thomas More, *Utopia*; birth of the future Mary I (18 February)
1517	Luther pins his 'Ninety-Five Theses' on the door of the church in Wittenburg and thus initiates the Reformation
1520	Field of the Cloth of Gold (celebrated meeting of Henry VIII and Francis I in France to arrange an alliance)
1521	Luther excommunicated by Diet at Worms; Pope Leo X awards Henry VIII the title 'Fidei Defensor' in recognition of his book entitled *Assertio Septem Sacramenortum* (*Defence of the Seven Sacraments*) which refuted Luther's attack on the seven sacraments
1526	William Tyndale prints the first Protestant New Testament in English
1529	Fall of Cardinal Thomas Wolsey (also Archbishop of York and Prince-Bishop of Durham); Thomas Cromwell becomes chief minister; Thomas More becomes Lord Chancellor
1531–3	Series of acts passed by Parliament paving the way for England's break with Rome (e.g., Act for the Conditional Restraint of Annates (1532), which restricts payments of annates to Rome)
1532	Thomas Cranmer becomes Archbishop of Canterbury
1533	Cranmer obtains an annulment for Henry (23 May); Henry marries Anne Boleyn secretly; Cranmer declares Henry's marriage of Catherine of Aragon illegal; Henry's marriage to Anne declared legal; Anne Boleyn crowned queen consort; Act of Restraint of Appeals passed, which provides the legal underpinning for the break with Rome as it brings all legal disputes under the jurisdiction of the King; birth of future Elizabeth I (7 September)
1534	Act of Restraining Payments of Annates and Concerning the Election of Bishops passed, which cuts off all financial payments to Rome; Henry VIII breaks with Rome and establishes the Church of England by declaring himself the Supreme Head of the Church

1535	Thomas More (b. 1478) executed (6 July) at Tower Hill; Laws in Wales Act, an act which introduces the norms of the legal administration of England to Wales; Thomas Coverdale's translation of Bible
1536	Death of Catherine of Aragon (7 January); Anne Boleyn (b. c. 1501) executed (19 May); Henry marries Jane Seymour (20 May); first Suppression Act (the beginning of the dissolution of the monasteries, which occurs over a four-year period); Pilgrimage of Grace, a popular rising in York protesting against Henry's break with Rome and the dissolution of the monasteries; William Tyndale burned to death in the Netherlands
1537	The future Edward VI born (12 October); death of Jane Seymour (24 October)
1538	Henry excommunicated by Pope Paul III
1539	Second Suppression Act (further dissolution of the monasteries)
1540	Henry marries Anne of Cleves (b. 1515, d.1557) on 6 January, but she is never crowned queen consort and the marriage is later annulled (9 July); Henry marries Katherine Howard (b. c. 1523) on 28 July; Thomas Cromwell executed; formation of the Society of Jesus (Jesuit order)
1542	Katherine Howard executed 13 February; accession of Mary Queen of Scots to the Scottish throne
1543	Henry marries Katherine Parr 12 July
1545–63	Council of Trent, the nineteenth ecumenical council that signalled the beginning of the so-called Counter-Reformation, or the Catholic Reformation. It sought to define doctrine clearly in answer to the Protestants and to foster reform in the Church
1547	Death of Henry; Edward VI accedes
1549	The Act of Uniformity unifies the liturgy along with the publication of *The Book of Common Prayer*
1552	Birth of Edmund Spenser
1553	Death of Edward VI; Lady Jane Grey reigns from 10 July to 19 July (b. 1536/7); *Forty-Two Articles* published
1554	Jane Grey executed (12 February) aged 16/17 years; Mary I accedes; re-establishment of Roman Catholicism in England by Parliament

1555   Execution of Hugh Latimer

1556   Execution of Thomas Cranmer

1558   England loses Calais, her last French territory; death of
        Mary I; Elizabeth I accedes (d. 24 March 1603)

1559   Religious settlement in England (Protestantism re-estab-
        lished); second publication of *The Book of Common Prayer*

1560   Geneva Bible

1563   *Thirty-Eight Articles* published (*Thirty-Nine Articles* were
        published in 1571); John Foxe, *Actes and Monuments*; plague
        in London kills 20,000 people

1564   William Shakespeare (d. 1616) born in Stratford on 23
        April (St. George's Day)

Introduction: Reading Medieval English Literature

Beatrice Fannon

The Middle Ages embraces a wide period of history, and there is always a danger of labelling it simply as 'the medieval' or (worse) the 'Dark Ages', terms which suggest a false level of homogeneity about the period and its literature. Instead, and more profitably, we might think of the Middle Ages as a period of great variety and richness that can be best appreciated through its vibrant literary culture. As the essays in this collection show, medieval literature is wonderfully diverse in form but also deeply rich in ideas, history and meaning.

There are, as with any literary period, challenges for the reader of medieval English literature. The most obvious is that the language is not always in a recognizable form of English. English as we now know it developed from a Germanic base, inherited from the Vikings and later overlaid with Latin and French influences.[1] As one moves towards the High Middle Ages (1100–1400), English becomes more recognizable in form, and the works of seminal authors such as Langland and Chaucer can be read more easily and enjoyed by a modern audience, although a good edition with a glossary is still essential if one is to avoid misreading. Words do not always mean what they seem to mean. Reading medieval literature can never be a passive task.

A second challenge in approaching medieval literature is the unfamiliarity of its religious and cultural mores, both of which can make the medieval seem distant. The end of the medieval period (traditionally regarded as ending with the Battle of Bosworth in 1485) coincides both with the Renaissance, heralding the rebirth of classical learning amongst other things, and with the Protestant Reformation, which brought about a rupture with the religious cultural dominance of Catholicism. Often the achievements of the Renaissance overshadow those of the medieval world, even though there were in fact a number of renaissances during the Middle Ages, such as the Carolingian renaissance (late eighth to ninth century), the Ottonian renaissance of southern Europe (tenth century), and the twelfth-century renaissance of the High Middle Ages. The medieval period, however, was a time of great intellectual and scientific innovation, as well as economic

1

growth. A very tangible example of the sophistication of the Middle Ages can still be seen in the soaring cathedrals, and even the ruins of the great monasteries which are scattered throughout Britain attest to the artistic and architectural achievements of the period.

Nevertheless, there is always a tendency to see the Middle Ages as sliding towards the sixteenth-century Reformation. The idea that the Reformation was an inevitable consequence of ecclesiastical corruption is a view which was largely shaped by Protestant Victorian scholarship[2] until it was challenged in the twentieth century by a series of revisionist historians.[3] The current scholarly view acknowledges the cultural vibrancy and religious devotion of the age, as well as the dissonant voices that effected such great social change. In trying to understand the Middle Ages and its relationship to the Reformation, it is also important to recognize that the Reformation in England happened in a very different way from the Reformation on the Continent. Although there were various Protestant movements in England (the Lollard movement associated with John Wycliffe is a notable example), the country remained loyal to Rome until the controversy over Henry VIII's annulment reached its dramatic conclusion. Even after Henry separated from the Roman Church in 1534, however, it cannot truly be said that he embraced Protestantism. Indeed, towards the end of his reign, he introduced draconian legislation which reaffirmed the Catholic doctrines of transubstantiation and clerical celibacy, and any opposition to these was considered to be a felony punishable by death.[4] Religion pervaded every aspect of life in the Middle Ages and a recognition of the importance of Christianity, and specifically Catholicism, in the period is fundamental to understanding its culture and literature.

The present collection

If there are challenges of understanding posed by the alterity of the medieval world, this does not mean we need to adopt different reading strategies or to read uncritically. Indeed, the study of medieval literature has been much influenced by the wider shifts in English literary critical practice throughout the twentieth and early twenty-first centuries.[5] Medieval texts are, in fact, now approached from a variety of critical positions. Some of these have grown out of political agendas – Marxism and feminism are notable examples – or have been influenced by other disciplines, such as psychoanalysis. Most recently, the political concern with environmental issues has led to the growth of 'ecocriticism', a critical school that focuses on literary depictions of the natural world, and seeks to find solutions to contemporary environmental issues in literature. Such developments have not eclipsed the traditional interest in poetics, but rather have enriched these discussions. Similarly, debates about the materiality of texts – their making and meanings – have informed the resurgent interest in palaeography and manuscript studies. Meanwhile, the emphasis on the fifteenth century as a time of active literary production has challenged the traditional emphasis of medieval studies on 'Ricardian poetry', poetry connected to the reign of Richard II.

The intention of the present collection of new academic essays is to reflect this rich set of critical developments and critical viewpoints. The essays explore not only the most important writers of the canon, such as Langland and Chaucer, but also the key genres of the period as well as lesser-known authors. Throughout the collection the emphasis falls on close reading, on historical context, and on drawing on appropriate critical and theoretical perspectives, though not in any narrow, mechanical way. The essays themselves have been grouped into three parts: Part I: Reading Medieval Romance; Part II: Chaucer; and Part III: Religious Texts and Contexts. Each part contains a variety of essays and approaches, ranging from traditional criticism to more theoretically inflected readings. However, often a theme in one essay is touched upon elsewhere in the collection and it is hoped that readers will take on the challenge of reading across the volume as well as exploring individual essays.

Part I: Reading Medieval Romance

Part I of the volume offers a series of essays that examine medieval romance from diverse angles. The first essay by John Hines, entitled 'The Ownership of the Literature: Medieval Literature in its Historical Context', explores how literature can be considered both as a product of its historical circumstances and how it can provide insights into cultural history. The essay begins by considering the consequence of the Norman Conquest for both the English language and English literary culture and traditions and goes on to discuss the transmission of chivalric romance (a genre traditionally associated with the Norman cultural elite) into English, with particular reference to the Middle English lay *Sir Orfeo* and its manuscript variants. The variations exhibit different thematic concerns and seem to reflect the cultural values of the social groups for which they were produced much more accurately than do limited ideas of 'genre' that might be applied to texts. Other manuscript compilations similarly attest to the complexity of medieval readership. As well as examining the historical circumstances surrounding the production of these medieval manuscripts, the essay also considers the 'ownership' of literature by exploring the developing 'market' and the increasing value placed on authorship, especially by the London authors, Chaucer and Gower.

Raluca Radulescu's essay, 'Liminality and Gender in Middle English Arthurian Romances', examines encounters with liminal figures and 'the Other' in several Arthurian Gawain romances and the challenges that such encounters pose to the chivalric world and its values. The essay explores the (often gendered) political and spiritual boundaries in *The Awntyrs off Arthur*. It then goes on to discuss a very different outsider in the lesser-known romance, *Sir Gawain and the Carle of Carlisle*. The Carl, who has a brutal reputation, tests the courtesy of three of Arthur's knights, and, though the text appears to highlight class boundaries, in reality it demonstrates the flexibility of such boundaries which allow the absorption of a churl into the chivalric order. The discussion of *Sir Gawain and the Green Knight* focuses on the figure of the Green Knight, who is liminal not only because of his physical alterity, but also owing to the site of his abode which is on the margins of the Arthurian world. The essay concludes with a brief discussion of the transformation of the alienating political and geographical 'otherness' in the French Arthurian romances in Henry Lovelich's translations, and in the most famous of the Arthurian texts, Malory's *Le Morte Darthur*.

Gillian Rudd's essay 'Shifting Identities and Interpretations in *Sir Gawain and the Green Knight*' begins with a discussion of the poet's use of the coupling of the familiar geography of the North-west Midlands region with the mythic and other-worldly landscape common to romance. This is the first of a series of tensions that runs through the poem: the interweaving of the real and unreal worlds; the incongruity of the Green Knight and his beheading challenge which is at odds with the courtly world and usual chivalric adventures; and the uncertainty about Gawain's success and consequent lack of closure at the end of the poem. The essay then discusses the polysemous figure of the Green Knight, often associated with the devil or the Green Man, and the renewed focus on his connection with nature through the lens of ecocriticism. An examination of the figure of Gawain himself reveals further tensions and transitions, parallels and paradoxes that result in a poem that is both unsettled and unsettling.

The final essay in this first section, Stephen Knight's essay on 'Untraditional Medieval Literature: Romance, Fabliau, Robin Hood and "King and Subject" Ballad', identifies lordly romance and hagiographic narratives as the dominant discourses which reinforce the two medieval centres of authority: the court and Church. There are, however, subgenres that resonate with the increasing secularization and defeudalization that can be observed in the late medieval period, and which offer counterpoints to the dominant aristocratic and ecclesiastical voices of the period. The essay discusses some of these dissonant voices, including the narratives of Robin Hood, popular romance, the king and subject ballads, and some of Chaucer's tales, all of which offer a challenge to both secular and religious authority.

Part II: Chaucer

Part II is devoted solely to the works of Geoffrey Chaucer, and thus reflects the prominence of Chaucer as a poet in the Middle Ages, and the dominance of Chaucer Studies in the study of Medieval Literature, while demonstrating his diversity as an author. Helen Phillip's essay, 'Chaucer and Politics', examines Chaucer's engagement with political discourse in his extensive oeuvre. By contextualizing Chaucer's works within contemporary political theory and alongside Richard II's own behaviour and royal image, the essay observes how Chaucer is often evasive and ambivalent in his representation of accepted political models, monarchical rule and patterns of political government. The essay goes on to examine Chaucer's equally contradictory exploration of class, with his seeming ambivalence towards social mobility coupled with his frequent questioning of the accepted meaning of gentility and how one comes to possess 'gentilesse'. The essay ends with a discussion of Chaucer's own life and his reflections on the turbulence of fame and the problem of achieving that 'stableness' that is a king's duty to provide, but which he often fails to deliver.

Rob Gossedge's essay, 'The Consolations and Conflicts of History: Chaucer's "Monk's Tale"', is similarly interested in Chaucer's engagement with history and politics. It examines the different historiographical traditions that Chaucer sets in conflict in the 'Monk's Tale': medieval insular history, institutional chronicle, Boethian understandings of historical change and the more radical, secular modes of writing history that privilege logical causation over divine providence. The consideration of Chaucer's treatment of different historiographical models sheds light on the 'Monk's Tale's' complex relationship with contemporary politics and the politics of writing history. Read in the context of contemporary historical events – above all the deposition and execution of Richard II – the 'Monk's Tale' engages in the same radical discourse found in Boccaccio's exploration of the rise and fall of great men in *De casibus virorum illustrium*. In the half-remembered, fragmentary and purposefully insignificant tragedies, Chaucer questions the entire function of writing history, and frustrates any attempt to read the past through a single philosophical lens.

Like the previous essay, Lewis Beer's essay, 'Readers and Authors in Chaucer's *House of Fame*', examines Chaucer's engagement with one of the great medieval Italian writers. It considers the question of the location of authority in Chaucer's dream-poem, and whether the onus is on the author or the reader to make meaning out of a text. The essay seeks to clarify the distinction between Dante's and Chaucer's attitudes towards the complex relationship between author and reader. The essay argues that, whereas Dante appears confident in the establishment of authorial control while still encouraging active reader interpretation of his text, Chaucer's text seems to remove authority from both. Thus, Geffrey's apparent uncertain authorial position – the House of Fame is a dream vision (and therefore it does not originate with the dreamer) and throughout the narrative other stories (belonging to other authors) are retold (so Geffrey becomes a reader) – is coupled with repeated warnings about misinterpreting texts, actively discouraging the reader's critical engagement with the text. The essay concludes by contrasting one of Dante's addresses to the reader in the *Paradiso*, and Chaucer's enigmatic refusal to say where textual authority lies.

Ruth Evans's essay 'Tie Knots and Slip Knots: Sexual Difference and Memory in Chaucer's *Troilus and Criseyde*' considers the central tragedy of remembrance in the poem: Troilus cannot forget Criseyde, but Criseyde quickly forgets Troilus. The essay examines the gendering of memory in medieval arts of memory and memory treatises, and considers the gendered politics of memory in Chaucer's romance, but does not read Criseyde's faithlessness through gendered binaries. Instead, drawing on Jacques Lacan's work on sexuation, the essay argues that the poem's poignant exploration of remembrance and forgetting does not function as a condemnation of Criseyde but is rather a way of presenting the failure of the sexual relation and the conundrum of sexual difference.

Finally in this section, Valerie Allen's essay 'Chaucer and the Poetics of Gold' considers Chaucer's works from the perspective of the poetics of gold, aesthetics and poetic value. The essay examines Chaucer's reputation for bringing the ornamentation associated with medieval Latin and French poetry into the vernacular and so bejeweling the poetic form, in the sense of decorating language with descriptive passages, Latinate words and rhetorical devices, and mastering metrical form. By tracking the instances of references to jewels, precious stones, silver and gold in Chaucer's works, the essay reveals the texts' fascination with gold in particular – a preoccupation with its brightness, which connects gold with the question of beauty (rhetorical ornamentation) and purity/weight (value/moral weightiness). The essay thus demonstrates how poetic language behaves like gold, as well as showing that gold is a deep metaphor for poetry. The references to gold resonate particularly with Chaucer's lyric, *Complaint to his Purse*. Between its rhymes, repetitions, variations and double entendre, words become golden and heavy as they are made to do the referential work of three or four words at a time. Poetic language starts to become precious, in the sense of rarefied and elite, rather than simply jewelled. Metaphor gains in stature from being a relatively surface-level trope to being the heartbeat of poetry itself.

Part III: Religious Texts and Contexts

Part III of the volume examines an area that pervades the whole of medieval culture: religion. Beatrice Fannon's essay, 'The Torment of the Cross: The Representation of the Crucifixion in Medieval Lyric and Drama', explores the different approaches and perspectives from which the Crucifixion is depicted in medieval lyric and drama. The Crucifixion, the central event in salvific history, provides the devotional centrepiece of much medieval literature. As well as seeking to affect a devotional response to the Crucifixion, medieval literature has a didactic function as it engages with the theology of the event. The essay begins by discussing the innovative perspectives offered by medieval lyrics of the thirteenth, fourteenth and fifteenth centuries, which range from offering the more iconographically familiar image of Christ crucified to more unusual lyrical treatments of aspects of the Crucifixion narrative and theology. The essay goes on to discuss the function of the Crucifixion narratives in the Corpus Christi cycles, and then explores the very different and theologically complex approach that is found in the late medieval Croxton *Play of the Sacrament*, a creative, though often problematic, restaging of the Crucifixion, which offers important insights into sacramental theology.

Like several of the texts discussed in the volume, *Piers Plowman* exists in a number of different versions, which, as Catherine Batt's essay 'Encountering *Piers Plowman*' discusses, attests to the provisionality of the text. The essay considers the ways in which the religious dream-poem continually re-examines difficult theological questions by placing them in a social context, rather than offering a solution to the fraught question of individual responsibility and justification within the framework of salvation theology. Close reading of the opening lines of the dream vision in the B text reveals the text's preoccupation with the problem of poetic expression and interpretation. The essay shows how the opening lines anticipate the poem's complexities and ambiguities as it continually shifts between the real and unreal, the active and contemplative life, and the outer and inner landscapes. The dream frame provides the perfect narrative tool for this protean text as it explores the problem of social conscience, raising concerns, the essay suggests, as relevant to the twenty-first century as to the fourteenth.

Roger Ellis' essay, 'Work in Progress: Spiritual Authorship and the Middle English Mystics', examines the nature of medieval authorship in light of manuscript production and circulation: frequently, unfinished or unrevised texts were circulated, as well as those which had been revised or reworked by different authors. It considers the extent to which the Middle English mystics – Richard Rolle, Julian of Norwich, Walter Hilton, the anonymous writer of *The Cloude of Vnknowyng,* and Margery Kempe – could claim authorship over their works against a backdrop of increasing authorial assertion. The authority of the mystics, however, must always be ambiguous in light of the understanding that God is the ultimate *auctor,* and all works must be brought to perfection in Him. The essay represents these spiritual classics essentially as 'works in progress', because the central element of the various authors' own understanding of their literary activities is that the spiritual project is permanently unfinished, that is, until it is finished by God.

Sheila Fisher's essay, 'Women's Voices in Middle English Literature: Who Gets to Speak and How?', concentrates on late Middle English texts and examines the voices both of historical women in their own writings and of the women who speak from male-authored texts. The essay examines the prevalence of women's voices (both real and fictional) in Middle English literature in figures such as Margery Kempe, Julian of Norwich, and Chaucer's the Wife of Bath and Prioress. The essay discusses the continued importance of physicality in determining the voice, that is, the nature of the body from which the voices speak. The bodies create expectations and remain important for shaping identity; this is particularly evident in Chaucer's 'General Prologue', but also holds true for Margery Kempe and Julian of Norwich. Bodies also speak for themselves: the extremes of Margery's ecstasies, for example, contrast strongly with the calmness of Julian's revelations. The essay utilizes the trope of ventriloquism to consider what it means to articulate another – or an Other – and how the author's gender matters when it comes to voicing women, and in the case of the mystical writers, what it means for women to attempt to voice God. The essay examines not only who could have a voice in late Middle English literature, but also how a modern reader might understand these different voices.

Finally, Martin Coyle's reflections on the preservation of the Coventry Doom Fresco in his essay, 'History, Frescoes and Reading the Middle Ages: A Final Note', lead to a consideration of some of the ways in which we, as readers, approach medieval texts, which are both part of their age, but also come down to us through accidents of history and so can provide us with only a partial view of the period. The essay also looks at the periodization of the Middle Ages, and how the discussion of boundaries helps us to conceptualize an era, while also shaping our preconceptions in an often negative way. The essay ends by looking at the opening lines of *The Canterbury Tales* and how, instead of being a simple portrait of contemporary life, they can be read in terms of the medieval acceptance of the end of history.

Notes

1. For an in-depth examination of the development of the English language, see Albert C. Baugh, *A History of the English Language* (London and Henley: Routledge & Kegan Paul, 1976 [1951]), pp. 47–239.
2. For example, James Anthony Froude's *History of England* (1879). See Eamon Duffy, 'Introduction' to *Saints, Sacrilege and Sedition* (London: Bloomsbury, 2012), pp. 33–43.
3. For a discussion of the revisionist movement in the twentieth century, see Eamon Duffy, 'Introduction' to *Saints, Sacrilege and Sedition*, pp. 3–14.
4. See The Act of the Six Articles, 1539, in *Documents of the English Reformation*, ed. Gerald Bray (Cambridge: James Clarke & Co. Ltd., 1994), pp. 222–32.
5. For an introductory chronological discussion of the development of English Literature as a discipline, see Robert Eagleton, *Doing English: A guide for literature students* (London: Routledge, 1999).

Part I
Reading Medieval Romance

1

The Ownership of Literature: Reading Medieval Literature in its Historical Context

John Hines

It is always useful to consider literature in relation to the context in which it was produced. Such an understanding helps to elucidate more of what a text might mean: for example, which features and factors of contemporary life may be being referred to, and why and how they mattered to author or readers or both. Informed and well-focused 'historicism' will bring us closer to an understanding of how aspects of the literature functioned and bore meaning in the context in which that literature arose. It is especially important to appreciate that literature is part of cultural life and thus part of the cultural history of whatever age it originates in. Literature is thus just as much and just as good evidence for a period and place as practical documents, recorded events, archaeological finds, buildings, works of art and monuments.

After outlining the development of literature within the Middle English period, this essay will examine in what sense medieval English 'belonged' to any individuals or groups in its original context. This question opens up a range of matters from the diversity of identifiable readerships and audiences to issues such as the status of authorship, the possession and circulation of manuscript texts and even the emergence of a market for literature.

Changes in English after the Norman Conquest

Politically, England had largely acquired its current boundaries by the start of the Middle English literary period. Nevertheless, when Harold II acted decisively to defeat the Norwegian king Harald Hardrada and his invading army at the Battle of Stamford Bridge

(Yorkshire) in September 1066, political separation and the loss of the lands north of the Humber–Mersey line were still very real threats for the King of England. Within three weeks, however, Harold II and most of his English army were killed at the Battle of Hastings. The victory of William Duke of Normandy (William the Conqueror) over King Harold II in October 1066 closed a 50-year period in which the tenure of the kingship had been violently contested and changed hands in dynastic terms more than once. The outcome of the Norman Conquest was a lasting and profound change in the political order and the cultural complexion of England, including its literature.

There were, it can be argued, three principal consequences for English literary history. First, the shared identity of the English-speaking population was emphasized by the presence of an Anglo-Norman, French-speaking elite, who used French (often in its distinct Anglo-Norman dialect) as the language of government and high culture.[1] Medieval English literary culture was subsequently shaped primarily on a regional rather than a national basis. It would not have been this social dominance alone that allowed French and other continental literary developments to influence Middle English literature profoundly over the following centuries, but it certainly, and constructively, established a broad and diverse, diglossic interface between French literary culture and English literary traditions.

A subtle difference of emphasis is proposed in that last sentence between 'culture' and 'traditions', particularly because the violent truncation of the Anglo-Saxon social and cultural elite after the Norman Conquest probably both hastened and secured the demise of an elevated Old English literary tradition, the second consequence of the Norman Conquest. However, the Late West Saxon standardized language of a literature that flourished especially in the last quarter of the tenth and first quarter of the eleventh centuries had already grown increasingly unlike any form of the spoken language, and literary output had not been great in the three or four decades before 1066.[2] This slump in known English literary output continued until around the turn of the twelfth to the thirteenth century, by which time a very different Middle English language had developed, one which was written in several markedly different regional dialects, not a national standard.[3] Dialectal differences from the South through the Midlands to the North, and between East and West, eventually in Ireland too, show that changes in pronunciation varied greatly. Distinctive features also range from an extraordinarily late survival of the feminine grammatical gender in Kentish to an abundance of Old

Norse-derived vocabulary in Midland and northern dialects (itself often varying from area to area).

The third significant consequence of the post-Conquest disloca- tion is that these Middle English regions also nurtured distinctive literary traditions. The evidence for a survival of the Old English alliterative verse form in the West Midlands is particularly strong.[4] It is not unusual to find coherent and differential local references and local perspectives in literary works: a shining example is the romance of *Havelok*, set in Lincolnshire and serving as a foundation legend for the North Sea port of Grimsby.[5] The diverse foundations of Middle English literature were by no means a weakness, for by the later four- teenth century regional traditions were being brought together in situations ranging from rivalry to creative juxtaposition in an effective way that also began to re-establish a national literature. These develop- ments go some way towards explaining the otherwise highly arguable attribution to Geoffrey Chaucer, the great author of that period, of the title 'Father of English literature'.[6]

Assimilating romance

One literary-historical case of cause and effect that is beyond dispute is that the Norman Conquest of England in 1066, and subsequently of Wales, starting in earnest 25 years later, established the social and cultural preconditions for the emergence of one of the most distinc- tive and familiar genres of medieval literature: chivalric romance. Endemic warfare and the militarization of the social elite were any- thing but new in western European life, even if the eleventh century is regarded by some historians as such an exceptionally harsh age as to deserve the title of an 'Age of Iron'.[7] The military success of the Normans – which was not limited to England and Wales – was largely due to the fact that in Normandy they had developed especially efficient new forms of social control and exercise of force, involving cavalry warfare, the use of castle strongholds and a rigid hierarchy of personal ties of service and reciprocal patronage and protection which we usually describe as 'feudal'. This suite of practices was also very well suited to the holding and subjection of a large and populous territory in Britain, where the conquerors and native populations remained largely foreign and opposed to one another.

Medieval romance could hardly embody the ideals of this elite social class more obviously. In the best cases, it not only dramatizes those values but also reflects upon them; it may thus both question and refine the ideals. There are many fine examples of how the dual obligations and interests of the men of this exclusive social sphere in warfare on the one hand and in women and heterosexual love on the other are brought powerfully together in the texts: sometimes to produce tense conflicts, sometimes to motivate the noblest behaviour. *Sir Gawain and the Green Knight* and Chaucer's 'Knight's Tale' are pre-eminent examples. In the latter case, we also know the circumstances in which the work was composed; and although Chaucer moved in the circles of the royal court, he did so as a Londoner and primarily as a man who had made his way as a representative of the small but important urban professional class.[8] By the time the first section of the *Canterbury Tales* was put together, the linkage of the Knight as narrator and the tale that he tells – of the young prisoner-knights Palamon and Arcite and their love-rivalry for the beautiful Emily – is presented as a stereotype, and one that is placed for critical exami-nation in a gallery of genres and narrator-characters that is broad and diverse. The conservatism and the determinism of the Knight's automatic habits of thought are made plain, however sympathetic and perhaps even reverent their handling.

The setting and the characters of the 'Knight's Tale' are classi-cal and pagan. Palamon and Arcite, and indeed Duke Theseus, are noble, but also spiritually as well as humanly tragic figures. Alongside the historically more specific and secular characteristics of romance, Christian devotion is a powerful ideological feature. This is far from mere outward conformity to correct Christian sentiments and judge-ments, but quite fundamentally a determinative factor, for a knight's Christian virtue supplants the cunning of the earlier heroes as what guarantees his success.[9] In this respect, the ways and degrees in which art imitated life and life imitated art are impossible to disentangle and to assess. It has been proposed, in somewhat naïve terms, that the paired themes of war and love in the romance genre addressed a dual audience in the elite halls of castles or court: men and women respec-tively.[10] This suggestion is useful in highlighting not only the issue of gender relations but also the special contextual valency of this litera-ture in historical circumstances in which women's freedom and power were systematically and severely restricted, if not utterly quashed. There are a few historical cases of medieval women who were highly influential and acted through their own agency. But rather than romance merely offering women palliative stories of female characters of enviable physical beauty, and often of exceptional virtue too, who could thus command the devotion and direct the actions of adoring knights, the passion of amorous, romantic, sexual love could be con-flated with that of spiritual and divine love[11]: the former was a stage of experience that led eventually to experiencing and valuing the latter. This ideological configuration endowed women with a power and influence of a more general and systematic nature, at the same time as binding them all the more firmly within the value system of the age and its culture.

Whatever its contemporary relevance, nearly all romance was set in a past, allowing it to invoke and employ a former golden age to veil the discrepancy between the mundane and often brutal realities of its actual setting and its ideals. The chivalric court *par excellence* was that of the legendary British King Arthur, historically located in the immediately post-Roman period in fifth-century Britain, which also saw the earliest phases of Anglo-Saxon settlement and the origins of England and Englishness.[12] Wales and Cornwall were geographically marginal areas for the Anglo-Norman seigneurial elite, but the Arthurian realm was not an entirely fantasy world in either time or space. There are a few fragmentary early appearances of Arthur as both a supposed historical figure and as a literary character in Welsh sources. The great transformation in Arthurian literature, however, comes with *Historia Regum Britanniae* (The History of the Kings of Britain) written, or rather purportedly translated into Latin from a Welsh or Breton original, by the Cambro-Norman cleric Geoffrey of Monmouth around AD 1135. As a work of history, this source passed on through the Middle Ages in England and Wales in a substantial tradition of versions of what was known as the *Brut*, both verse and prose.[13]

Later in the twelfth century, primarily in the decades of 1170–90, it was a French poet, Chrétien de Troyes, who first authored definitive, rich, romance elaborations of stories set around Arthur's court, including, in *Perceval*, the appearance of *la Sainte Graal* (the Holy Grail). Chrétien knew, but was not demonstrably part of, the now Plantagenet-ruled French aristocratic sphere in England and Wales. An equally gifted and influential contemporary of Chrétien's was, exceptionally, an authoress, Marie de France, who certainly did move to England and produced both a collection of 'Breton lays' and one of fables; the latter, remarkably, is stated to have been translated from English in a period from which we have no surviving English works of that type or quality.[14] It is salutary to appreciate how clearly it was the case, then, that the adoption of romance as a genre for English literature was not only a matter of foreign influence upon native culture, or the gradual anglicization of an invasive elite and its dominant culture, but was also a stage in the popularization of the genre and its values. It could then be adapted to other purposes.

Sir Orfeo

These are issues we can illustrate well by looking in closer detail at a still widely read Middle English romance, the 'Breton lay' of *Sir Orfeo*. We have three medieval manuscript versions of the poem, labelled *A*, *H* and *B*. *A* is the earliest known copy, in the Auchinleck manuscript (c. 1330). The Auchinleck manuscript itself is the earliest known example of the compilation of many different texts into large, handwritten vellum codices to serve as 'household miscellanies': be that by direct commission from a patron or as a commercial venture by an early 'bookseller'.[15] Early in the 1400s, apparently in Warwickshire, another copy was written as the first of six items in a booklet that was ultimately bound up in what is now British Library Harley MS 3810 (*H*). The latest copy (*B*) was written on paper in what is now Oxford MS Ashmole 61. This compilation was gradually put together for a household in Leicestershire.[16] None of these versions of *Sir Orfeo* is the direct source or descendant of any other extant copy.

The earliest copy, *A*, can be adjudged qualitatively the richest and subtlest of the versions, yet it is intriguingly incomplete. Physically, the Auchinleck manuscript has at some stage suffered from harsh excisions and erasures, and a title and initial illustration are definitely missing from the start of its *Sir Orfeo*, together with lines constituting a prologue. These lines can be reconstructed, not only from the evidence of versions *H* and *B* but also by the remarkable fact that essentially the same prologue is used in the Auchinleck manuscript to introduce an English translation of Marie de France's *Lai le Fresne*.[17] This prologue primarily introduces these texts as examples of the 'Breton lay' and outlines the characteristics of that narrative sub-genre: lyrical in style, and diverse in subject matter, showing both good and evil; with a strong inclination towards the marvellous and tales of fairy; but:

> Of al þinges þat men seþ
> Mest o love, for-soþe, þai beþ.[18]

[Of all the subjects that are found, mostly, in truth, they deal with love.]

It is curious that, where the truncated *A*-text begins on folio 300 of the Auchinleck manuscript, it does so exactly at the start of the narrative proper: 'Orfeo was a kinge' (A 39). Both narratively and thematically the surviving text reads entirely satisfactorily without its prologue. The generic focus of the prologue is, however, neatly recalled at the end of the *A* version by a return to the story of Breton harpers adopting and transmitting the story (A 597–602).

Love and kingship are principal themes of *Sir Orfeo*. The core story is a reworking of the classical myth of Orpheus and Eurydice[19]: Orfeo loses his wife, Dame Heurodys, who is in this story stolen away by the King of Fairy. In the Middle English story, unlike the classical myth, Orfeo eventually brings her back, having wandered and suffered in the wilderness for years but finally charming the King of Fairy with his harping. Orfeo's love for his wife is intense and pure, and parting from her is therefore like death:

> Þe king unto his chaumber is go,
> & oft swooned opon þe ston,
> & made swich diol & swiche mon
> Þat neiʒe his liif was y-spent.   (A 196–9)

[The king went to his chamber and often swooned upon the stone floor, and made such lamentation and sorrow that his life was almost gone.]

As he does, however, live on, the only appropriate setting for his desolation is the wilderness (A 209–14), although in political terms his decision to go into exile is presented as being enacted through careful and correct procedure: Orfeo deputes his royal authority to his steward, and directs that when he is finally known to be dead, Parliament should choose a new king (A 204–18).

In his abdication, Orfeo does not divest himself of royal authority to sink in social status to another conventional and culturally defined role, that of a peasant, but rather to become a fictional figure, a wild man of nature.[20] In the ultimate happy resolution of the tale, Orfeo is fully brought back to himself, recognized, re-tired and re-installed as king (ll. 575–94). It is particularly significant that Orfeo's first and most serious challenger in the narrative, the King of Fairy, also has the status, character and attributes of a king:

> Þe king hadde a croun on hed;
> It nas of silver, no of gold red,
> Ac it was of a precios ston. (A 149–51)

[The king had a crown on his head; it was not of silver or of red gold, but made of a precious stone.]

This king is eventually tracked down in a castle, which is 'riche & real & wonder heiʒe' ('rich and royal and wondrously high', A

355–76). The ideal king, be he Orfeo or the King of Fairy, is the epitome of aristocratic nobility: in fact Orfeo's attention is drawn to the castle by his educated and retained pleasure in observing and following the fairy ladies' hunting party. After Orfeo has requested Heurodys as a reward for his beautiful minstrelsy, the king first demurs as an expression of his refined taste:

A sori couple of ʒow it were,
For þou art lene, rowe & blac,
& sche is lovesum, wiþ-outen lac. (A 458–60)

[You would make a sorry couple, for you are scrawny, rough and black, and she is lovely, without a flaw.]

However, because it would be yet more unconscionable for a king to fail to keep his word, he grants the request (A 463–72).

In light of the Fairy King's determination not to be guilty of speaking a 'lesing' (a falsehood: A 465), a moral question concerning deceit and fidelity emerges as an engrossing ambivalence in this poem. Orfeo may arguably never actually lie, but he certainly deceives others about who he is. He gains entrance to the castle claiming to be a minstrel (A 379–86) and insists to the King of Fairy that he is 'nothing but a poor minstrel' (A 429–30). On returning to Winchester with Heurodys, he acts the anonymous visitor to the town, borrowing the clothes of the beggar, and, still with his harp, confronting his deputy, the steward (A 475–514). To the latter's great credit, the steward responds with a love he bears for every harper for his lord Orfeo's sake, and is grief-stricken when Orfeo further feigns that he had picked up the harp in the wilderness having come across Orfeo's dead body there (A 515–49). Ironically, from a strictly or simply moral point of view, Orfeo thus recognizes the steward as a 'trewe' (faithful) man, and loves him for that (A 554–5). He then recounts the actual story, still not as a narrative account but in the conditional mode, promising the loyal steward his due reward: 'If all this had happened' (A 556–74). The steward does indeed succeed Orfeo when the latter's life ends, long afterwards (A 595–6). The practical moral scheme of the poem is that Orfeo's deceptions act for the best by testing and proving the virtue of the King of Fairy and of the steward just as the cruel loss of Heurodys tests him; his own virtue as a noble lover in finding his life in the royal court untenable without his beloved wife is likewise matched and repaid by the nobility of the King of Fairy and the fidelity of the steward. That goodness can grow and multiply, and that even in the most testing of circumstances essential virtue ultimately begets reciprocal generosity and happiness, can be counted a recurrent theme of the Breton lay.

Versions of *Sir Orfeo*

The recognition by the critical reader of such an ethically inspiring ambivalence as a startling and major quality of *Sir Orfeo*, and particularly of its most effective version, *A*, renders some differences of the *H*- and *B*-versions all the more striking. *H*, the next dated copy, has nibbled away at the focus on Orfeo's kingship. This is perhaps reflected most clearly in Orfeo's less military attempt to prevent Erodys (her name in this text) being taken by the fairies. In *A* he goes with a thousand knights, who form a defensive wall (using the technical military term *scheltrom*: 'shield wall', 'phalanx'); in *H*, he goes with two hundred knights who 'make watch on every side' (H 177–90). The *H*-text's interest in Orfeo's state in the wilderness is also reduced (H 239–48): the passage primarily describes the situation and its bodily effects on Orfeo, not dramatically imagining how he lived. Most fundamentally, the *H*-recension also appears to reflect an attempt to relax the moral tension over Orfeo's deceit: he does not tell the Fairy King that he is nothing but a poor minstrel, and indeed is described by that king as 'a trewe man' (H 431). Even more directly, in the dénouement, Orfeo reveals his true identity to the steward as soon as he has assured himself of the latter's fidelity (H 456–95). The *H*-text then concludes quite summarily in just fifteen further lines.

The *B*-text has moved even further along this path. In several respects we can characterize its particularities in terms of greater conventionalism – beginning with a 'merry time of April' invocation at the very start (B 1–6). It uses 'King Orfew' as a title, and presents the king and his knights in a more stereotypical way when they actually do make battle and shed their blood attempting to prevent the taking of Meroudys (as she has become in this version) (B 191–2). Where Orfeo previously fell in a swoon in his chamber in grief, here, more piously, he falls to his knees (B 199). Orfeo's final self-revelation to the steward is simply blundered. The conditional clause found in *A* commences but is not grammatically continued:

> ȝiff j were Orfeo þe kyng –
> Ther-for, stewerd, lystyns to me:
> Now þou may þe kyng her se. (B 552–3)

> [If I were Orfeo, the king – therefore, steward, listen to me: now you can see the king here.]

It proceeds to a crudely worded assertion of kingly power and of the threat immanent in the tests:

And if þou have of my deth blyth
Thou schuld be hangyd also swyth. (B 568–9)

[And had you been glad at my death, you should have been hanged without delay.]

All three versions conclude with a prayer: this occupies one line in *A*, five in *H* and seven in *B*.

To assess these texts as sources that may provide insights into cultural history at the same time as being explained by historical circumstances, there is a set of key questions to be considered. Are the differences between them, and the changes made in the poem, reflections of different readerships being targeted, products of different times or just the symptoms of historical drift and degradation over time and through transmission? It is not a matter of any historical controversy to state that the diminution of the scope and celebration of a very refined nobility evident in the versions later than the *A*-version is congruent with social, economic and ideological changes during the period from the earlier fourteenth century to the fifteenth which essentially showed ever greater concern for an equitable economy of exchange, 'quid pro quo', in interpersonal dealings.[21] Likewise, that personal religious piety was cultivated and expressed by lay folk both in public and at home more and more regularly and materially is abundantly attested.[22] At the same time, the slow ebbing of the dramatic quality of the *A*-version in the later copies can also be held characteristic of a coarsening effect of time and repetition; an interesting idea, though, to which we shall briefly return by the end of this essay, is that it is also a symptom of a literature that was coming more to be read rather than to be imagined.

Readership and audience

With more information about the circumstances and character of the patrons for whom the manuscript compilations containing *Sir Orfeo* were produced, and of their connections with the various compilers and scribes, we might be able to make more specific suggestions about interests which the different adaptations of the text may have been designed to meet. It is clear, for instance, that the Auchinleck manuscript is the grandest of the three, and easy to associate with a more 'aristocratic' tone in the Breton lay. Without making risky assumptions, however, we can be satisfied with a more general perception of how groups of readers, particularly in household units, were caught up in historical processes which the literary record reflects, embodies and bears witness to.

Sir Orfeo and its manuscripts are anything but alone in this respect. From close to the date at which we find our earliest witness to *Sir Orfeo*, there are two well-studied manuscripts that are exceptionally illuminating, not least because their historical and archaeological contexts are so well understood.[23] Oxford Bodleian Library MS Digby 86 is the earlier of the two, its compilation starting in the early 1280s. Calendar entries recording the death dates of family members, and practice signatures by a later owner, place the manuscript in the fourteenth century at the farm of Underhill in the parish of Berrow, south-west Worcestershire. Unlike the suggested commercial production of the Auchinleck manuscript, this manuscript was apparently compiled and completed within the household itself, with at least half of the work being done in a period of 15 months. In this collection, the texts were originally produced as a set of folded vellum booklets, initially kept (we infer) in a sort of wallet but soon ingeniously joined together into what then became a book.

The background of the Underhill household in this area deep within the Welsh Marches shows that it was a household that had risen, socially and culturally, from peasant origins, through economic success and, apparently, ambitious and opportunistic marriage alliances. Much of the contents of Digby 86 is in French or Latin rather than the English vernacular; the range in the character of the texts is quite broad, and a distinct change in focus is discernible from more conventionally serious French and Latin texts to diverse and often frivolous works, plus other Middle English pieces, between two initially separate collections that were joined in the final codex. It is impossible to tell whether it was the result of an ambition to collect a diverse and representative library or of the random availability of a wide range of exemplars, but the conscious anthologizing of various genres of literature is apparent in the compilation. Especially interesting is the copy of the earliest extant Middle English fabliau, *Dame Sirith*, a risqué, bawdy tale that was apparently written first in a separate booklet and, notably, was marked up for performance – either by four individuals or by one successively declaiming the parts of two women, a lustful clerk and a narrator.[24] However, it is in the lyrics, in short stanzaic songs, that we can perceive the richest and most persistent opportunities for readers to engage with the texts.

Much of the historical context of the composition of the second of the two manuscripts, British Library MS Harley 2253, is known: it was compiled and written in the Ludlow area of Shropshire a few years before the Black Death struck in 1346, by a priest who was probably a victim of that terrible plague. The scribe's work is well known, not only in Harley 2253 and two other major codices but also in a large number of dated legal documents from the area. Harley 2253 may have been commissioned by a rich wool merchant, Sir Lawrence de Ludlow, of the still standing Stokesay Castle, but this cannot be proved. Local allusions and interests are copiously reflected in this manuscript – as in the scribe's other work. Harley 2253 also contains far more French texts than Latin or English. It includes a version of a Middle English romance, *King Horn*, but is best known as the source of the Harley Lyrics, which range from Christian and devotional poems to love songs and political and satirical pieces of contemporary relevance.[25] The love lyrics consistently portray frustrated, unrequited love, in a misogynistic and pessimistic tone, quite explicitly contrasted with the permanence and dependability of Christ's love. This is particularly evident in one pair of parallel texts known as 'The Way of Woman's Love' and 'The Way of Christ's Love':

> Ever & oo, for my leof icham in grete þohte;
> y þenche on hire þat y ne seo nout ofte.[26]

> [All the time, for my love, I am in heavy thought; I think on her whom I do not see often at all.]

> Ever & oo, nyht and day, he haueþ vs in is þohte;
> He nul nout leose þat he so deore bohte.[27]

> [All the time, night and day, he has us in his thought; he does not wish to lose what he so dearly bought.]

Amongst the Harley Lyrics, the dialogue between a clerk and a girl titled 'De clerico et puella' re-enacts a vignette concerning forbidden desire and temptation that is reflected in a more shamelessly vulgar manner in *Dame Sirith* in Digby 86. In nine stanzas the clerk and the girl speak alternately, four times each: the clerk repeatedly pleads his love in conventional terms of an unrequited love-sickness; the girl verbally dismisses him to begin with, but subsequently reveals her fear of retribution for them both because she is jealously guarded by her father and family. We then learn that she has already fallen for the clerk and kissed him through the window; in the end her pity for his declared suffering overcomes her reticence and she pledges:

> Fader, moder, & al my kun ne shal me holde so stille
> Þat y nam þyn, & þou art myn, to don al þi wille.[28]

[Father, mother, and all my kin shall not hold me so tightly I shall not be yours and you be mine, to do all you desire.]

Simple though it is, this fundamentally 'dramatic' lyric not only reflects real identities within and around a household such as that to be found at a distinguished house like Stokesay Castle, but also positively invites the exercise of imaginative empathy with (or apprehension for) individuals in the situation portrayed. The heterogeneous quality of the Harley manuscript, containing lyrics that are both sacred and profane, demonstrates the complexity of the nature and reading practices of the medieval household and the impossibility of restricting certain literary genres to particular social classes.

The genre many see as the inverse of romance, the scurrilous fabliau, has, in the course of a hundred years of scholarly study, been attributed to every major division of medieval society: the urban bourgeoisie, the seigneurial and aristocratic elite, the peasantry and the literate clerks.[29] The humbler social background of the household to which MS Digby 86 belonged might initially seem to agree with the proposition of a humbler social origin for this literature: besides *Dame Sirith*, Digby 86 also contains a copy of a popular French fabliau, *Les quatre souhaits Saint Martin*.[30] Harley 2253, however, is equally important in terms of literary history for containing four Anglo-Norman versions of fabliaux.[31] 'Ownership' can be created or asserted through appropriation, and while one could not claim that literary appropriation and adaptation are necessarily easy undertakings, we can definitely see that this was an opportunity taken advantage of more and more in English culture from the late thirteenth century onwards. It does not automatically involve subversion: conventional piety and religious orthodoxy, as in the Harley Lyrics, dominate the material. However, the social diffusion of access to religious imagination and dramatization, as well as of the skills required for authorship and thus claims to authority, did come to pose a challenge to structures of power and their ideology.

Authorship as 'ownership'

Association with a text as an author is, of course, another form of literary 'ownership'. In our own times, this is arguably the most prominent aspect of a proprietorial connection to literature. There is an interesting contrast between Chaucer, the most widely appreciated of the London authors,[32] and John Gower, on the one hand, and the author of *Piers Plowman* ('Will Langland') and the *Gawain*-poet on the other. Langland's work enjoyed considerable popularity – there are many manuscript copies[33]; the *Gawain*-poet was an artistic genius, though his work has survived in just one modest manuscript.[34] The latter remains anonymous; Will Langland is effectively a *nom de plume*. Langland and the *Gawain*-poet variously assert and reflect the regional associations characteristic of earlier Middle English literature; their alliterative verse-style is provincial and traditional. Chaucer and Gower, the 'known' authors of the London scene, insert themselves quite differently as narrator-characters, '*personae*', in their English works. Gower, indeed, had himself memorialized as an author, his carved effigy lying on his tomb pillowed by his three major works (in Latin, French and English respectively): *Vox Clamantis*, *Mirour de l'omme* and *Confessio Amantis*.[35]

Curiously, the peak of achievement represented by the generation of Chaucer, Gower, Langland and the *Gawain*-poet did not bring about an immediate and substantial re-orientation of English literature. The traditions carried on: like *Sir Orfeo*, romances were copied and adapted in the fifteenth century. But the old relevancy and concomitant authority of the texts were ebbing away; Malory's 'Tales of Arthur' are far more consciously regretful and nostalgic for a lost chivalric world than was apparent before.[36] Fifteenth-century Middle English literature is, rightly, now appreciated as far more than a sad testimony to the failure of creativity and an Age of Dullness, but there was a falling off.[37] The inherited modes could no longer even irreverently be treated with the confidence they previously had. The next great surge in productivity, originality and quality came when the Elizabethan playhouses and printing presses provided quite a new market and role for genuinely entrepreneurial authors in the later sixteenth century. A watershed had been crossed to render literature a full-blown commodity and readers its customers – supporting agents, publishers and impresarios as well as authors. That, however, was yet another adaptive twist, not the consolidation of a process of recrudescence.

Material, technical, social and economic circumstances all modify the very nature of literature. The medieval texts we can read, enjoy and study are usually very variable entities – modulating through the processes of manuscript copying and transmission, and certainly through processes of adaptation, more or less subtle in execution. Much Middle English literature was not really meant to be read in private, as became the norm in the modern era; the texts we have represent readings and performances that belonged to and interacted with social and material contexts. It is illuminating to recognize, for instance, that the change of Orfeo's queen's name to Meroudys in the Ashmole version of *Sir Orfeo* can be best explained as an aural misinterpretation of the phrase 'Dame Heroudys'. In our own time, authors are increasingly making use of multimedia facilities and rapid social network communications to engage groups of readers in the composition of variable texts. Film and television, from adaptations of literary 'classics' to works specially written for the media, in some ways offer us a good analogy to what the real connection was between medieval literature and its public in that period. Reading the preserved written texts is rather like looking only at the script of a drama intended for broadcast and audiovisual recording. That is, of course, where we must start, but we can do much more besides merely reading. By appreciating the context of medieval texts, we can re-enact a genuinely medieval mode of experience, taking our own form of 'ownership' of the texts.

Notes

1. Richard Ingram (ed.), *The Anglo-Norman Language and its Contexts* (Woodbridge: Boydell, 2010); Jocelyn Wogan-Browne et al. (eds), *Language and Culture in Medieval Britain: The French of England c. 1100-c.1500* (Woodbridge: Boydell, 2009).
2. Norman F. Blake, *A History of the English Language* (Basingstoke: Macmillan, 1996), pp. 75–131.
3. Blake, *A History of the English Language*, pp. 132–71; Hans Frede Nielsen, *From Dialect to Standard: English in England 1154-1176* (Odense: University Press of Southern Denmark), pp. 1–47.
4. Thorlac Turville-Petre, *The Alliterative Revival* (Cambridge: Brewer, 1977); Ralph Hanna, 'Alliterative poetry', in *The Cambridge History of Medieval English Literature,* ed. David Lawton (Cambridge: Cambridge University Press, 1999), pp. 488–512.
5. G. V. Smithers (ed.), *Havelok* (Oxford: Clarendon Press, 1987); John Hines, 'From **AnleifR* to Havelok: the English and the Irish Sea', in *Celtic-Norse Relationships in the Irish Sea in the Middle Ages 800–1200*, eds Jón Viðar Sigurðsson and Tim Bolton (Leiden: Brill, 2014), pp. 187–214.
6. The precise phrase appears to have been used first in 1700 by John Dryden, *Fables, Ancient and Modern,* Preface; the term 'Father Chaucer', however, appears already in Robert Greene's *Greenes Vision*, 1592.
7. John Gillingham, 'Thegns and knights in eleventh-century England: who was then the gentleman', *Transactions of the Royal History Society*, Sixth Series, 5 (1995), pp. 129–153; Robert Bartlett, *England under the Norman and Angevin Kings 1075-1225* (Oxford: Oxford University Press, 2000).
8. Derek Pearsall, *The Life of Geoffrey Chaucer* (Oxford: Blackwell, 1992).
9. Sidney Painter, *French Chivalry* (New York: Cornell University Press, 1964), pp. 65–94.
10. Painter, *French Chivalry*; W. J. Barron, *English Medieval Romance* (Harlow: Longman, 1987), pp. 25–9.

11. The classic text on this subject is C. S. Lewis, *The Allegory of Love: A Study in Medieval Tradition* (Oxford: Oxford University Press, 1936).
12. Leslie Alcock, *Arthur's Britain* (London: Allen Lane, 1971); Alan Lane, 'The End of Roman Britain and the Coming of the Saxons: an Archaeological Context for Arthur?', in *A Companion to Arthurian Literature*, ed. Helen Fulton (Oxford: Blackwell, 2012), pp. 15–29.
13. Ad Putter, 'The Twelfth-century Arthur', in *The Cambridge Companion to the Arthurian Legend*, eds Elizabeth Archibald and Ad Putter (Cambridge: Cambridge University Press, 2009), pp. 36–52.
14. Marie de France, *Fables* ed. and trans. Harriet Spiegel (Toronto: University of Toronto Press, 1994).
15. Laura Hibbard Loomis, 'The Auchinleck Manuscript and a Possible London Bookshop of 1330–1340', *PMLA*, 57 (1942), 595–627. A facsimile of this manuscript with a transcription has been made available on-line by the National Library of Scotland: *http://auchnileck.nls.uk/*
16. George Shuffelton (ed.), *Codex Ashmole 61: A Compilation of Popular Middle English Verse*, (Kalamazoo, MI: Western Michigan University Press, 2008); Lynne Blanchfield, 'Rate revisited: the compilation of the narrative works in MS Ashmole 61', in *Romance Reading on the Book: Essays on Medieval Narrative Presented to Maldwin Mills*, eds Jennifer Fellows et al. (Cardiff: University of Wales Press, 1996), 208–220.
17. A. J. Bliss, 'Introduction' to *Sir Orfeo*, ed. A. J. Bliss (Oxford: Oxford University Press, 1966), pp. xlvi–xlviii.
18. *Sir Orfeo*, ed. A. J. Bliss (Oxford: Oxford University Press, 1966), *A* 11–12; cf. *H* 11–12; *B* 17–18. All further references to the three different versions (*A, B* and *H*) are from this edition and are given parenthetically in the main body of the text.
19. See Virgil, *Georgics*, IV, 453–527; and Ovid, *Metamorphoses*, Books X and XI.
20. Cf. A. C. Spearing, '*Sir Orfeo*: madness and gender', in *The Spirit of Medieval English Popular Romance,* eds Ad Putter and Jane Gilbert (Harlow: Longman, 2000), pp. 258–72.
21. See Christopher Dyer, *Making a Living in the Middle Ages: The People of Britain 850–1520* (New Haven and London: Yale University Press), esp. 265–362; Pamela Nightingale, 'Knights and merchants: trade, politics and the gentry in Late Medieval England', *Past & Present,* 169 (2000), 36–62; Roger A. Ladd, *Antimercantilism in the Late Medieval English Literature* (London: Palgrave Macmillan, 2010).
22. Nicole R. Rice, *Lay Piety and Religious Discipline in Middle English Literature* (Cambridge: Cambridge University Press, 2008).
23. Marylin Corrie, 'The compilation of Oxford, Bodleian Library, MS Digby 86', *Medium Ævum,* 66 (1997), 236–49; Carter Revard, 'Scribe and Provenances', in *Studies in the Harley Manuscript: The Scribes, Contents and Social Contexts of British Library MS Harley 2253*, ed. Susannah Fein (Kalamazoo, MI: Medieval Institute Publications, 2000), pp. 21–109; John

John Hines 29

Hines, *Voices in the Past: English Literature and Archaeology* (Cambridge: D.S. Brewer, 2004), pp. 71–104.

24. John Hines, *The Fabliau in English* (Harlow: Longman, 1993), pp. 43–70.

25. G. L. Brook, *The Harley Lyrics*, 3rd edn. (Manchester: Manchester University Press, 1964); *Medieval English Verse*, trans. Brian Stone (Harmondsworth: Penguin, 1964), pp. 175–212.

26. 'The Way of Woman's Love', Brook, *The Harley Lyrics*, no. 31; *English Lyrics of the Thirteenth Century*, ed. Carleton Brown (Oxford: Clarendon Press, 1962 [1932]), pp. 162–3, ll. 7–8.

27. 'The Way of Christ's Love', Brook, *The Harley Lyrics*, no. 32; *English Lyrics of the Thirteenth Century*, ed. Carleton Brown (Oxford: Clarendon Press, 1962 [1932]), pp. 161–2, ll. 7–8.

28. 'De clerico et puella', Brook, *The Harley Lyrics*, no. 24; *English Lyrics of the Thirteenth Century*, ed. Carleton Brown (Oxford: Clarendon Press, 1962 [1932]), pp. 152–4, ll. 35–6.

29. Joseph Bédier, *Les Fabliaux: Études de literature populaire et d'histoire littéraire du moyen âge*, 2nd edn. (Paris: Publisher, 1895); Per Nykrog, *Les Fabliaux: Étude d'histoire stylistique medieval* (Copenhagen: Ejnar Munksgaard, 1957); Marie-Jane Stearns Schenk, *The Fabliaux: Tales of Wit and Deception* (Amsterdam: John Benjamins, 1987); Hines, *Fabliau in English*, pp. 23–7.

30. Wilhem Noomen and Nico van den Boogard (eds), *Nouveau Recueil complet des Fabliaux littéraire* (Assen/Maastricht: van Gorcum, 1982), vol. 4, no. 31.

31. Ian Short and Roy J. Pearcy (eds), *Eighteen Anglo-Norman Fabliaux* (London: Anglo-Norman Text Society 14, 2000); Hines, *Fabliau in English*, pp. 37–42.

32. Helen Cooper, 'The frame', in *Sources and Analogues of the Canterbury Tales, Vol. 1,* eds. R. M. Correale and Mary Hamel (Cambridge: D.S. Brewer, 2002), pp. 1–22; Helen Cooper, 'London and Southwark Poetic Companies: "Si tost c'amis" and the *Canterbury Tales'*, in *Chaucer and the City,* ed. Ardis Butterfield (Cambridge: D. S. Brewer, 2006), pp. 109–28.

33. Ralph Hanna, 'The versions and revisions of *Piers Plowman*', in *The Cambridge Companion to 'Piers Plowman'*, eds Andrew Cole and Andrew Galloway (Cambridge: Cambridge University Press, 2014), pp. 33–49.

34. Ad Putter, *An Introduction to the Gawain-poet* (Harlow: Longman, 1996).

35. John Hines, Nathalie Cohen and Simon Roffey, '*Iohannes Gower, Armiger, Poeta*: Records and Memorials of his Life and Death', in *A Companion to Gower*, ed. Siân Echard (Cambridge: D. S. Brewer, 2005), pp. 23–41.

36. Catherine Batt, *Malory's Morte Darthur: Remaking Arthurian Tradition* (New York: Palgrave, 2002).

37. David Lawton, 'Dullness and the Fifteenth Century', *ELH*, 54 (1987), 761–99.

2

Liminality and Gender in Middle English Arthurian Romance

Raluca Radulescu

Belonging to the fellowship of the Round Table is, by definition, in any Arthurian romance the greatest honour. In establishing a set of recognizable features of the Arthurian world and its chivalric code, romance authors aligned their stories with accepted models of aristocratic behaviour, subsequently woven into narrative patterns that brought popularity to the genre. By building the context of *aventure* [adventure] and setting its parameters (in other words, the cycle of departure – challenge/obstacle – (painful) gain – return), authors worked with their audiences' expectations of a world in which ideals are enacted and deviations from the 'norm' are corrected.[1] It is not surprising, therefore, that Arthurian romance revels in opposites – characters are either 'in' (belonging to) or 'out' (not belonging to) of the Arthurian fellowship and court – defining and classifying types of noble behaviour and those who do/do not exhibit it. Thus modern critical approaches focusing on the marginal or liminal and the 'Other' can provide profitable avenues for the investigation of Arthurian texts.

Such approaches have been applied to a small group of Middle English Arthurian romances, though usually only those deemed by scholars to be sufficiently sophisticated to warrant examination. Among the Middle English Arthurian verse romances, the text that receives most attention is *Sir Gawain and the Green Knight*, while among the prose romances Sir Thomas Malory's *Le Morte Darthur* takes centre stage. In these analyses, the study of liminality sometimes touches on aspects connected to material culture, although the postcolonial approach is prevalent. Materiality, however, features prominently in romances written across linguistic and geographical areas and across centuries; by analysing the way that it is presented in the context of encounters with liminal figures, new facets of these texts can be uncovered, as will be demonstrated in the following essay.

In the corpus of insular romance, Gawain, Arthur's nephew, plays a unique role as the quintessential Arthurian knight. Hence he is the protagonist in the body of verse romances that have been labelled the 'Gawain romances'. These (mostly late medieval) romances revolve around some form of testing, not only of Gawain's prowess in arms, but also of the Arthurian values or ideals that he represents. In all of the extant Gawain romances, emphasis is placed on the spatial dimension (borders and territories, as well as challenges to these), courtesy (is Gawain, the notorious womanizer of French romance, going to be put to the test?) and (political) integration of the outside challenger, usually a border lord or foreigner who initially challenges the court, but ends up joining the Round Table fellowship.

Spiritual and political borders: *The Awntyrs off Arthur*

Among the romances that form the Gawain corpus one of the most problematic (but also fascinating for this reason) is *The Awntyrs off Arthur*. Extant in four separate manuscripts,[2] *Awntyrs* presents an ideal starting point for a discussion about materiality in relation to encounters with the Other in a liminal space. *Awntyrs* is a peculiar Arthurian poem in that its title announces a link with Arthur but the adventures are hardly Arthur's at all. As a bipartite poem, in which two different, though not totally unrelated, stories are recounted, *Awntyrs*, in its current form, can perhaps be said to appeal to its readers' desire to engage with the ideals of the Arthurian world. It explores the extent to which the exercise of chivalry and courtly mores plays a role not only in this life, but also in the next. First, a brief reminder of the plot is necessary. In the first part of the poem, Arthur goes hunting with a large courtly company including Gawain and Guenevere. In the forest of Tarn Wathelene, Guenevere and Gawain become separated from the rest of the company and experience an encounter with the world beyond, in the shape of a ghostly appearance, which turns out to be none other than Guenevere's mother. The ghost warns Guenevere about the dangers of fleshly sin and warns Gawain of Arthur's downfall. Guenevere asks what she can do to alleviate the ghost's pain, and she is told to give alms and pay for Masses. In the second part of the poem, Gawain fights Galeron of Galloway, a knight outside Arthur's jurisdiction, over lands which Galeron claims Gawain controls unlawfully. Arthur brings about resolution and Galeron joins the Round Table, while Guenevere arranges for Masses to be said for her dead mother.

In *Awntyrs*, liminality is expressed in a range of ways, from the space where the encounter with the ghost of Guenevere's mother takes place (in a forest, during a hunt) to the characters themselves (the ghost, Galeron and perhaps even Guenevere herself). The experience of liminality is mediated by the construction of opposites which define at least three types of boundary: that between the living and the dead; that between the Arthurian fellowship and those outside it; and that between types of spiritual reform required in the economy of salvation. Each of these boundaries merits further investigation. The first boundary, between the living and the dead, is described in strikingly sensationalist language for those accustomed to Arthurian romance, though it would not have been perceived as unusual by a medieval audience familiar with the tradition of popular devotion on which it is based (e.g. *The Mass or Trental of St Gregory*). It is characterized by a raw materiality that is alien to chivalric romance, which then translates into an uneasy message to both Guenevere and Gawain, on the one hand, and the audience of the text, on the other. The moaning voice of the ghost 'yauland and yomerand' ('howling and wailing')[3] is coupled with a grotesque but almost tangible description of the body:

Bare was the body and blak to the bone
Al biclagged in clay uncomly cladde. (ll. 105–6)

[The body was naked and completely dark black / Clotted with earth, foully covered.]

Emphasis is placed on the materiality of the appearance, gruesome in detail, thus effecting fear and repulsion in the audience, urging dread of eternal damnation and thus inducing a desire to do penance. Yet the first two components of the description are purely physical: one is the body that does not stir when Gawain pulls his sword ('the body bides'; 'the corpse stands still', l. 122), and the other is the voice:

hit stemered, hit stonayde, hit stode as a stone,
hit marred, hit memered, hit mused for madde. (ll. 109–10)

[it stammered, it was stunned, stood as a stone, / it grieved, it murmured, it groaned as a mad person.]

The punishment endured by Guenevere's mother is understandably proportionate to her sin (identifiable as luxury, given the gruesome tortures of the body), thus leading to the ugly decay of the body and the torment of the soul within. It forewarns Guenevere and the audience of the penalty in store for those guilty of the same sin, but it also draws attention to the raw realities of death and its imminence in medieval experience, in typically medieval *memento mori* fashion. As this voice – and the corpse from which it speaks – requests Masses and almsgiving to improve its state, the soul of Guenevere's mother is identified as languishing in purgatory; souls in hell cannot benefit from the suffrage of the living. It is noteworthy, however, that, in the wake of A. C. Spearing's influential reading of the poem as a diptych which speaks to the medieval audience of ways to bring together life and death,[4] the most recent editor of the text, Thomas Hahn, observes:

> [...] in both its halves, *Awntyrs* presents a view of social and spiritual interdependency that reflects common medieval notions of society as a unified political and sacred body. *Awntyrs* assumes, and gives vital expression to, a sense of corporate religiosity, in which the living and the dead are directly in touch with each other, so that those in heaven, on earth, and in hell (or limbo) act together in securing their mutual welfare.[5]

The unity and fluidity of the boundaries between the living and the dead that Spearing and Hahn mention seem to draw even more attention to the liminal space inhabited not only by the ghost, but also by her daughter Guenevere. The ghost does not identify itself immediately, and the poem's author does not even note her gender straight away. As Laura Haught insightfully notes, the ghost is identified first as a woman, then as a former queen, by her own words about status; thus, 'in death, the ghost is not only property-less, she is also kinless and community-less'.[6] The ghost is certainly not identified by Guenevere, nor is it forthcoming in naming Guenevere as its daughter. Indeed, this lack of clarity directs attention away from the association of the two women, suspending the moment and the characters in some form of time loop where kinship associations do not function in expected ways. In other words, the incident or *awntyr* points to the space and timeframe of the encounter being liminal, and so outside the usual cause-and-effect rationale of normal daylight experience.

Gendered liminality in *The Awntyrs off Arthur*

Guenevere, too, is outside the hunt, separated from the adventures by a storm, and excluded from the world of championship that Arthur's knights inhabit. Her association with Gawain, the pinnacle of chivalry, points to 'courtliness' as Guenevere is thus protected from the violent pursuits of hunting. The situation also reveals that chivalry and perhaps courtesy too are about to be tested through the most representative figures of both genders, Guenevere and Gawain. Arthur, therefore, may not be the easily identifiable protagonist of the *awntyrs*, but he is certainly the one whose chivalric values are recognizable through his best knight and his queen. The audience could imagine that Gawain alone can display the necessary detachment to mention the raw realities of chivalry to the ghost while remaining fearless in the face of whatever the ghost might reveal, while Guenevere's presence in the episode brings a nuance of the familiar and the everyday associated with religious practices surrounding death and the departed.

In addressing the ghost, Gawain does not merely talk about his knightly way of life, but also asks for an insight into the future – in a scene that, to my knowledge, has no equivalent in any other known Arthurian romance. Gawain's question is couched in terms relating to the material world of chivalry and its rewards rather than the ideals of honour and courtesy to which it aspires:

> How shall we fare, quod the freke, that fonden to fight,
> And thus defoulen the folke on fele kings londes,
> And riches over reymes withouten eny right,
> Wynnen worship in werre thorgh wightnesse of hondes? (ll. 261–4)

In this text, Gawain acknowledges violence as the foundation of knightly enterprise, aligning his presentation of the lived experience of knighthood with late medieval perceptions and representations of knightly violence.[7] None of the idealism so frequently encountered in romances is present here, nor does Gawain display any enthusiasm for or defence of the knightly way of life that he describes. Indeed, this is a unique moment of piercing insight into the nature and reality of medieval chivalry, and, more specifically, Arthurian chivalry as explored in the Middle English romances. Gawain includes himself in the group of those who 'defoulen the folke on fele on kings londes', pointing to the practice and showing how his fellow knights are not concerned about those that they defeat in battle, the poor or any of the ideals of knighthood so often rehearsed in the romances and chivalric treatises.[8] It seems that Gawain is more anxious to gain an insight into the fate of knights after death; his question is justified by the logic of the plot. The dialogue with the ghost thus brings together both genders in their concern with salvation. It could be argued that Gawain's words anticipate the actions described in the second part of the poem, where he fights Galeron over lands to which Gawain himself is not entitled by right.

Given the openness of his initial question to the ghost, however, Gawain's reaction to the ghost's reply is surprisingly muted. The ghost's warning is troubling: it presages Arthur's downfall, brought about by someone within his household. At this point, the poem's audience faces a striking change of tone, which requires some recalibration of response. There is a visible gap between Guenevere's and Gawain's concerns, which are presented along gender lines. Guenevere wants to find out how to alleviate the anguish that her mother is suffering beyond death and learns about the role of almsgiving and Masses in the economy of salvation. Gawain's question, however, follows the male-centred interests of Arthurian chivalry, and the answer that he receives switches the register of the poem from religious duty to political reality. Gawain is forewarned, in the manner of fortune-telling, of the political collapse of Arthur's reign at the hand of one within the king's circle. On the personal front, the ghost refers to salvation within the ritualized performance of penance and obtaining forgiveness, while on the general front it ignores all potential salvation or opportunities to remedy the situation, only giving out a grim forewarning of future disaster.

The religious dimension of the encounter may, at first sight, appear to temper the violence of the otherwise male-dominated adventure of the poem's second part. The message delivered by the ghost lends the romance an air of prophetic message. The ghost predicts the end of Arthur's reign with an abundance of heraldic (material) detail that surprises the reader:

> Sir Arthur the honest, avenant and able [honourable, gracious and powerful]
> He shal be wounded, iwys [indeed] – wothely [lethally], I wene.
> And al the rial rowte [royal company] of the Rounde Table,
> Thei shullen dye on a day, the doughty [brave ones] bydene [together],
> Suppriset [overcome] with a suget [subject]: he beris hit in sable [black coat of arms],
> With a sauter engreled [cross with a notched edge] of silver full shene [bright].
> He beris hit of sable, sothely to say (ll. 302–8)

There does not seem to be any doubt over how the identity of the usurper might be revealed: the heraldic device is described in enough detail to suggest a particular individual. The language employed goes beyond the coded nature of political prophecy, where ambiguity allows room for interpretation; here there is an aura of both mystery and openness that puzzles the receiving audience within the poem and outside it.

It is all the more surprising, therefore, that Arthur and his court do not take heed of the warning, nor ponder the words, at least to the extent that Gawain's account of his encounter with the Green Knight in the eponymous poem (discussed in the following pages) warrants pause and reflection on the part of the Arthurian court. In *Awntyrs*, there is no such moment of acknowledgement of the political nature of the warning, nor is there any recognition of the fact that the ghost claimed to be none other than Guenevere's own mother. Guenevere's experience is relegated to the margins of chivalric existence encounter, showing how her own status might be high as a queen, but remains marginal as a woman: she is part of but always outside the world of the fellowship and chivalric adventure. Her religious duty is restricted to looking after the fate of her mother's soul; thus, the mother–daughter pair is relegated to the margins of male society. There is no indication that Masses or prayers will be arranged to prevent what the ghost has predicted for Arthur and his knights. Guenevere at least does engage with the ghost's message and performs the requested service, though not to the letter – she forgets about almsgiving. No mention, however, is made of Arthur and his knights trying to understand or act upon the message that Gawain brings from his encounter.

The second part of *Awntyrs*: political margins

The poem's second part displays 'amnesia' in that Arthur and his court show no concern over the revelations that Gawain and Guenevere share with them, but rather unquestioningly continue their courtly life. Sir Galeron of Galloway arrives at Arthur's court with his lady during a feast. At this juncture, the rich descriptions of material culture remind the reader of the splendid complexity of both *Sir Gawain and the Green Knight* and the *Alliterative Morte Arthure*, thus pointing to the author of *Awntyrs* as an accomplished writer and fine observer of courtly life and literary decorum. Both Galeron and his lady are described in detail, almost as a pair who mirror in some way the unwitting association of Guenevere and Gawain in the ghost encounter. Galeron's affiliation and lands are listed in detail as he challenges Gawain over their governance. Galeron is

> the grettest of Galwey of greves and gyllis,
> Of Connok, of Conyngham, and also Kyle,
> Of Lomond, of Losex, of Loyan hilles. (ll. 418–20)

The rest of the poem focuses on the adjudication of territorial rights between Galeron and Gawain, bringing to the fore the *realpolitik* of Arthur's kingship in acting as a fair judge. Galeron's political position, territory control and noble status combine to present him as an honourable and worthy opponent rather than a frightening Other, in a way that does not quite fulfil the expectation that an intruder or marvel usually interrupts a courtly feast to challenge Arthur and teach the court a lesson in courtesy or prowess or both. From the point of view of liminality, therefore, Galeron is a 'familiar enemy', a recognizable potential opponent whose noble status is reassuring and whose claims can be easily settled due to his and Arthur's court's shared understanding of the values of courtesy and political compromise. The materiality of the description in this part of the poem brings about familiarity and reassurance.

By contrast, the *awntyr* of the encounter with the ghost merely puzzles Arthur's court, as it does the poem's audience, given its unusual positioning in the context of the romance genre. The anonymous author of the poem (or the one responsible for conflating two stories, if we take the view that these are two stories) seems deliberately to draw a veil of mystery over the events by introducing an 'adventure' that is alienating and alluring at the same time. Nevertheless, it does not seem entirely fortuitous that the Other in this poem is represented as both female (the ghost) and male (Galeron), yet it is only the latter that can be recognized and 'processed' or integrated into the Arthurian way of life. The ghost signals the marginality of female experience to the fellowship, yet also points to its vital role in performing the all-important rituals that ensure the salvation of the soul. The male intruder confirms that knighthood is alive and well, and Arthur's political society can carry on with its practices for as long as it is allowed to endure.

Class boundaries: *Sir Gawain and the Carle of Carlisle*

Another text in which materiality plays a role in the encounter with the Other is the less sophisticated, and lesser known, popular romance *Sir Gawain and the Carle of Carlisle*. In this text, an outsider, in appearance a fearsome Other, is brought into the fold of the Arthurian fellowship. Although this romance survives in only one manuscript,[9] it contains elements that would have been familiar to audiences of vernacular Arthurian romance: the chastity test, the uncouth opponent who turns out to be courteous and knightly, the happy ending, here the wedding of Gawain to a beautiful young lady. The strength of the Arthurian tradition in Middle English is evident in this text through numerous intertextual references, such as the list of names of Arthurian knights at the beginning of the story (ll. 34–90) and later the traditional test of Gawain's virtue through temptation by a married lady at the instigation of her own husband (ll. 445–80); the latter is reminiscent of the better-known romance *Sir Gawain and the Green Knight*.

   The plot of *Sir Gawain and the Carle of Carlisle* is relatively uncompli-
cated: the adventure occurs after a preamble consisting of a royal hunt in
the forest, after which Gawain, Kay and Bishop Baldwyn (protagonists
of the other popular Gawain romance, the *Avowing of Arthur*) decide to
lodge with the Carl of Carlisle, despite being forewarned of the Carl's
bad reputation as an anti-chivalric champion. However, the challenges
presented by the Carl to Gawain and his fellow knights are, in typical
fashion, only designed to show how even the best knights at Arthur's
court can behave in less than courteous ways. The reactions that Kay
and Baldwyn display in the test might be justified by the 'Otherness'
of the Carl; he is preceded by his reputation and his whole character is
defined both through his appearance and the strange, liminal space that
he creates around himself by entertaining wild beasts in his company:

> Then the lyon began to lour
>   And glowyd as a glede,
> The ber to ramy, the boole to groun,
> The bor he whett his toskos soun
>   Fast and that good spede.
>
> The Carle the knyghttus can beholde,
> Wytt a stout vesage and a bolde.
>   He semyd a dredfull man:
> Wytt chekus longe and vesage brade;
> Cambur nose and all ful made;
>   Betwyne his browus a large spane;
> Hys moghth moche, his berd graye;
> Over his brest his lockus lay
>   As brod as anny fane;
> Betwen his schuldors, whos ryght can rede,
> He was two tayllors yardus a brede.
>   Syr Key merveld gretly than.[10]

Such a man can only inspire dread, especially when his outlandish
ways are matched by eating and drinking habits on a par with his large
physical stature; the description of his table manners is reminiscent
of Dame Ragnelle of the other popular romance, *The Wedding of Sir
Gawain and Dame Ragnelle*, not least in that he displays a gargantuan
appetite (ll. 290–7).
   The Carl tests all three knights by placing his foal in the same shed
as their war horses. Kay and Baldwyn fail to display courtesy and put
the foal outside because they do not deem it sufficiently noble to
share the shed with their own horses (ll. 300–30). Gawain, the para-
gon of good manners, treats the foal well, showing that his practice

of chivalry and courtesy is not superficial, but extends across all social strata. The Carl's courtesy test indicates that he is more subtle and sophisticated than Arthur's knights give him credit for, despite his bad reputation. The development of the plot also suggests there is more to the tests than merely establishing superiority in courtesy and proving the noble status that the Carl deserves; in Sean Pollack's words:

> [the poem] remains notable for its treatment of identity and its connection to sovereignty. Borders and boundaries constitute the permeable limits and meanings of social, political, and cultural identity. [...] like *Sir Gawain and the Green Knight*, [it] advocates the crossing of borders as a necessity for the understanding of identities.[11]

In other words, the poem highlights the processes by which a complex personal, social and political identity can be shaped, then revealed and ultimately recognized within the parameters that a late medieval audience would be familiar with. By the end of the story Gawain has shown obedience to his host, the Carl, when asked to sleep in the same bed as the Carl's wife, and has been rewarded with sexual favours by the Carl's daughter. Gawain then marries the young lady, who is said to be as accomplished as any of the ladies at Arthur's court. In the logic of the plot, the Carl behaves in a manner suited to a vassal in any romance: he tests the noble guest and, finding him above reproach, offers his own daughter as a reward, thus securing a profitable alliance for both parties. At this point, on a personal as well as political level, the story has achieved its aims, integrating the Carl into the Arthurian 'fold' as a worthy knight and confirming that this alliance with someone who controls territories at the borders of Arthur's kingdom is prudent and mutually beneficial. Yet the Carl's final offer of courtesy is surprising. The economy of the plot does not indicate at any point that generosity in the area of church building or almsgiving is required in order to further confirm the Carl's access to nobility:

> A ryche abbey the Carle gan make
> To synge and rede for Goddis sake
>   In wurschip of Oure Lady.
> In the towne of mery Carelyle
> He lete hit bylde strange and wele;
>   Hit is a byschoppis see.
>
> And theryn monkys gray
> To rede and synge tille domysday,
>   As men tolde hit me,
> For the men that he had slayne, iwis. (ll. 654–63)

The reparation element – penance for the 'men that he had slayne' – as well as the material side of the Carl's generosity (spending for a good cause; leaving a visible monument in the locality) point to the Carl's entrance into Arthur's society as an event celebrating his sense of responsibility for the community that he leads and should now protect, rather than oppress, as he had previously done. In other words, the foundation of a Cistercian abbey in 'mery Carelyle' thus marks the Carl's official gesture of entering Arthurian political society by acting as a noble and responsible leader of his community, and looking after the moral and spiritual welfare of his subjects.

As a sort of 'contest for nobility' story, *Sir Gawain and the Carle of Carlisle* shows that the Carl needs not be seen as the Other, a threat from the borders of Arthur's kingdom, but rather as a reminder that the boundaries of Arthur's kingdom, and of Round Table fellowship (real and virtual) are forever drawn and redrawn, allowing entrance into the ranks of knighthood to those who display a shared understanding of the individual and group values entertained by Arthur's knights.

The Other in *Sir Gawain and the Green Knight*

No discussion of the role played by the Other within a rich description of material culture in a liminal encounter can ignore the masterpiece of Middle English Arthurian romance in verse, *Sir Gawain and the Green Knight*. A poem quintessentially concerned with the encounter with a liminal figure, *Sir Gawain* presents the testing of Gawain within a framework designed to inspire (courtly) debate over the conflict of duty and the values placed at the centre of Arthurian chivalry against a detailed landscape of courtly life in late fourteenth-century England. In *Sir Gawain*, the audience witnesses a carefully orchestrated encounter with the Other in the person of the Green Knight, who interrupts Arthur's courtly Christmas and New Year celebrations by proposing a deadly game of chopping heads. The Green Knight might be presumed to be an uncivilized intruder, but the challenges that he poses to the Arthurian fellowship, and to Gawain as its representative, display a refined command of courtly manners and knowledge of chivalric duties. He shocks through his large stature and unusual clothing, horse, choice of weapons (rather lack thereof, since he holds a Danish axe and a branch of holly) and colour green (his body as well as his horse), but he is recognizable as a knight through his demeanour and understanding of chivalry and the importance of *trouthe*.

The materiality conveyed in the description of both the Green Knight and his (liminal) abode are relevant to the present discussion because the poem points to the same interest in combining *realpolitik* with religious responsibility as seen in the popular Gawain romances, albeit in much more sophisticated and multi-layered narrative. The 'half-cleric, half-courtly' anomymous author of the poem[12] uses religious symbols to point to the underlying spiritual test Gawain will be subjected to, quite apart from the threat to his life and the shame of breaking his *trouthe*, his initial pledged word to the Green Knight, and his subsequent exchange-of-winnings game with the lord at the castle. Material objects – Gawain's pentangle and his shield with the image of the Blessed Virgin Mary painted inside – take on symbolic value. Their presence in the poem points to fourteenth-century knightly piety, reminding the audience of the two sides of a knight's life: the inner religious life of the chivalric hero, and the social and political duties of the soldier. Similarly, Gawain's enforced piety on his journey – accompanied by the image of the Blessed Virgin Mary and God on the path of suffering – provides a contrast with his youthful exuberance at the initial feast in the first scene in the poem, when like everyone else there (and indeed the poem's audience), he is feasting his eyes on the court and its ladies (among whom Guenevere features most prominently) as well as later, while feasting at Bertilak's court, in the presence of Bertilak's lady.

In the liminal space represented by Bertilak's castle, the temptations are linked to all five senses: materiality is experienced through sight, smell, hearing, touch and taste, while the moral and spiritual nature of the challenge retains its paramount importance in the overall test of chivalry. The materiality of the story, especially the alluring delights of the descriptions and the suggestive content of Gawain's bedroom temptations, are, however, presenting another temptation – this time to the poem's audience. Through the thinly veiled mask of an encounter with a liminal figure (Bertilak or the Green Knight) in a liminal space (the castle, but even more so the Green Chapel), the poem shows that its edifying message is intended not just for Gawain or Arthur's knights, but for the reader as well. The journey of discovery follows the symmetry of bedroom and hunting scenes, inevitably drawing the audience into the web of symbolic associations between the outside actions and the inner trials of the hero. However, at no point in the story is the reader allowed to forget the wealth of courtly detail, be it in costume, language, gestures or actions. Gawain's refusal to join his host on the hunting expeditions would be surprising for audiences familiar with aristocratic pursuits, who would recognize the importance of physical exercise for the knight. In chivalric treatises such as that of Ramon Lull, it is clearly stated that 'the knight should exercise his body continually – by hunting wild beasts – the hart, the boar and the wolf'.[13] Gawain's sojourn in bed, enforced by his host, instead of being allowed to join the hunt during his stay at Bertilak's castle might suggest a moment of pause during which Gawain can ponder impending death or at least the challenge of his demise promised by the game that he willingly entered into with the Green Knight a year before. It has also been argued that this might suggest a neglect of duty, a spiritual state of apathy, or even a sign of the sin of sloth.[14] That being said, the peerless nobility of the hero hardly ever allows the reader to consider him quite so harshly – this would certainly look more like the clerical judgement than the knightly or courtly one. Through this literary journey, a medieval audience not only discovers more about the difference between the realities lived through by fourteenth-century knights and the ideals suggested by the 'cleric' side of the discourse in *Sir Gawain*, but also about the temptations that literary texts present to the mind and soul.

The Vulgate Cycle and Malory's *Le Morte Darthur*

Another type of engagement with materiality and liminality is evident in the work of the translators of the Old French Vulgate Cycle. To take a late medieval example, Henry Lovelich, London skinner and translator of the first two branches of the Vulgate, the *Estoire de Merlin* (The History of Merlin) and *Estoire del saint Graal* (The History of the Holy Grail), attaches a visibly material and concrete context to the otherwise distant past described in his sources. The plain landscapes of French romance become the vivid cityscapes of fifteenth-century London, as Roger Dalrymple, Michelle Warren and Ambra Finotello have demonstrated.[15] An emphasis on almsgiving and the foundation of religious establishments is also noticeable. In the depictions of the courtly scenes in Lovelich's *History of Merlin*, emphasis is placed on the communal and 'democratic' appeal of Arthurian ideals, while in his *History of the Holy Grail*, the spiritual level is shown to materialize in forms of religiosity connected to fifteenth-century practices.[16] Thus the alien and alienating geography of the lands described in the original *Estoire del saint Graal* – lands populated by people from far away and long ago – is rendered relevant to a fifteenth-century audience through familiar gestures and locations. The Other of prophecy and pseudo-biblical legend is thus made familiar but remains obscure, luring an audience more accustomed to romance entertainment into a story that is exotic and edifying in equal measure.

Finally, an essay dedicated to the exploration of materiality and liminality in Middle English Arthurian romance has to at least gesture towards Thomas Malory's *Le Morte Darthur*, the best example of prose romance produced in the English vernacular at the end of the period. Analyses of liminality and materiality can shed light on sensitive issues in Malory's fictional world. He reworks his French and English chronicle and romance sources to recreate the Arthurian landscape, famously assigning recognizable names in the English countryside to all the major locations of the story. In *Le Morte Darthur*, Arthur's Camelot is Winchester, Elaine's Ascolat is Guildford, Lancelot's stronghold at Joyous Garde is either Alnwick or Bamborough.[17] This process anchors his Arthurian world into the political and geographical landscape of his fifteenth-century contemporaries.[18] Liminality is also present in Malory's work, though its complex manifestations are too numerous to list or categorize here. The world beyond, be it magic or spiritual, the familiar or unfamiliar, the usually threatening outsider or female agency, are all treated by Malory in a manner that enriches our understanding of late Middle English Arthurian romance.

Notes

1. For a more detailed examination of Arthurian ideals, see Elizabeth Archibald, 'Questioning Arthurian ideals', in *The Cambridge Companion to the Arthurian Legend*, ed. Elizabeth Archibald and Ad Putter (Cambridge: Cambridge University Press, 2009), pp. 139–53; and Elizabeth Archibald, 'Malory's ideal of fellowship', *Review of English Studies* n.s. 43, 171 (1992), 311–28.
2. These are: Oxford, Bodleian Library, MS Douce 324; London, Lambeth Palace Library, MS 491.B; Lincoln, Cathedral Library, MS 91 (the Lincoln 'Thornton manuscript'); and Princeton, New Jersey, Ireland Blackburn MS.
3. *The Awntyrs off Arthur*, l. 86, in *Sir Gawain: Eleven Romances and Tales*, ed. Thomas Hahn (Kalamazoo, MI: Medieval Institute Publications, 1995). All further references are to this edition and given parenthetically in the text.
4. A. C. Spearing, '*The Awntyrs off Arthure*' in *The Alliterative Tradition in the Fourteenth Century*, eds Bernard S. Levy and Paul E. Szarmach (Kent, OH: Kent State University Press, 1981), pp. 183–202; A. C. Spearing, 'Central and Displaced Sovereignty in Three Medieval Poems', *Review of English Studies*, 33 (1982), 247–61, esp. 248–52; and A. C. Spearing, *Medieval to Renaissance in English Poetry* (Cambridge: Cambridge University Press, 1985), pp. 121–42.
5. Hahn, 'Introduction' in *Sir Gawain: Eleven Romances and Tales*, ed. Thomas Hahn (Kalamazoo, MI: Medieval Institute Publications, 1995), p. 171.
6. Leah Haught, 'Ghostly Mothers and Fated Fathers: Gender and Genre in *The Awntyrs off Arthure*', *Arthuriana* 20:1 (2010), 3–24.

7. See Richard Kaeuper, *Chivalry and Violence in Medieval Europe* (Oxford: Oxford University Press, 1999).
8. For a discussion of the relationship between Christian ideals and chivalry in medieval romance, see Raluca Radulescu, 'How Christian is Chivalry?' in *Christianity and Romance in Medieval England*, eds Rosalind Field, Phillipa Hardman and Michelle Sweeney (Cambridge: D. S. Brewer, 2010), pp. 69–83.
9. Aberystwyth, National Library of Wales, Brogyntyn 2.1 (also known as Porkington 10).
10. *Sir Gawain and the Carle of Carlisle*, ll. 237–58, in *Sir Gawain: Eleven Romances and Tales*, ed. Thomas Hahn (Kalamazoo, MI: Medieval Institute Publications, 1995). All further references are to this edition and given parenthetically in the text.
11. Sean Pollack, 'Border States: Parody, Sovereignty, and Hybrid Identity in *The Carl of Carlisle*', *Arthuriana* 19:2 (2009), 10–26 (p. 22).
12. I borrow the phrase from A. D. Putter, *Sir Gawain and the Green Knight and the French Arthurian Tradition* (Oxford: Oxford University Press, 1997), p. 210.
13. The original quotation reads: 'to hunte at hertes, at bores & other wyld bestes'. Ramon Lull, *The Book of the Ordre of Chyualry, translated and printed by William Caxton from a French version*, ed. Alfred T. P. Byles EETS OS 168 (London: Oxford University Press, 1926), p. 31.
14. This idea is explored in V. J. Scattergood, 'Sir Gawain and the Green Knight and the Sins of the Flesh', *Traditio*, 37 (1981), 347–71.
15. Roger Dalrymple, '"Evele knowen ʒe Merlyne, jn certeyne": Henry Lovelich's *Merlin*', in *Medieval Insular Romance: Translation and Innovation*, ed. Judith Weiss et al. (Cambridge: D. S. Brewer, 2000), pp. 155–67. See also Michelle R. Warren, 'Lydgate, Lovelich and London Letters', in *Lydgate Matters: Poetry and Material Culture in the Fifteenth Century*, eds Lisa H. Cooper and A. Denny-Brown (Basingstoke: Palgrave Macmillan, 2008), pp. 113–37; Michelle R. Warren, 'Translation', in *Middle English*, ed. Paul Strohm (Oxford: Oxford University Press, 2008), pp. 51–67; and Ambra Finotello, 'Three Middle English Translations of the *Estoire de Merlin*: *Of Arthur and of Merlin*, Henry Lovelich's *History of Merlin* and the Prose *Merlin*', unpublished PhD thesis, Bangor University, 2014.
16. See Chapter 3 of Raluca Radulescu, *Romance and Its Contexts in Fifteenth-century England: Politics, Piety and Penitence* (Cambridge: D. S. Brewer, 2013).
17. A classic study of Malory's method of historicizing Arthur through associations to a recognizable material landscape in late medieval England is Felicity Riddy's 'Reading for England: Arthurian Literature and the National Consciousness', *Bibliographical Bulletin of the International Arthurian Society*, 43 (1991), 314–32.
18. The most recent study that takes this view is Dorsey Armstrong and Kenneth Hodges, *Mapping Malory: Regional Identities and National Geographies in 'Le Morte Darthur'* (London and New York: Palgrave Macmillan, 2014).

3

Shifting Identities and Landscapes in *Sir Gawain and the Green Knight*

Gillian Rudd

The anonymous poem *Sir Gawain and the Green Knight* survives in only one manuscript, British Library MS Cotton Nero A.x. Normally this would indicate a text with little general appeal (contrast with the multiple manuscripts and variations of *Piers Plowman* or *Canterbury Tales*), but *Sir Gawain* has been popular with academic readers since the manuscript's rediscovery by Henry Madden in 1839 and reached a new and wider public audience with Simon Armitage's poetic translation in 2006. Prior to that, it had undergone numerous translations and editions, including being adapted for children (most recently by Michael Morpurgo in 2004) and transformed into an opera by Harrison Birtwistle in 1991. The phenomenon of its popularity has been noted by Glen Olsen in his preface to the online Cotton Nero A.x project; on his count, ninety-five editions and translations of the poem have appeared since Madden brought the manuscript to light and this number does not include editions available in several formats, such as the Norton edition, which offers the translation by Marie Borroff, or compilations such as *The Broadview Anthology of British Literature: the Medieval Period*, which uses James Winney's verse rendition which is also available as an independent, parallel-text edition of the poem. In short, *Sir Gawain and the Green Knight* has become one of the best-loved medieval texts, popular with both scholars and general readers.

Setting the scene

This achievement is all the more remarkable because the English that the poem uses is that of the North-west Midlands and as such is one further remove from contemporary English than that used by Chaucer, Langland and Malory. For many readers it is the power of

45

the plot that helps them overcome any difficulty posed by the language and it is this plot which surely accounts for much of the poem's success. It combines many elements that we now associate with the medieval world of literature: Arthurian knights, magical events, strange quests, beautiful (and seductive) women, castles, forests and, perhaps most importantly, a sense of taking place in the mythical time of romance. Yet if the time is mythical, the setting is not, or at least not consistently so. True, the action of the poem begins in Camelot and the poet refers to Logres (l. 691), which is the customary but unspecific location for Camelot in Arthurian romances, but after that the poem moves through the highly specific and very real geographical landscape of the northern Welsh borders, Anglesey and Wirral as Gawain rides out seeking the Green Chapel.[1] This geography is in keeping with the poem's North-west Midland English, but it also links this romance with a clutch of other Gawain romances which relate similar adventures to this poem and which associate Gawain with Celtic borderlands.[2] Its emphasis on setting allows the poem to explore the contrasts and connections between the human and non-human natural world, between individual identity and community ideals, and between the different codes of conduct expected or elicited by different surroundings, demonstrating that where you are may influence who you are. The different places and spaces of the poem thus offer a good place to start any exploration of the text as a whole.

The poem opens with a brief summary of how Britain acquired its name (ll. 1–35), which establishes a link between the story that follows and the history and geography of the country itself. It is a land named after Brutus, the great-grandson of Aeneas, who is referred to here as Felix Brutus, perhaps hinting that not only was Brutus happy or lucky (both possible meanings of the Latin term *felix*) to arrive on the island after a life of early misfortune, but also that Britain is fortunate in having been named after such a figure. This, the poet asserts, is a land where more marvels have occurred than in any other (ll. 23–4) and in whose long line of kings, Arthur is without doubt the noblest. The scene is set for a tale which blends the mythical world of Arthur and his knights with the actual landscape of the North-west Midlands region, and, according to some critics, the politics of Richard II's court.[3] But before moving on to the locations of the poem's action, it is worth noting that the poet tells us that the story that he is about to recount is one that he 'in toun herde' (l. 31). Phrases such as this are not uncommon in the opening lines of lais[4] and it may be that the poet is deliberately invoking the elements of enchantment, fairy other worlds (frequently Celtic), the cast of lords, knights, ladies, and deeds of love and courtly endeavour that are features of this genre. Such associations prepare us for the mixture of real and unreal that we are about to encounter as the poet introduces us to Arthur and his court during a Christmas feast in Camelot, but the passing mention of a town as a place where one hears such tales is a subtle hint that the more mundane world which we ourselves inhabit may also have some bearing on our understanding of this poem.

As already indicated, *Sir Gawain and the Green Knight* sets great store by where things happen from the start. That opening summary rehearsing how Britain was established manages to imply that it is closely linked to Troy, without actually saying so. We are reminded first of the siege of Troy, from which Aeneas fled, and then told that his kinsmen went on to settle almost the whole of the West:

> Hit watz Ennias þe athel, and his highe kynde,
> Þat siþen depreced prouinces, and patrounes bicome
> Welneʒe of al þe wele in þe west iles.[5] (ll. 5–7)

Following traditions, most of which can be traced back to Geoffrey of Monmouth's rather inventive *Historia Regum Britanniae* (History of the Kings of Britain, c.1135), the poet goes on to remind us that Romulus founded Rome and Tirius Tuscany, Langaberde gave his name to Lombardy and Felix Brutus gave his to Britain. All these lead up to Arthur's Camelot, which provides the first location of the poem. It matters less that we know who these people are (and indeed there is some question over Tirius)[6] than that we absorb the linked association of people and place. Each of these men can be regarded as heroic models who established powerful and respected civilizations and so they have reputations as leaders as well as fighters. Arthur, as the greatest king of England, is their natural inheritor, but he is also a figure who marks the shift from an epic hero, such as Aeneas or Brutus, to a chivalric one. In this poem, Arthur is famed as much for his manners as his prowess, and his court and companions reflect this: the knights are the best known ('the most kyd knightes', l. 51), the ladies the 'lovelokkest' (l. 52), and Arthur himself the 'comelokest' (l. 53). In short, Camelot is the finest court and the knights of the Round Table the most refined as well as the bravest in the land. A good feast, such as the one at the start of the poem, is not merely a matter of plentiful food, but also of dainty dishes brought in with due ceremony and served to well-dressed diners seated at elegantly dressed tables. Three stanzas of the poem are devoted to describing this scene (ll. 60–129), not because such detail is new, but because we are expected to recognize such richness as part of what Camelot is. This is the Camelot of medieval romance, familiar to the *Gawain*-poet's audience from the French tradition, which also supplied the tradition of Arthur's custom of not beginning to eat at feasts until some marvel had been recounted or some wonder occurred. We are thus plunged into a scene of celebration and confidence, but also of anticipation as we, like Camelot, are left waiting for one of the famous adventures to begin.

The Green Knight

The form that the awaited marvel takes on this occasion is that of a large green knight riding into the hall, mounted on an equally green horse, bearing in one hand an axe and in the other a holly branch. This figure resonates with associations. His greenness means he has been linked to the Celtic otherworld, to the devil, to the legendary Green Man and more generally to the natural world. Whichever association is chosen, the simple presence of this figure sets up a dichotomy between all that Arthur and his court stand for and all that this greenest of knights epitomizes. And he is green – the poet cannot stress that enough; bright green all over in fact ('oueral enker grene', l. 149). It is not just his clothing, but also his hair and even his skin that are green. One common way to read this initial confrontation is as the cosy, feasting, codified human world of Camelot being rudely reminded of the harsher, harder, unruly world of nature beyond its walls. The carefree space of Arthur's Camelot is here invaded by an other-worldly figure who is repeatedly described as not human: an 'aghlich mayster' (l. 136), whose green hue understandably evokes wonder (ll. 233–4) and leads to the conclusion that he is either phantom or fairy (l. 240) – it is worth remembering that fairies at this date are powerful tricksters far from the benign, tiny creatures that they have since become. For the most part we see this weird interloper through the eyes of Arthur's court. The voice of the poem is a little more circumspect and a little less quick to insist upon the alien nature of this green knight, declaring 'Half etayn in erde I hope [believe] that he were' (l. 41). The hesitancy that the word 'hope' allows over whether or not the Green Knight is literally half-giant is further underlined in the next line which asserts the humanity of this figure: 'Bot man most I algate mynne him to bene' ('But at any rate I judge him to be the biggest man', l. 141). The alliteration of 'man' and 'most' stresses that however unusually powerful or tall ('most' covers both meanings) he may be, this figure is yet surely that of a man.

The belief and emotive reaction of 'hope' is balanced by the more rational verb of judgement 'mynne' in a movement of response and counter-response that becomes a principle of the whole poem. Even the outcome of the challenge and Gawain's quest is subjected to a series of interpretations that leaves the reader unsure of whether or not Gawain can be said to have succeeded or lost.

But we are leap-frogging ahead, much as one season overlaps another at the start of the poem's second fitt. We should return to this massive green figure on his green steed brusquely demanding to speak with the leader of the company before declaring his purpose: to challenge this court, so renowned for being made up of the bravest and most courteous knights in the land, to a simple game. The challenge is explicitly not one of combat – hence the lack of weapon or shield – but an exchange of blows, using the axe he carries. Moreover, it is to take place in the hall itself, then and there in fact, as the Green Knight offers his opponent the first blow, which he will accept unarmed and without defence. This is a far cry from the challenges and quests that require the knights to travel away from the court, or at least step outside to a tournament ground. As such it is also a contrast to the set-piece tournaments and jousting, the 'rych reuel oryȝt and rechles merþes' which Arthur's court have been spending their time playing, and which helped set the scene during that initial description of Camelot (ll. 40–3). Whatever this Green Knight is, he is bringing his challenge right to the heart of chivalry, testing it at its core not just by his appearance, but also through displacing the weapons of courtly entertainment, the lance and the sword, with an implement of either battle or woodmanship (the axe). The image created here is complex and intriguing as everything about this Green Knight resonates with the world outside the man-made walls of Camelot. Not only are green skin, hair and beard most unnatural for a human, but they are also details unique to this poem, marking a difference between the Green Knight of this story and green knights found in other romances, such as Malory's *Tale of Sir Gareth*. In this latter, Gareth spends some time fighting a series of coloured knights including a knight who is designated 'green' because that is the colour of his livery and the drapes that cover his horse, not because rider and horse alike possess green skin, hair, hide and mane, as is the case for our poem's mysterious interlopers.

While this saturating green hints at fairy or devilish associations,[7] the decoration on the saddlecloth offers other connections. Made of green silk with gold threads, it is embroidered with birds and butterflies (l. 166) and while the gold thread and green beadwork indicate how rich the decoration is, the subject matter suggests that this strange figure may also be regarded as a knight of Nature. Although it is inaccurate and over-simple to identify this figure as the Green Man of legend, however tempting such identification may be,[8] the poem is nevertheless inviting us to make some kind of connection between this Green Knight and the natural world. The connection is only enhanced by the fact that as well as carrying an axe he also carries a holly branch, which, as the poem reminds us, seems greenest when the woods are bare (l. 207). It is almost as if this one figure embodies everything that Camelot is not: he is solo rather than part of a company; he is unknown rather than named; and his affiliations seem to be with the worlds of magic and nature rather than those of courtly behaviour, feasting and games that occupy Camelot as they keep the harsh realities of winter at bay.

Read in these terms, it becomes possible to regard *Sir Gawain and the Green Knight* as a text which debunks human centrality through the figure of the giant green knight who rides into Arthur's court unannounced, issues a beheading challenge and then defies all expectations by not being killed when his head is sliced from his body. This apparent disregard for the laws of nature is in fact revealed as being thoroughly in tune with the natural cycle of the year, as the second fitt of the poem picks up on the end of the first and slightly recasts it to remind us that spring follows winter, life shoots up from apparently dead wood and the natural processes begin anew. But new beginnings are not the same as repeated actions. The flowers that spring up after winter are not the exact same flowers that died the previous year; renewal involves change, a point made by one of the most frequently quoted lines in the poem: 'A ȝere ȝernes ful ȝerne and ȝeldez neuer lyke' ('A year passes very quickly and never produces the same thing', l. 497). The line is both threat and promise as it points out that the time will quickly elapse before Gawain must stand a blow in his turn but with potentially very different consequences. As Gawain himself is to put it with wry humour later, he cannot restore his head if it is struck off onto the stones: 'þaȝ my heded falle on þe stonez / I con not his restore' (ll. 2282–3). Given the regenerative power of the Green Knight and this later rueful admission by Gawain that mere humans have no such power, it is not difficult to see why the poem has been read as challenging human-centred and Christian values by reminding its readers of other versions of power and other value systems. The view that the poem champions a pro-natural and pre-Christian pagan world has proved repeatedly popular since its earliest suggestions in the work of Jessie Weston and E. K. Chambers and further articulation by John Spiers in 1947.[9] Despite Brewer's best attempts, this way of reading the Green Knight has been given new impetus by the recent rise of ecocriticism. Now, however, the Knight is a more complex figure, as the very concept of the natural world being embodied in a human knight raises difficulties for a critical school invested in highlighting the fraught relations between humans and nature, and which often wishes to find hints in literature as to how our current imbalance between humans and the rest of the world could be righted.

Reading Green

A recent foray into this now burgeoning area of green studies seeks to present Gawain and the Green Knight/Bertilak as representing two ways that humans relate to the natural world. Gawain's attitude is epitomized as 'militaristic dominance' where Bertilak's is regarded as stewardship.[10] Bertilak's attitude is preferred, but it is not an ideal-ized relation in which humans, animals and the vegetative world live in perfect harmony, free from predation or consumerism of any kind; such a reading would be impossible, given how much of the text is given up to detailed descriptions of Bertilak and his hunting. Rather readings of this kind suggest that the danger Arthur and his court run is in not accepting their responsibility as part of a cycle which requires risk as well as feasting, and serious endeavour as well as courtly game – a cycle that requires them to accept responsibility for the good government of their resources, not the unthinking exploita-tion of them. In this context, the fact that the Green Knight carries his challenge right into Camelot and furthermore enacts the first part of the beheading game right there serves to highlight both the need for humans to understand our relations to the rest of the world and our habit of ducking the demands and consequences of such relations. That paradox is revealed by the poem to be integral to what it means to be human. Like Gawain, we are flawed, simultaneously wishing to live up to high ideals and yet eager to employ measures that will save us from having to accept the apparently inevitable consequences of those ideals. For Gawain that conflict is presented in the form of a girdle which he can easily refuse to accept as a love-token, but can-not turn down as a life-preserver. His indignation when it is revealed that his opponent not only knows of the girdle and suggested the attempted seductions that accompanied it, but also regards it as an understandable and easily forgivable failing to have decided to save one's life, only highlights the conflicts and cross-currents that make up our human character. That in turn contributes to the sense of unresolved questions with which the poem ends: can we say Gawain succeeded in his quest? Would he have lost his head without the girdle, or escaped totally unharmed, without even a nick in the neck? Are the ideals of courtly life endorsed or revealed as deeply flawed? For some, such lack of resolution is a productive lack of closure, which echoes the yearly cycle that gives the tale its framework, but for others the lack of closure creates an echoing hollow which reveals a poet saddened by the sham of courtly conduct, which has been found wanting, despite all its ornate display and intricate code.[11]

In this light, the Green Knight's entrance is not simply a disruptive, yet desired, result of the gathering in Camelot. His challenge goes beyond a game and becomes a trial which both threatens and justifies Arthur's court by testing not only its ability to live up to its reputation, but its ability to incorporate and adjust to the changes such a challenge must bring. If the court is the social, decorous world, then the Green Knight may well be the natural world, but crucially he is also the human face of that world, the natural world as we like to think of it and as we create and manage it. It thus speaks volumes that Camelot's reaction to their imposing visitor is first fear, then to cut off its head, then fear again as that head is retrieved and speaks before riding back to the unknown, at which point Camelot reverts to feasting and laughter. The poem accepts this state of affairs, commenting that although the company initially lacked topics of conversation when they first went to eat, now they have more than enough to talk about: 'Thaȝ hym wordez were wane when þay to sete wenten, / Now are þay stoken of sturne werk, staf-ful her hond' (ll. 493–94). There is a slight menace in these words as the term 'sturne werk' indicates difficult and serious matters, while the alliterating 'stoken' and 'staf-ful' imply an almost vengeful, crammed, handful; but such connotations are not dwelt upon, allowing us readers to relax and enjoy ourselves, like Arthur and his court, knowing we have a good story to entertain us whose deeper implications we may choose to ignore.

Gawain: knight errant or courtly guest?

It is only Gawain who has his hands full, leaving the rest of the court carefree, if a little sad at his departure just short of a year later. Here, close to the beginning of the second fitt, we again see Arthur's court with its knights and ladies feasting and laughing. There are, though, some differences; it is not a simple replication of the previous year, not least because this time rather than waiting for some adventure to come to them before they eat, they feast before sending Gawain out on adventure on their behalf. In an opposite but not quite equal motion, Gawain takes up and reverses the position of the Green Knight: where that Knight was the unknown entering the known, Gawain is the known entering the unknown. This opposite but not quite equal paralleling is irresistible, made all the more so as we see Gawain being armed. Where the Green Knight was dressed in green, Gawain is dressed in gold; where the Knight was spurless, Gawain displays his gold spurs with pride (l. 587); like the Knight's, though, Gawain's clothes are trimmed with ermine, his horse decked in as much splendour as he and his helmet bands studded with gems (l. 599). Significantly, the embroidery decorating Gawain's silk also features birds, but these are specifically parrots and turtledoves, rather than the generic 'bryddes' of the Green Knight, and instead of flowers he has love knots. This is Nature rendered as symbol and the preference of the court for symbol over object is epitomized by Gawain's shield which features on the outside a pentangle, the sign of fidelity invented by Solomon, and on the inside an image of the Virgin Mary. The meaning of the pentangle is explained at some length in the poem,[12] but the core point is that each aspect of fidelity is linked with the others, just as the points of the pentangle are interwoven: fail in one, fail in all. The poet asserts that the device is known as the 'endeles knot'(l. 630) but it appears that this is his own term, invented doubtless to foreshadow the girdle Gawain receives later in the poem and *unknots* in a rage of shame and frustration at the end of his second encounter with the Green Knight (l. 2376).

The arming and departure of Gawain is a set-piece at the end of which Gawain claps his spurs to his steed and gallops away. The whole is highly performative and as such not only recalls the Green Knight's magnificent performance the year before, but also demonstrates how much of our identity is socially constructed and bestowed upon us. Camelot has made Gawain into the epitome of knightly valour, devoted to Mary and Christ, setting out alone to fulfil his promise and lamented (rather prematurely as it turns out) as a great loss, and as a leader and nobleman. This version of Gawain prevails as he rides through Wales and the Wirral, now almost a pilgrim figure undertaking a quest in God's name ('on Godez halve', l. 692) through lands and people that are themselves as good as godless (ll. 701–2). It is fitting, then, that he cries out to Mary to find him some shelter where he might hear Mass on Christmas Eve and no surprise that the next thing he knows he finds himself looking at a castle which is an answer to a prayer. Gawain has become the knight that Camelot has made him; having begun the poem simply as Arthur's nephew and, by his own account, the least of the knights in Arthur's house (ll. 354–6), he arrives at this unknown castle as a knight errant, and is greeted as such by the gatekeeper and so gains entrance.

Once inside the castle gates, Gawain is first divested of his mail and clothes and then dressed in rich robes before being given plenty of good food. These actions are both cordial and reverse the feasting and arming scene enacted by Camelot to mark Gawain's departure, but there is more to it than simple hospitality to a travel-worn stranger. As he is welcomed into the castle, Gawain undergoes a transformation in two stages. We have just read of him journeying alone across winter wastes, sleeping outside in his armour (l. 729), braving hardships alone and defeating foes too numerous to mention (l. 719). That Gawain was a man of arms, 'duȝty and dryȝe' (l. 724) and he retains something of that doughty persona as he enters the second castle of the poem, being greeted with honour and respect by men of rank (knights and squires) as well as servants. He hands his helmet, sword and shield to servants, but is still in full armour as he enters the hall (l. 831), thus presenting himself as a man of combat. Here he is welcomed by the lord of the castle and as we see Gawain take in this man's appearance we may also detect the beginning of a further transformation from weary knight errant into courtly guest (ll. 860–74).[13] The terms Gawain uses as he surveys his host progress rapidly from the neutral 'gome' (l. 842) through 'bolde burne' (l. 843) to 'hoge hathel' (l. 844) before finally arriving at the conclusion that such a man is well fitted to be the leader of a noble company. We are seeing this lord through Gawain's eyes and, with such a man as this before him, there is no place and no need (or perhaps no hope) for Gawain to retain the image of lone champion knight with which he entered Hautdesert. The role of hardened warrior is so evidently fulfilled by his host that Gawain cannot be similar, and so when he chooses a robe from those offered to him (l. 864), he complies with a second transformation and becomes the epitome of a different kind of knight – the consummate courtly man of words, a man of 'courtesie'.

It soon becomes apparent that in taking up this role Gawain has fulfilled the identity by which he is known to this company. He may not know this castle, but its inhabitants know him by reputation as the man whose fame exceeds all others (l. 914), but not, it swiftly transpires, for deeds of arms or bravery, nor even as one of Arthur's knights, but for his manners and unrivalled skill in 'luf-talkyng' (l. 927). This is not an attribute of Gawain we have seen before in this poem, but shortly after he has been credited with it we see

Gawain being approached by the lady of the castle and her attendant women. He has become an object worthy of view, it seems,
and through this observation his new persona is confirmed. Courtly,
charming, the epitome of fine manners, this Gawain will stay flirting
with the ladies at home while the lord and his men go hunting. It is
tempting to read this as a feminized Gawain, but it is important to
remember that such accomplishments as dancing, good conversation
and indeed flirting were proper attributes for the kind of courtly
knight that we find depicted in Chaucer's *Book of the Duchess*, for
example, and indeed the relevance of the courtly lyric tradition
for *Sir Gawain* has been demonstrated by William Hodapp.[14] With
Gawain thus re-clothed and recast, the poet goes on to treat us to a
perfectly twinned and intertwined depiction of these two very different aspects of knighthood as the host, Bertilak, is seen outside the
castle engaged in hunts which demand physical skill and stamina,
while Gawain is caught up in a game of words and manners with
Bertilak's lady in the castle.

Parallel worlds: courts, hunts and the Green Chapel

The three hunts and three seduction attempts have been frequently
paralleled[15] and in general Hautdesert has been presented as a mir-
ror-image of Camelot in which the boyish King Arthur is reflected
in the mature, manly Bertilak whose energetic hunts, described in
such detail, present a marked contrast to the jousts and tournaments
fleetingly mentioned as part of Arthur's Christmas entertainments. In
fact, Hautdesert is less a reflection of Camelot than an enlargement
of it: everything is bigger, louder and more vigorous. It is becoming apparent that the poem as a whole operates around a system of
reflections which are not direct equivalents. Instead, the process is
more organic as each action leads not to an opposite and equal reaction but to response and change. We have already seen the beginning
of this process as Gawain rode out from Camelot and we find a
similar substitution at work when Gawain arrives at Hautdesert and
we see the unexpected intrusion of the Green Knight into Camelot
become Gawain's courteous request for entry to Hautdesert. Where
the Green Knight 'hales in at þe halle dor an aghlich mayster'
(l. 136), Gawain hails and is greeted by a pleasant porter who answers
his call and then takes a message inside before finally opening the
gates (ll. 807–14). Significantly this follows two stanzas describing the
castle and its grounds, moat and drawbridge – there is no possibility
of just riding into the main hall of this castle, as appears to be the

case with Camelot. We are clearly invited to compare the two courts but, while paralleled, they are not direct contrasts of each other and, as a result, the poem also prevents us from creating an easy binary opposition between the human, civilized realm of the court and the animal, unregulated world of the woods. The intertwined relation-ship between human and non-human is most readily seen in the way hunting scenes parallel the seduction scenes. Although it may appear that we are being presented with a marked contrast between out-door pursuits and indoor entertainments, and we may even wish to read this third fitt of the poem as a presentation of the ways that the (presumed) opposing forces of nature and civilization may be kept in balance, such simple opposition breaks down under further scrutiny. As is well established, the hunted animals do not all have the same kind of relation to humans: the stag and boar are not simply noble, wild beasts who also have heraldic association, they are also animals deliberately bred and encouraged in land that is tended in order to provide suitable environments for them. The fox, on the other hand, is outside such care: a creature designated as 'vermin', his role is solely to be eradicated. Yet, as the narrative makes clear, his attributes are the most useful and necessary of the animals. It is his wit and wile that Gawain needs to get him out of a tight spot with his host's wife and it is the purely instinctual, animal response of wanting to save one's own life that is cited as an acceptable excuse for breaking the rules of both the exchange-of-winnings game and the code of honour of the exchange of blows during the final dénouement at the Green Chapel.

The meeting of Gawain and the Green Knight at the Green Chapel is the moment the poem has been building towards and yet so many shifts and substitutions have occurred before we get there that it should come as no surprise when the long-awaited encoun-ter is not quite what we were led to expect. In a now recognizable principle of the poem, what was supposed to be a straightforward tit-for-tat exchange of one blow for another segues into a series of feints which balance not just the original single swing of the axe in fitt 1 but the three days of exchange of winnings of fitt 3. Once again, the expected simple mirroring has become an amplification. Once again an expected direct exchange of equivalents is transmuted into a process of response and change. This fact is explicitly mentioned by the Green Knight, who remarks, 'Here are no renkes vs to rydde, rele as vus likez' (l. 2246). With no lords to part them, they may act as they please, an observation which invites some kind of covert re-writing of the rules of engagement. In fact, it soon transpires that such re-writing has already occurred as the full-strength, head-severing blow delivered by Gawain is transmuted into two feints and a mere nick in the neck given by the Knight. This odd and unequal return of blows is then explained not as fulfilling the original agreement made in Arthur's court, but as a response to the three exchanges of winnings enacted in Hautdesert. The Green Knight is revealed as Bertilak, lord of Hautdesert, transformed by Morgan le Fay and sent to Camelot to scare Guinevere to death. The green girdle, so carefully kept back and hidden from the exchange of winnings, is now worn openly by Gawain and recognized by Bertilak as woven by his wife. However, because Gawain accepted it as a charm to save his life, it no longer matters that he failed to declare it as a winning. Just at the point when we might expect all to be resolved, nothing is matching up now as both Gawain and the reader are forced to re-assess all the events of the poem in the light of the new information the now fully conflated figure of Bertilak/Green Knight presents. Gawain's response is to embark on a series of further redefinitions of the girdle. Having accepted it not as love-token but as life-preserver, he is quick to redefine it again first as a sign of man's fragility and later as a badge of personal failure as he struggles to comprehend the meaning of his own quest story.

The reader, too, may be struggling between regarding Gawain as a brave but mortal and so flawed man who has fulfilled his quest and been rewarded with his life, or as a man unable to accept his own human frailty who returns to Camelot chastened and not much the wiser. We are not helped by the laughter that greets his return – is this relief and delight at the return of a hero, or merriment at the sight of a young knight persisting in taking himself too seriously? The poem relentlessly refuses to come to rest on any single version of events and so it is fitting that the final stanza returns us to a reprise of the first, which is not quite a simple repetition. Once again we are referred to the list of heroes who have defined our country and the siege of Troy, but now, even with the laughter of Camelot ringing in our ears, we are also reminded of Christ and thus offered a further way to read Gawain as we sit back and review the text in our minds. The poem, like the year, has turned full circle and, as foretold in line 499, the beginning has not quite matched the end. Nevertheless, this is the natural process of life unfolding and in this case the natural process of narrative as well, which reaches an end that can also be a new beginning, whether that new beginning is taken in terms of religious understanding, personal endeavour, cycle of life or simply a good story told well.

Notes

1. The poet's level of detail has allowed many scholars to match actual landscape to that described in the poem. See Ralph Elliott, *The Gawain Country* (Leeds: Leeds Texts and Monographs ns 8, 1984) and 'Landscape and Geography' in *A Companion to the Gawain-Poet*, ed. Derek Brewer and Jonathan Gibson, Arthurian Studies XXXVIII (Cambridge: D. S. Brewer, 1997), pp. 105–118. For suggestions that Bertilak's castle and grounds at Hautdesert may be based upon actual castles, see Michael Thompson, 'The Green Knight's castle', in *Studies in Medieval History Presented to R. Allen Brown*, eds C. Harper-Bill, C. Holdsworth and J. L. Nelson (Woodbridge, 1989), pp.317–26 and 'Castles' in Brewer and Gibson, pp.119–30.

2. See Thomas Hahn (ed.), *Sir Gawain: Eleven Romances and Tales* (Kalamazoo, MI: Medieval Institute Publications, Western Michigan University, 1995), pp. 30–3.

3. See Michael J. Bennett, *Community, Class and Careerism: Cheshire and Lancashire Society in the Age of 'SGGK'* (Cambridge: Cambridge University Press, 1983) and his chapter 'The Historical Background' in *A Companion to the Gawain-Poet*, pp. 71–90; John. M. Bowers, *The Politics of 'Pearl': Court Poetry in the Age of Richard II* (Cambridge: D. S. Brewer, 2001) and Leo Carruthers, 'The Duke of Clarence and the Earls of March: Garter Knights and *Sir Gawain and the Green Knight*', *Medium Aevum*, 70.1 (2001), 66–79.

4. Lais, or lays, are short romance tales, normally around 800–12,000 lines long, which often identify themselves as being written versions of ancient Breton or Celtic tales which are performed to the accompaniment of a harp, which some take to explain why they are normally written in rhyming and rhythmic verse. Marie de France is credited with codifying the genre in the mid-twelfth century in a collection that was evidently popular in both England and France. The Welsh setting of some of her lais and the association of lais generally with enchantment are particularly relevant for *Sir Gawain and the Green Knight*. A good overview of the form may be found in the 'General Introduction' to *Medieval English Breton Lays*, eds Anne Laskaya and Eve Salisbury (Kalamazoo, MI: Medieval Institute Publications, Western Michigan University, 1995).

5. *Sir Gawain and the Green Knight* in *The Poems of the Pearl Manuscript: Pearl, Cleanness, Patience, Sir Gawain and the Green Knight*, ed. Malcolm Andrew and Ronald Waldron, revised 5th edn (Exeter: University of Exeter Press, 2007). All quotations from the poem are taken from this edition.

6. The manuscript seems to read Ticius, a name unknown to scholars, but it is possible the poet refers to Tyrrhenus (sometimes written Tirius) who appears in some commentaries as the father of Tuscus, the alleged founder of Tuscany. See *Sir Gawain and the Green Knight*, ed. J. R. R. Tolkien and E. V. Gordon revised 2nd edn ed. Norman Davis (Oxford: Clarendon Press, 1967), p. 71 n. 11.

7. See Derek Brewer 'The Colour Green' in *A Companion to the Gawain-Poet*, pp. 181–90.

8. The association of this Green Knight and the Green Man who appears as a foliate head in medieval church carvings is succinctly dismissed by Derek Brewer in 'The Colour Green', pp. 181–2.

9. John Spiers, 'Sir Gawain and the Green Knight', *Scrutiny*, 16 (1947), 274–600.

10. Michael George, 'Gawain's struggle with ecology', *The Journal of Ecocriticism* 2.2 (July 2010), 30–44.

11. See J. J. Anderson, *Language and Imagination in the Gawain-Poet* (Manchester: Manchester University Press, 2005).

12. See Richard Green, 'Gawain's shield and the quest for perfection', *English Literary History* 29 (1962), 121–39; Ross G. Arthur, 'Gawain's shield as *signum*' in *Text and Matter: New Critical Perspectives of the Pearl-Poet*, eds Robert Blanch, Miriam Miller, Julian Wasserman (Troy, NY: Whitston, 1991), pp. 221–27; Gerard Morgan, 'The perfection of the pentangle and of Sir Gawain in *SGGK*' in *Essays on Ricardian Literature in Honour of J. A. Burrow*, eds A. J. Minnis, C. Morse and T. Turville-Petre (Oxford: Clarendon Press, 1997), pp. 252–75.

13. This shifting of mode fits well with Judith Butler's point that gender and identity are matters of performance rather than of innate being, but the point has been explored in more depth with regard to the role codes of conduct have to play in this particular poem by Jonathan Nicholls, *The Matter of Courtesy: Medieval Courtesy Books and the Gawain-Poet* (Woodbridge: D. S. Brewer, 1985).

14. See William F. Hodapp, 'Make we mery: lyric as context for courtly life in *Sir Gawain and the Green Knight*', *Comitatus*, 281 (1997), 36–44.

15. See J. D. Burnley, 'The hunting scenes in *Sir Gawain and the Green Knight*', *The Yearbook of English Studies* 3 (1973), 1–9.

4

Untraditional Medieval Literature: Romance, Fabliau, Robin Hood and 'King and Subject' Ballad

Stephen Knight

Beyond court and church

Speaking as it does for a culture basically controlled by court and church, medieval English literature, like its European avatars, is for the most part concerned with appreciating the behaviour and values, and reflecting the problems, associated with the continued authority of aristocrats and priests. In lordly romance and saintly *vitae*, secular and religious moralities are propounded and the interesting dangers of deviations are illustrated – lust and malice threaten both court and church, while cowardice and disloyalty haunt the chivalric activists, and sins of the flesh and the spirit stalk the world of the aspirant Christian.

But there was also room in the period for a distinctly different domain, for quite other forms of ethical problems and narrative tensions. This was recorded in some medieval literature, mostly deriving from the later period when texts were more often written down and preserved, and when new social forces which had no central commitment to the world of court or church were recognized and developed as new forms of cultural self-analysis. Stories emerged which were focused on the lower gentry, on the free agents called yeomen, and on people who made a living by plying trades or providing services. These innovative personnel emerge in uncertain relationships and with unclear status, both ethical and social, so that something like a coalition of new foci and voices is to be seen in English literature in the new sub-genres of popular romance, fabliau, outlaw narrative and the 'king and subject' ballad. These formations have usually been noticed, if at all, merely as separate variants of the dominant modes of literature, but they deserve consideration as a group of texts bearing both some interconnections and representing the kind of formation that Raymond Williams identifies as an 'emergent structure of feeling',[1] one that responds to the increasing secularization and defeudalization of late medieval English society and its self-realizing culture, a force most firmly and memorably realized in the Robin Hood material.

Popular romance

The first signs of innovative themes come in unusual versions of the most fully recorded secular medieval English literary form, the romance. Not being the medium of either religious or social authority, the English language frequently brought to its versions of the romance genre a certain mundanity – nothing matches the high courtesy of Chrétien de Troyes, and the English version of *Sir Percival* has no mention of the Holy Grail, though there are positives – only in English does Isolde's dog lick the love-potion cup and remain devoted to the lovers for life. But more structural are themes in some English romances that take a wider social view of the context and ethics of the hero and his interlocutors, where the early French materials are mainly focused on court and church.

The English romances are more widely given to uncourtly issues. As Helen Cooper has shown, in the fifteenth century many of them move away from what she calls 'a fantasy of high chivalry' to issues like 'civil strife' and 'father-killing', which she identifies as being 'not a note that is sounded in the metrical romances of the fourteenth century, nor in the dramatic romance of the Renaissance, but it is one that carries a particular resonance in the troubled close of the Middle Ages'.[2] She discusses as major examples *Melusine*, and – their medium itself suggesting an innovative position – the prose *Alexander* and Malory's own lengthy prose reworking of the Arthurian story. To that category can be added a number of other late medieval English romances which deal with family tensions focusing on mothers and sons, family-based romance stories of separation and final, if often incomplete, reunions, as in the fairly early *Sir Eglamour of Artois* (mid-fourteenth century) and also *The Erl of Tolous*, *Le Bone Florence of Rome*, *Sir Triamour*, *Octavian* and *Sir Degaré*.[3]

These romances which replace aristocratic male angst and glory by telling of families disrupted by either internal errors or external malice are extensions of the problems of those early romances where the hero like Yvain in *Le Chevalier au Lion* falls from his elevated status, but regains it by a rigorous application of chivalric values. But there are late English hero-alone romances that are inherently hostile to traditional authority, royal or feudal. In the late fourteenth-century popular romance *Sir Launfal*, the hero, mistreated by Guinevere, becomes an exile from court, and is then mistreated by a status-conscious town mayor. He only wins happiness matching his inner qualities when he leaves both worlds forever with the queen of the fairies – who blinds Guinevere as they leave. A reverse path to happiness from isolation via fantasy and brutality is achieved in the mid- to late fourteenth-century *Gamelyn*, where the youngest son is cheated out of his limited inheritance and then bullied by his eldest brother. The middle brother sympathizes, but has no impact, and Gamelyn triumphs through the direct methods of the outlaws, whom he has joined in the forest and whose leader he becomes. He invades the court that seems about to execute the middle brother, breaks the judge's cheekbone and arm, and then hangs him, the sheriff, the twelve jurymen and his bad brother. His good brother takes the estate and the king appoints Gamelyn as a chief justice of the forest. This romance has clear links to the outlaw narrative, as will be discussed below.

Fabliau

If romance can move towards the popular, there can also be popular contexts and concerns at the heart of high medieval English literature. Chaucer, among his many remarkable achievements, was the only English poet to undertake the form of the fabliau – it is hard to find any other example in English. That makes it all the more striking that seven of the twenty-four *Canterbury Tales* are essentially fabliaux – and, suggesting Chaucer's purposeful interest in the genre, six of the first ten tales are in that form. Miller, Reeve and Cook all offer classic sexual fabliau stories (as later will the Shipman),[4] Friar and Summoner have the slightly less common anti-clerical mode, and the Merchant melds fabliau-style marital misadventure with a parodic treatment of romance in a way that seems, largely unnoticed by Chaucerians, to refer back to the opening Knight–Miller collision of socially and tonally extremely different accounts of passion versus authority.

Chaucer's decision to make three of his first four tales fabliaux, with the Miller offering a barrage of vulgar response to the story told by the evident social leader on the pilgrimage, the Knight, is thematically purposeful. The fabliau, as shown by Bédier in his

ground-breaking study of the form,[5] was by then no longer popular
in France, and though it had been re-used by Boccaccio in his recent
Decameron, that does not seem a primary source for Chaucer. Not, as
was once thought, because he did not know the work, but, as Donald
McGrady suggests, because if Chaucer had followed the *Decameron*
more closely 'such a dependence upon a single work might have
appeared unseemly to the poet and his contemporaries'.[6] It had not
seemed so in *Troilus and Criseyde* or indeed the 'Knight's Tale' itself,
and the most recent study of Boccaccio's use of the fabliau shows
an uncanny resemblance to Chaucer's deployment of them – Brown
counts twenty-seven of the hundred tales as based on fabliaux,[7] a
good deal more than other scholars have, but almost exactly the same
percentage as Chaucer's; and the *Decameron* also bunches them for
enhanced effect, as Chaucer does. Although Chaucer was aware of
what Boccaccio was doing and used a similar structure, but did not
follow him in detail, it is most likely that Chaucer's purpose is simply
different from Boccaccio's.

Boccaccio uses fabliau stories as elements in his exposition of social
attitudes to behaviour. The stories do not deal in social conflict, and
the only sign of conflict between tellers, or even complexity between
teller and tale, is when some of the seven ladies object to the sexual
nature of tales told by some of the three gentlemen. Boccaccio's stories shape a wide-ranging account of human ethics and interactions,
and scholars have found deeper meanings at times in the symbolic set-
tings of the frame, or *cornice* – one powerful reading suggests that the
drive of the whole work is to show how Reason can contain Anger
and Lust when aided by the seven classical and Christian virtues, as
personified by the seven ladies.[8]

Chaucer, realizing a much more socially dynamic understanding
of what his narrators represent, makes the fabliaux into instruments
of social challenge, as the drunken Miller insists on a political reading of
the Host's invitation to 'quite' the Knight's tale, which he evidently
only meant as matching it in terms of taste and quality. Chaucer
will continue this disruptive rather than expressive mode when the
Summoner and Friar exchange hostile anti-clerical fabliaux and the
Merchant and Franklin juxtapose popular stories riddled with aspi-
ration: the first a fabliau of ill-based social and sexual assumption,
and the second a tale of wonder threatened with fabliau–style sexual
connivance that ultimately fails in the face of moralized aspirational
values – effectively creating an anti-fabliau. Social challenge is built
into the Miller's threat to 'quite' the Knight, but then the Reeve's
angry response to the incursive artisan creates disabling dissent among

the insurgent social forces and imposes some closure on the Miller's energy. In this the Reeve speaks for his position of petty authority within the existing system.

Having raised through the Miller a socio-cultural challenge to the Knight's tale, Chaucer diminishes its status and value through the Reeve. This evaluative deterioration of the churls' narratives appears to continue as the Cook, enjoying the Reeve's anti-Miller spirit, insists – with the Host's support – on telling a 'jape', evidently to focus on sexuality: its last words are that the 'joly prentys' who is apparently to be the central figure has a friend who has a wife who 'heeld for contenance / A shoppe, and swyved for her sustenance'.[9] Later practice by Chaucer (in the case of the Monk, of his own tale of Sir Thopas and possibly that of the Squire) suggests that someone was going to interrupt the Cook's tale on the basis of its verbal offensiveness. Indeed, the sequence of tales certainly takes a sober turn, with the 'Man of Law's Tale' drawing on the riches of Christian ethical learning, completing a usually unnoticed court and church frame around the fabliaux – he was the second listed, and so senior, among the non-gentry, non-clerical pilgrims. His incorporation with those elevated figures effectively closes the disruptions of the opening group in conservative orderly terms.

But there is another possible development of the Cook's tale beyond this firm authoritarian closure. In the sizeable *cd* group of manuscripts, which stems from the very early and apparently un-edited Corpus text, and also in the early (though textually eccentric) Harley 7004, there is a second Cook's tale. This is none other than *Gamelyn*, which puts outlaw violence behind the hero's re-establishment against corrupt authority. These manuscripts lack accepted authority, and the clumsy style and unnuanced voice of *Gamelyn* make it unbelievable as Chaucer's work, but some scholars have thought Chaucer had it among his papers to work up into a second Cook's tale. It is, however, naïve to state, as does the *Riverside Chaucer*, that *Gamelyn* 'does not seem at all appropriate to the Cook'.[10] Making strange-seeming tales fit uncannily, revealingly, is part of Chaucer's exploration of his storytellers, as with the Wife of Bath or the Nun's Priest. Chaucer himself changes tales from silly to sober, as the Cook might also have done. There are also points of contact: Gamelyn says to his brother 'I will not be thi coke',[11] and then uses a large cook's pestle as a weapon. Whatever might be the full meaning of the Cook–*Gamelyn* juxtaposition, it evidently links the fabliau incursion into the *Canterbury Tales* to popular romance: both present a social challenge to authority and its cultural self-realization.

The first fragment fabliaux can also be read as Chaucer's displaced recognition of the disorderly social forces of his own period. A miller was identified memorably in the widely distributed John Ball letter as a mythical leader of the social disorder of 1381.[12] Though this was more recently named the Peasants' Revolt, most leaders were not peasants but artisans, small landowners and town-dwellers, not unlike Chaucer's fabliau narrators, but none seems to have been a reeve, the one who introduces damaging dissent to the popular voice. Other possible links exist. The forces of disruption in 1381 moved from country centres into London as do the first three fabliaux; minor officials of the church were often involved, as they are in the disruptions of these stories. The whole event was seen as a breach of traditional obedience and the Miller handles this last connection in comic reversal. Nicholas's deployment of Noah's Flood for his private purposes can be seen as a farcical displacement of the great biblical punishment for disobedience, which in the period (and notably in the miracle plays mentioned in the tale) was usually focused as lechery; and like Noah one man shows fidelity to his duties, albeit now only a stupid credulous artisan. While Noah's wife dissented from entering the ark, Alison is keen both to enter and leave it – though only with Nicholas. In Chaucer's hands, the fabliau is resurrected both for entertainment and for complex socio-political purposes.

Medieval Robin Hood

The popular texts discussed so far are all re-formations of existing structures, but new forces also generate new genres and new figures, and the richest, most varied and longest-lasting of these late medieval recognitions of a changing world of people, relationships and their cultural realizations is to be found in the tradition of Robin Hood. The outlaw is first heard of in two separate, but parallel, anti-authoritarian domains. One is oral tradition, which records, from the early fifteenth century on, passing references to a yeoman hero resisting local authority, whether civil or clerical, sheriff or abbot. There are proverbs and place-names that refer to him and widespread casual comments:[13] in 1429 a judge ruled that 'Robin Hood in Greenwood Stood' was legally obvious, that is, an assertion whose basis was so well-known it did not need proving in court. This figure of popular resistance was both against the law – there are early records of criminal activities in his name, including as a poacher's alias – and also seen as hostile by the church. The mid-1380s version of *Piers Plowman* presents Sloth as a lazy priest who is ignorant of his Paternoster but knows well 'rymes of Robyn hood'; from about 1460 a comic poem uses the same motif when 'a sow sat on hym bench and harpyd Robin Hood'.[14] Parallel to these passing references are some mid-fifteenth-century literary narratives about the outlaw hero. Though in ballad metre, they are too long to be sung and are recorded in manuscript anthologies with other popular material and also serious moral texts, collections without primary links to either church or court.[15]

The two earliest outlaw poems are effectively a matching pair of narratives.[16] 'Robin Hood and the Monk' (c.1465) tells how Robin is trapped in town by the sheriff when he is identified by a monk whom he and his men have previously robbed: the sheriff's men breach sanctuary to take him, and Robin's higher Christian standards are evident because he is in town to attend mass, having a special devotion to Saint Mary. Little John and Much the Miller's son respond to Robin's capture by trapping the monk whom the sheriff has sent to the king for instructions. They kill him and his boy – early outlaws can be hard-handed – and impersonate them before the king, returning with the royal seal sent to bring Robin to court and punishment, but they free him, killing the jailer in the process. The poem opens with Robin arguing about money that John has won in a shooting contest, which is why Robin was alone in town and also why finally he not only thanks John for saving him, but offers him leadership of the band. John demurs; and outlaw activity and celebrations continue.

'Robin Hood and the Potter' (1468) again has John entangle Robin in a dangerous situation, but this time the hero saves himself. A potter arrives in the forest and John, knowing how dangerous a fighter he is, encourages Robin to oppose him. They fight a draw, Robin exchanges clothes with him, goes into town and sells the pots extremely cheaply, including to the sheriff's wife, who invites him to dinner – they exchange notably courteous language. The sheriff is interested in the quasi-potter's talk of cattle in the forest, and Robin displays his archery skill; then they head for the forest, the sheriff dreaming of wealth from livestock, but he is trapped and loses all his money – Robin sends a horse home with the sheriff as a present for his wife.

A third poem, 'Robin Hood and Guy of Gisborne', can be associated with these two. Though it is only preserved from the 1640s in Thomas Percy's famous manuscript anthology, its language seems quite early and it includes a scene found in a short play that survives from about 1475. After Robin and John again argue and separate, John is trapped by the sheriff. Robin recuses him after he meets the sheriff's bounty-hunter Guy of Gisborne, dressed in a horse skin, with 'topp', apparently the head, attached. They compete in games, and then when Robin reveals his name they fight fiercely. Robin wins, with some difficulty, and beheads his enemy. He dons the horse-costume, joins the sheriff while pretending to be Guy, and, as a reward for having killed Robin, asks to kill the captive John. He releases him instead, and John shoots the sheriff dead as he runs away. There may be some sensational elaboration here to match the later date of survival, but the mix of ferocity and trickery, and the determined aggression towards the civil authorities is consistent with the fifteenth-century ballads; the three realize consistently a figure hostile to the agents of the church and the civil law.

The origin of this very popular figure who lives vigorously in both oral referential tradition and in substantial early texts is by no means clear. A coalition of archival historians and popular journalists would like there to be a 'real Robin Hood' whose crimes were converted into popular myth, and some have scoured the records, finding a few minor criminals called Robert Hood or with similar nicknames. While this may please modern interests in both individuality and factitiousness, it recognizes neither that real figures like Jesse James and Ned Kelly have a very restricted range of activities and locations quite unlike Robin Hood, nor yet that there is another, different, late medieval Robin Hood. This is a non-criminal figure who leads so-called 'play-games', public celebrations which occurred in May-time, mostly at Whitsun, and usually in small sea-ports in south-western England (later spreading more widely, including to lowland Scotland). There was a procession and collection of money for civic purposes, like mending the roads or the church tower, culminating in a celebration with sports, games and a 'Robin Hood Ale'. No songs or plays survive, though they must have been involved – detail that is recorded about the play-games is usually financial, mostly their costume costs.

This is another late medieval popular cultural function without benefit of church or aristocracy: the local priest is not involved in organizing events, and the south-western ports where the play-games first occur are noticeably not those where royal or aristocratic power was strong.[17] There is only one mention in the play-game records of a sheriff, because he wore a green costume like Robin and John, which may suggest his forest residence in 'Robin Hood and the Potter'. Overall there are no anti-authority elements in the play-games; indeed, this Robin is a version of organic local authority. Without any link to the petty criminals traced in the north of England by the reductive archivists, the figure appears to look back to the French thirteenth-century lyrics which feature Robin, sometimes surnamed de Bois, 'of the wood'. In these *pastourelles* there is Marian, a *pastoure*, or shepherdess, who is sexually harassed by civic or clerical authorities, wandering knights or clerics. She usually resists and quite often her boyfriend, the young peasant Robin, helps her. But he more often appears in *bergerie* poems where he is a leader in simple peasant celebrations, much like the play-games found in English ports connected to France by the wine trade, which also went to France-friendly southern Scotland. Play-game Robin does not often have a named partner, though Marian appears in some late instances. In England he gains the surname Hood in the play-games. Then a major change occurs in the oral references and the early texts when he becomes a determined outlaw, opposed strongly to the authority of church and state.

The Hood surname presumably functions as a social marker (a hood is a poor man's hat), and if it already has some sense of disguise, the play-games do not energize that in terms of social resistance, as the outlaw stories will do consistently. The turn against authority for the representative of yeoman identity appears to be linked to the negative experience of the fourteenth century in England. The mid-century plague and its recurrences hit hard a people already weakened by weather that drastically deteriorated soon after 1300. At least a third of the population died, and the ratio was higher among the lower classes; when this created a severe shortage of labour, government action was taken to retain ordinary people in their servile status and in their traditional locations, and also to hold down the resultant rise in wages. These circumstances led to widespread distress and anger: 1381 was only the major moment of social dissent. Outside both the cultural domain and the authoritarian control of the aristocracy and the church, the mythic representative of the ordinary people turned to resistance.

Late medieval Robin Hood

The idea of the elusive strength of ordinary people did not escape the unfavourable notice of authority in the sixteenth century, when centralizing control of long-standing popular activities led to recurrent containment of the celebrations that had grown from the play-games: in Edinburgh in 1561 the banning of a Robin Hood event by the council prompted citizens to break open the Tolbooth prison, free the inmates and lock up the magistrates. A notable example of literary policing was the idea that Robin Hood was in fact the noble Earl of Huntingdon, mistreated and exiled by bad Prince John, but reinstated by King Richard on his return from the crusades, an idea enshrined in two plays by Anthony Munday in 1598–9, *The Downfall of Robert, Earle of Huntingdon*, and *The Death of the same noble outlaw*. So this Robin only resisted wrongful authority, and was fully loyal to true authority – going to the forest was actually his 'downfall', and the link to Prince John was first made then to enable this startling re-orientation of the outlaw. Gentrification had limited effect on the myth in general, mostly because noble exile Robin just sat around moping until his restoration, and almost none of the exciting tricksterish action of the yeoman tradition was redeployed. But the conservative idea that Robin was only a moral, not a social, radical and was essentially from above the yeoman class remained attractive and can often be found in modern versions, especially from Hollywood.

There were other, more popular, sixteenth-century elaborations of the late medieval literary yeoman. Around 1500 appeared *The Gest of Robin Hood*, a lengthy poem found only in print and probably assembled for that mode. Much early printing had lofty chivalric concerns, realizing the false consciousness of an audience whose urban mercantile status meshed with this new market-oriented form of production. 'Gest' as a title referred to Latin *res gestae*, 'things done', and the poem is a mini-epic, a set of Robin Hood adventures – some familiar, some innovative – giving the narrative the extended structure and shape of a hero's life, ending with his death and fame, so suggesting a social and cultural status somewhat higher than he normally possessed. The opening shows Robin instructing his men in their principles, sending some off to collect money and seek an interesting guest for dinner – the latter request makes the outlaw leader seem a forest version of King Arthur. Some of the stories are familiar, but there are also new strands of narrative, which frame and change the direction of the usual outlaw operations against church and state.

The first sequence of the poem is about a poor knight the outlaws meet, who has had to pay a fine because his son killed a man in a joust. This classic romance problem is coupled to the hostility towards the Church, as an abbot has lent the knight money for the fine and is about to foreclose on the lands given as security. So Robin lends the knight £400 and, improbably adopting a feudal lord's status, re-equips him with a horse, clothing and even a servant, Little John (before he works for the sheriff). The knight then outfaces the greedy monks and returns in a year's time to repay Robin, bringing him a present of bows and arrows – and along the way, he stops to help a yeoman who is being bullied. When he arrives, Robin has just stolen £800 from some monks and gives the knight back the £400 – again, a quasi-feudal hyper-generosity to show Robin's positivity in religion: the knight's only surety has been Robin's favourite, Saint Mary. This opening, and so emphasized, sequence links Robin and his values to true nobility, suggesting a morally based coalition against the corrupt church. The connection will later turn against the sheriff when he arrests the knight and the knight's wife appeals to the outlaws for help. Briskly, they shoot and behead the sheriff and free the knight.

But just as Robin reveres Mary, so is he (as was clear in 'Robin Hood and the Monk') no enemy to the king, only to his officials. In the lengthy final sequence of the *Gest*, the king comes, disguised as an abbot, to the forest to confront this notorious outlaw. Because this abbot gives a true account of the money he carries, they become friends and enjoy robust sports – something of the play-game spirit is enacted at the level of national loyalty. The knight arrives and recognizes the king, who forgives Robin and takes him off to court, so incorporating him to authority. But Robin, finding it costly and unexciting at court, negotiates, with some difficulty, a short period of leave. He never returns, staying for years in the forest until he is betrayed by his relative the Prioress, who is the lover of a knight hostile to Robin and so acts for both church and gentry. The ending, leaving Robin outside and against the power of state and church, is in keeping with the anti-authority basis of the medieval hero, but the positive contact with the knight and, for the most part, the king, and the recurring instances of Robin's apparent feudal power, such as his generosity and his possession of horses, all tend to make him a less aggressive, less socio-culturally challenging figure. He seems at times well on the path to gentrification, and much of the incident of the *Gest* can be linked to *Fulk Fitz Warren*, a poem about a real noble outlaw who was exiled by King John, as Munday was to make Robin himself;[18] but the knight and king also perform the work of foreclosure that Chaucer achieved through the hostility of the Reeve and the degraded attitude of the Cook.

In the *Gest*, Robin the Yeoman has been moved closer to the gentry but his status is modified, not actually changed: he is not yet true gentry like the knight, and still hates the overweening sheriff. Their status is shown by recurrent formulaic adjectives: Robin is 'gode' (14 times), the knight 'gentyll' (19 times) and the sheriff 'proude' (20 times), and these adjectives can cluster to emphasize these archetypal values. Somewhere between yeoman disruption and gentrified incorporation, the *Gest* was frequently reprinted in the sixteenth century, but then seemed to fade from interest until it was repositioned in modern times as the major medieval outlaw text. This may itself have

been the result of its somewhat elevated status: the few fully gentrified texts did not thrive, like Munday's soon forgotten plays, Ben
Jonson's fine but unfinished, *The Sad Shepherd* (c. mid-1630s), and a
late seventeenth-century ballad, in which Robin is the exiled earl and
Marian seeks him disguised as a boy – they fight, recognize each other
and settle down forever in the forest. What did survive in considerable strength was the yeoman tradition, now taking the form of short
printed ballads, sold as 'broadsides', with a tune indicated: fortunately,
collectors like Samuel Pepys and Anthony à Wood gathered them
carefully.

Among the thirty-two surviving broadside ballads reprinted by
F. J. Child,[19] the only close connection with earlier material is 'Robin
Hood and the Butcher', which simply changes the trade from Potter
and condenses the story, and there are two later ballads cut out of
the *Gest*; familiar in spirit are ones about robbing bishops and rescu-
ing men from the sheriff's gallows. As far as the other broadsides are
concerned, the earlier they survive the more likely they are to be anti-
authority, even fiercely so, like the popular 'Robin Hood's Progress to
Nottingham' where the fifteen-year-old Robin meets fifteen forest-
ers. One refuses to pay when Robin wins a bet on his archery skill,
so Robin shoots the man dead, then kills all his colleagues and takes
to the forest. In the seventeenth century, the church becomes a more
common enemy than the sheriff, and several ballads appear which are
basically pro-authority, such as 'Robin Hood and Queen Katherine'
where, without being gentrified, Robin is friendly to royalty and
shoots at court for the queen. The largest single category, though,
is mainly apolitical, just telling how Robin 'meets his match', that
is, fights someone in the forest, agrees a draw and often gets him to
join the band. In the broadside ballads, Robin may be a simple leader
of simple men, or against the Catholic Church, or decreasingly, yet
still at times strongly, opposed to the social systems, but he is in this
highly popular mode almost never gentrified: the values and interests
of church and court remain foreign to the outlaw tradition.

King and subject

The Robin Hood material also looks towards other elements of
late medieval popular realization. A connection to popular romance
occurs in the broadside 'Robin Hood and Will Scarlet' (also known by
the market-oriented title 'Robin Hood Newly Revived'). The hero
meets a well-dressed stranger, fights him and agrees a draw, but then
innovatively finds that Will is his own cousin, a man of the gentry

with the family name Gamwell: this name and story appear to be connected to the popular romance *Gamelyn*, where a well-born hero also joined the outlaws. More closely linked with another sub-genre is Robin's meeting with the king in the *Gest*, which is a version of a little-known but highly original sub-genre known as the 'King and Subject' ballads: the texts are still hard to find, but Child provided synopses of the main ones in his headnote to 'King Edward the Fourth and a Tanner of Tamworth'.[20]

The idea of a monarch evaluatively adrift without the support of his power apparatus has long been of interest, but in the late medieval period it recurs as a way of reflecting on the interface of royal power with a new type of social entity, the self-sufficient person who does not depend on a lord for standing and income. The pattern is that the king is alone, often lost, and meets the 'subject' in a wild or natural setting, outside the orderly domain of court, church or town. The king and the subject spend time together, often engaging in sports, even a drinking ritual; there is some exploration of their differences and the ways in which the subject is effectively independent of royal power, and there will be a final resolution of the differences, almost always at court, usually involving some incorporation of the subject.

The resolutions can vary: in one of the earliest poems, 'King Edward and the Shepherd' (c. 1450), the terrified shepherd, realizing that he has met, as if an equal, with the king – whom he knew as 'Joly Robyn' – begs for mercy, but receives no response. Conceivably an end is missing, but that seems unlikely and this poem appears to offer a challenging statement of the real nature of authority. Most others have an incorporative outcome. In 'The King and the Barker' (c. 1400) the money-oriented barker, or salesman, is given 100 shillings in cash, but later survivals are more generous. 'King Edward IV and the Tanner of Tamworth', apparently in existence by the mid-sixteenth century, ends with the simple subject being made an esquire and given possession of Plumpton Park (where the king in the *Gest* had been losing his deer). The interestingly named subject John de Reeve (in a ballad only found in Thomas Percy's Folio manuscript of the 1640s) is knighted, as is one of his sons, and provided with a suitable income, while in the early seventeenth-century 'King James I and the Tinker' the subject is rewarded massively with a knighthood and land worth £3000 a year. Most of the independent and to some degree dissenting subjects are, like these, absorbed into the power structure through charity and appointment. That is the king's intention in the *Gest*, but Robin avoids it, which is unusual. At the end of the para-Robin Hood ballad *Adam Bell* (c. 1536), the three

Cumberland outlaws are made forest officials by the king, and that process, located in Sherwood, is also the outcome of 'King Henry II and the Miller of Mansfield', which only survives from Percy, though its language seems at least sixteenth century. 'King William III and the Loyal Forester' from the late seventeenth century has the same theme, though, perhaps because of the troubled times, it sees the forester's opposition to poaching as unusual.

Other 'king and subject' texts are focused on a churchman and the king, largely avoiding social forces. In Gerald of Wales' early thirteenth-century Latin story about Henry II and a Cistercian abbot, the king eventually favours the abbot's interests without social standing being considered; Child felt this structure was basically a different story, where the king sets an allegedly clever man a riddle, but it is solved by a simpler man. He treated 'King John and the Bishop', first found in Percy's manuscript, as the base text of this form,[21] but it also shares the 'king and subject' pattern of royal alias, threat and positive outcome; further, the churchman has a half-brother who is a shepherd, a simple subject: he solves the riddle, and both are rewarded. However, by the time of 'King Henry VIII and the Abbot of Reading', a later seventeenth-century survival, anti-Catholicism seems to have led to the abbot-subject being imprisoned and fined rather than rewarded and absorbed.

If the 'king and subject' sub-genre can drift away from the theme of social innovation and the strains it places on authority, it does as a whole testify to recurring attempts to realize the presence in late medieval England of such new forces. Very noticeable is the overlap with the broader reaches of the Robin Hood tradition. In his forest wanderings recorded in broadside ballads, Robin fights a 'meets his match' encounter with a Tanner, a Tinker, a Shepherd and a Ranger (i.e. a Forester), all subjects also met by the king. In these forest-fight stories, Robin himself seems to rework a 'king and subject' model, without the assumption of authority (perhaps linked to King Edward's claiming the alias 'Joly Robyn'). The Miller of Mansfield operates in Robin Hood territory, and comes to rule Sherwood; poaching and enjoyment of natural delights are shared by the outlaws and the subjects met by the king. Further, Robin is himself directly involved in an extensive and ultimately eluded engagement with royal authority, and his own interaction with abbots and other monks is recurrent though, like the 'king and abbot' versions of the genre, it may in part be the product of post-reformation anti-Catholicism.

There are more connections throughout this group of popular texts – Gamelyn's assertion of his right in response to oppressive authority is an outlaw-like mix of loyalty and sheer violence, the response frequently feared by the king when meeting alone his surprisingly independent subject. The encounter Chaucer constructs between Knight and Miller is in narrative terms one between authority and someone who just ignores it, like that between king and subject. However, these deep-laid links do not suggest the popular literary sub-genres are a carefully integrated plot against textual and by extension social authority. Rather they suggest that each of these elusive late medieval sub-genres, working in separate but parallel ways, relate to and realize new English social and political forces: in Raymond Williams's terms, an 'emergent structure of feeling' that in the consciously acculturated world of mercantilism and individualism, and in a market for literature, will eventually generate the novel. What in the late medieval period are variant and dissenting forms of English literature point the way ahead to a social and cultural world of story with a context and an audience far wider than the medieval court and the church.

Notes

1. See Raymond Williams, *Marxism and Literature* (Oxford: Oxford University Press, 1977), pp. 128–35.
2. Helen Cooper, 'Counter-romance: civil strife and father-killing in the prose romances', in *The Long Fifteenth Century: Essays for Douglas Gray*, eds Helen Cooper and Sally Mapstone (Oxford: Clarendon, 1997), pp. 141–62 (pp. 143, 162).
3. See Stephen Knight, 'The social function of the middle English romances', in *Medieval Literature: Criticism, Ideology and History*, ed. David Aers (Brighton: Harvester, 1986), pp. 99–122.
4. Kolve has questioned if there was enough of the tale to predict its future to be that of a fabliau, but there is enough to show it was headed for vulgarity and the final words point clearly enough to sexual comedy: V.A. Kolve, *Chaucer and the Imagery of Narrative: The First Five Canterbury Tales* (Stanford, CA: Stanford University Press, 1984), p. 275.
5. Joseph Bédier, *Les Fabliaux* (Paris: Champion, 1893).
6. Donald McGrady, 'Chaucer and the "Decameron" reconsidered', *Chaucer Review*, 12 (1977), 1–26 (p. 15).
7. Katherine Brown, *Boccaccio's Fabliaux: Medieval Short Stories and the Function of Reversal* (Gainesville, FL: University of Florida Press, 2014). See Appendix, Table 2, '*Decameron novelle* and fabliaux analogues', pp. 171–2.
8. See Victoria Kirkham, 'An allegorically tempered *Decameron*', *Italica*, 62 (1985), 1–23.
9. *The Riverside Chaucer*, General Editor Larry D. Benson (New York: Oxford University Press, 1987), p. 862, ll. 4421–2.

10. *Riverside Chaucer*, p. 853.
11. 'The Tale of Gamelyn', in *Robin Hood and Other Outlaw Tales*, ed. Stephen Knight and Thomas Ohlgren, TEAMS Middle English Texts Series, 2nd edn. (Kalamazoo, MI: University of Western Michigan Press, 2000), pp. 184–226; see p. 196, l. 92.
12. See Rodney Hilton, *Bond Men Made Free: Medieval Peasant Movements and the English Rising of 1381* (London: Methuen, 1976), p. 223.
13. See Stephen Knight, *Robin Hood: A Complete Study of the English Outlaw* (Oxford: Blackwell, 1994), pp. 262–88.
14. See Stephen Knight, *Reading Robin Hood: Content, Form and Reception in the Outlaw Myth* (Manchester: Manchester University Press, 2014), p. 18.
15. See Thomas Ohlgren, *Robin Hood: The Early Poems, 1465-1560: Texts, Contexts, and Ideology* (Newark, DE: University of Delaware Press, 2007).
16. See *Robin Hood and Other Outlaw Tales*, note 13.
17. See Stephen Knight, 'Robin Hood: the earliest contexts', in *Images of Robin Hood: Medieval to Modern*, ed. Lois J. Potter and Joshua Calhoun (Newark, DE: Delaware University Press, 2008), pp. 21–40.
18. See Knight, 'Robin Fitz Warren: the formation of *The Gest of Robin Hood*', in *Reading Robin Hood*.
19. See F. J. Child (ed.), *English and Scottish Popular Ballads*, 5 vols, reprint edition (New York: Dover, 1965: originally published 1888), vol. 3, p. 154.
20. Child, no. 273, vol. 5, pp. 67–75.
21. Child, no. 45, vol. 1, pp. 403–14.

Part II
Chaucer

Part II

Chaucer

5

Chaucer and Politics

Helen Phillips

The Middle Ages did not conceptualize the political as a distinct sphere of human activity as readily or extensively as we do today. Political issues are often subsumed in moral or religious discourse in Chaucer's writings, which additionally often display a tendency towards oblique, multivalent, conflicted – at times evasive – treatments of deep or controversial subjects. Chaucer eschews simple single narratives to interpret complex questions about life; perhaps that is why many of his compositions remain unfinished, or present a diversity of voices, or include phrases or speeches within their narratives which open up disconcerting or contradictory viewpoints, or causes for human protest, counteracting received views of how society and the universe are governed.

Nevertheless, Chaucer provides many statements of central contemporary political principles. Two basic assumptions were kingship, as the source of government, and hierarchical order, which descended from the heavens through Creation, realms and households, and which if correctly observed guaranteed harmony and stability. The most revered secular virtue was 'truth', meaning loyalty, fidelity – between rulers and subjects and in civil and personal relationships – a virtue deemed essential to individual honour and social coherence.

Kingship

The citizen participation that drives modern political structures (policy formation, political discourse, parties and securing power) was absent from medieval society. Government issued from the king, acting – in theory – with counsel from his lords. Political theory was accordingly often couched as advice to princes. The widely

79

known *De Regimine principum* (The Rule of Princes, c. 1280), written by Giles of Rome for the young future Philip IV of France, first
instructs how a king must govern himself morally, and then addresses
questions of government, pronouncing that all authority, including
law-making, lies with a king. A good king rules for the common
good, peace and stability, and listens to counsellors. The worst king
is a tyrant.

A less absolutist understanding of kingship appeared in the
Coronation Oath of Richard II (crowned aged 10 in 1377). With
each new monarch, the precise wording of such oaths was the site
of power struggles between royal authority and the great lords. An
embryonic notion of contract, with respective obligations binding
king and people, is evident in his magnates' arrangement that first
Richard swore to rule with justice and mercy for the common profit
(long-established tenets in such oaths) and in accordance with both
existing and future laws, and only thereafter did the lords swear alle-
giance. Richard's subsequent attempts to by-pass the magnates' power,
by policies of centralization aimed at creating his own networks of
administration and adherence, by choosing and promoting his own
advisers, protecting his own prerogative and acting at times unilater-
ally, for example in levying taxation, were major causes of his 1399
deposition and a threatened deposition in 1386. One accusation in
1399 was that he claimed that the laws were in his own mouth, a
theory in line with Giles of Rome but clashing with the developing
fourteenth-century English view that kingship involved obligations
as well as power.

Mirroring trends in certain continental monarchies, Richard
programmatically promoted a royal image of splendour and
divinely granted authority: through the magnificence of his
court, through rituals of respect and through the arts. The Wilton
Diptych now in the National Gallery, London, depicts the Virgin
handing a banner of England to Richard, angels bearing Richard's
personal badge of the White Hart and Richard himself flanked by
two sainted English kings, Edmund and Edward the Confessor,
and St John the Baptist, who is associated with Richard's birthday,
6 January, Christ's baptism and the Epiphany. The parallel between
Richard's own royalty and the court of heaven is clear; here his
authority is given by heaven, and the relationships he appears to
be involved in as king are with the spiritual realm, not with the
troublesome parliaments, magnates, conflicts and financial exigencies of his real-life situation.

The qualities of a true king are showcased, positively and negatively, by Chaucer in several passages. The 'Squire's Tale' praises Cambyuskan as an ideal king. Besides adhering to his religion, he was

> hardy [brave], wys, and riche,
> And pitous and just, alwey yliche [consistent];
> Sooth [true] of his word, benigne, and honourable,
> Of his corage [heart] as any centre stable;
> Yong, fressh, and strong, in armes desirous
> As an bacheler [young knight] of al his hous.
> A fair persone he was and fortunat,
> And kept alwey so wel roial estat
> That ther was nowher swich another man.[1]

Note the age-old requirement that a king should be a warrior, and the traditionally twinned justice and mercy, in 'pitous and just'. 'Roial estat', the concept of royal rank and the honour innate in royal identity, central to Richard's royal image-making, is present here as a principle the ideal king upholds. (We shall see Chaucer exploiting it tactfully as a handle, often when he essays advice about improving royal behaviour.) The wording also exemplifies the late medieval emphasis on 'stableness', a king's duty of being stable in behaviour and ruling in ways that bind his kingdom with order and peace.

Chaucer's ballade *Lak of Stedfastnesse* laments a decline in the world today of stability and loyalty, and an increase in oppression. Its envoy addresses the King specifically and, as often, Chaucer uses praise as a vehicle for veiled warning:

> O prince, desyre to be honourable,
> Cherish thy folk and hate extorcioun.
> Suffre nothing that may be reprevable
> To thyn estat don [to be done] in thy regioun.
> Shew forth thy swerd of castigacioun,
> Dred God, do law [carry out the law], love trouthe [fidelity] and worthinesse,
> And wed thy folk agein to stedfastnesse.[2]

'Worthinesse' often meant prowess, as well as general high standards of behaviour. The approval of firm 'castigacioun', though reflecting the assumption that a good king must be strong and control his subjects, perhaps dates specifically to 1388, when, in response to complaints by the Commons about the liveried retainers of great lords terrorizing some areas, the King agreed to cut back his own liveried retainers. Yet the trope that Richard should castigate others to curb 'extorcioun', like the appeal to him to avoid anything likely to lay his royal 'estat' open to reproof, perhaps shows Chaucer using respect for kingship to proffer a warning. Similarly, the ending twists the often used image of king and subjects as husband and wife so that the ostensible admonition is that Richard must redirect the *people* to act in ways that will restore stable government: he must re-marry *them* to the 'stedfastnesse' required for a well-run kingdom.

The same appeal to 'roial estat' appears in the *Legend of Good Women's* Prologue, where Queen Alceste reproves a God of Love who seems in part to represent Richard II: both positively in his splendour and cultivation of a glorious, godlike royal image, and negatively in his tendency to ire and self-will. It is an important political speech. In the earlier F Prologue,[3] the speech seems to refer to the 1386–1388 hostilities between Richard and his lords, when the Appellant ('accusing') lords removed his favourites, curbed his court expenditure, forced him to re-swear his Coronation Oath and reminded him that Edward II had been deposed. The longer G version perhaps also reflects Richard's so-called tyranny of the late 1390s, with his 1397 vengeance against his enemies, the Dukes of Gloucester and Norfolk, and the Earls of Arundel and Warwick, followed in 1398 by his exiling of Henry of Lancaster, John of Gaunt's son, who was soon to replace Richard in a 1399 coup as Henry IV.

Chaucer's wording is a tour de force of canny and intricate political admonition couched in terms of enhancing royal dignity while daringly pointing to actions that break the obligations of a true and good ruler. Addressing him 'as ye ben a god and ek a kyng' (G. 421), the Queen (probably obliquely representing Queen Anne) asks for royal mercy. The fourteenth century tended to see the role of a good queen as offering wise counsel and petitioning the king to show mercy (the heavenly parallel was Mary, in her typically late medieval role as Queen of Heaven, pleading for mercy for sinners). The *Legend's* plea for royal mercy is for Chaucer, who is deemed to have offended Love by writing about an unfaithful woman, Criseyde. The situation may belong to the world of courtly fantasy but her teaching about kingship speaks cogently to the crisis of the late 1390s and Richard's alleged faults of tyranny, unlegislated taxation and acting in accord with his personal will:

> This shulde a ryghtwys lord han in his thought,
> And not ben lyke tyraunts of Lumbardye
> That usen wilfulhed and tyrannye.

For he that kyng or lord is naturel[4]
Hym oughte nat be tyraunt and crewel
As is a fermour [tax-collector], to don the harm he can.
He most thynke it is his lige man [sworn subject],
And that hym oweth [it behoves him], of verray [true] duetee,
Shewen his peple pleyn [complete] benygnete,
And wel to heren here [their] excusacyouns,
And here compleyntes and petyciouns,
In duewe tyme [promptly], whan they shal it profre.
This is the sentence [teaching] of the Philosophre [i.e Aristotle],
A kyng to kepe his lyges in justice;
Withouten doute, that is his office [duty of his position].
And therto is a kyng ful depe ysworn
Ful many an hundred wynter herebeforn;
And for to kepe his lordes hir degre [rank and dignity].[5]

Reminding the king about his Coronation Oath, described here as centuries old, the speech urges just treatment of Richard's lords. The argument strikingly extends to them the quasi-divine authority which, according to the King's own absolutist views, set apart a born king: 'For they ben half-goddes in this world here' (l. 373). The speech admonishes the god-king to heed petitions (petitions were the main vehicles of parliamentary and individuals' attempts to propose or influence royal policies); to observe due procedure in judging men; to act compassionately towards his poor as well as rich subjects; and – the dominant burden of the plea – a king must 'evere han reward [regard] for his owen degre' (l. 385), that is, demonstrate true royal nature by tempering anger with mercy. The lion, king of the beasts by birth, does not lower himself to take revenge for a fly's bite: true 'genterye' [high birth], 'maystrye' [authority] and 'noble corage' are shown by temperate, considered action (ll. 377–86); and it is only 'for a lord, that is ful foul to use' ruthless condemnation of a supplicant (ll. 387–90).

The 'Tale of Melibee', allegorically depicting a wise wife teaching a rich and powerful man to avoid foolish vengeance and resist unreliable counsellors, addresses moral questions generally without any specific allusion to Ricardian politics but, though it is otherwise a careful translation from French it makes one perhaps significant alteration. It removes (at VII. 1199) a quotation from Ecclesiastes, 'Woe to the land that has a child as lord and whose lord dines in the morning': perhaps contemporaries might have seen here a cloaked allusion to Richard II's youth and his perilous impulses for vengeance? Yet the message of 'Melibee' would also have encouraged Richard's policy of pacificism towards the French (unpopular with the magnates).

Tyranny, order, common profit

The medieval concept of tyranny, as the abuse of power in a system where authority was vested in an individual, included many aspects of bad rule. The *Legend* speech above associates it with cruelty, wilfulness and illegal extortion of taxes. More directly, the 'Monk's Tale' offers cautionary tales of rulers who offended against the duties of kingship: Nero, for example, developed monstrously luxurious tastes (often seen as paralleling excessive exercise of power), ruled tyrannically, executed Seneca for stating 'an emperour moot nede / Be vertuous and hate tirannye' (VII. 2507–8), and was overthrown by Fortune and his own people.[6] The 'Manciple's Tale' states bluntly that the only difference between a tyrant and a lowly outlaw is that the royally born oppressor has a bigger force of men to do harm (IX. 223–34).[7]

The subject's prime duty was obedience: Chaucer's works present this as a virtue even in endurance of oppression, as in Constance's acceptance of a series of unjust, life-threatening, royal actions against her in the 'Man of Law's Tale'. It extended to the marital hierarchy: the wife's obedience to her husband as 'lorde' (X. 921–36), which is a duty that Griselda in the 'Clerk's Tale' takes to heroic extremes; and to the Christian's submission to God, of which Griselda's obedience is presented as an allegory (IV. 1142–62).[8] Chaucer's writings also – though frequently in a complex and problematizing way – invoke obedience in conjunction with how we all should respond to miseries caused by natural forces such as time, nature, mutability (and also by sexual desire, which in theory should bring harmony, fruitfulness and joy but often brings conflict, loss and misery).

The 'Knight's Tale' demonstrates both obedience from royal women under the patriarchal rule of the conqueror Theseus, and also a doctrine, voiced by Theseus, that earthly adversity must be endured as a form of cosmic obedience, because time itself has been imposed by eternal heavenly power on humans. Like political disobedience, complaining against life's vicissitudes is condemned by Theseus as rebellion against God as ruler:

> Thanne is it wysdom, as it thynketh me,
> To maken vertu of necessitee,
> And take it weel that [what] we may [can] nat eschue,
> And namely that to us alle is due [especially what happens to us all].
> And whoso grucceth ought [grumbles at all], he dooth folye,
> And rebel is to hym that al may gye [can ordain].[9]

The 'Knight's Tale' is Chaucer's most extensive treatment of a vision of political order, imposed here by Duke Theseus, as an extension of celestial order. Its human characters' experiences are presented as strongly directed by gods, planets and Fortune. The text's aesthetics, its style (especially key verbal repetitions), imagery and choice of material convey this vision of order and control as divinely ordained bringers of harmony as effectively as explicit statements of the doctrine do. Both the royal marriages in it are masterminded by the conqueror's fiat. First he conquers the land of Femenye and then marries its queen, all in the same line (I. 866). When he proposes that Emily should marry Palamon, he uses the term 'accord', foregrounding ideas of submission to a contract (with himself: she shakes *his* hand) and of stability – not love or passion – for this dynastic marriage. He defines it in hierarchical terms: she 'shul [...] taken [Palamon] for housebonde and for lord' (ll. 3071–2) with the matching hierarchical inducement that Palamon belongs to the ruling class: 'He is a kynges brother sone' (l. 3084). Similarly one consolation Theseus offers for young Arcite's death derives from his rank: a knight's death at the peak of his warrior reputation should prevent his friends grieving (ll. 3047–56).

The other consolation is Theseus' exposition of divine order that dismisses emotional misery. The First Mover, the Creator, designed the universe as a 'fair cheyne of love', a metaphorical combination that claims that control and hierarchy ('cheyne') equate to 'love', which in this tale means lord–subject harmony. Seeing how the world works, Theseus asserts:

Thanne may men by this ordre wel discerne
That thilke Moevere stable is and eterne. (ll. 3003–4)

It is part of that benign plan that the world of temporal experience is of little significance. Yet Chaucer's text earlier contained an outcry from Palamon refusing to believe in a benign rational design or good 'governance' – because of the injustice and misery encountered in that temporal experience:

O crueel goddes that governe
This world with byndyng of youre word eterne [...]
What is mankynde moore unto you holde
Than is the sheep that rouketh [cowers] in the folde?
For slayn is man right as another beest, [...]
What governance is in this prescience [providence],
That gilteless tormenteth innocence? (ll. 1303–14)

No reassuring answer is provided in the text.[10] Chaucer allows similar questionings of the notion of divinely benevolent ordering of natural and human events to be voiced in *Mars* (ll. 218–44)[11] and the 'Franklin's Tale' (V. 865–92)[12] – where, as with Palamon's protest, the question is cautiously left for theologians to decide (l. 890). The Boethian answer, of course, of which Theseus' Prime Mover speech above offers a version, is that the lower world of fleshly temporal experience is inherently inconstant, untrustworthy and unworthy of a wise man's concern (this world is only a thoroughfare full of woe) and explains another great speech in the 'Knight's Tale' urging acceptance of the divine design (ll. 2847–9). The claim that heavenly order underpins political government tends to be accompanied by a doctrine that it is best not to take earthly (secular) life too seriously: arguably a consolatory personal and spiritual worldview but not one readily usable as a basis for discussing political issues.

A magnificent Boethian hymn translated in *Troilus and Criseyde* (III. 174–71) hails the divine order (again as 'Love') that controls nature as also bringing harmony to kingdoms and marriage.[13] Yet both Trojan parliamentary politics and the vagaries of his lover's heart, as well as forces of chance and inconstancy, bring Troilus to a point of despair where he refuses to believe in free will (an essential tenet of both Christian and Boethian worldviews) and no longer wishes to live in this world. His escape (once in the heavens) into a happy disregard for earthly existence (V. 1814–25) is a parallel to the individual mental retreat from concern about public success celebrated in *Truth* and *Fortune*: it is best to 'Flee fro the prees' and turn away from ambition ('climbing', the 'wrastling for this world', *Truth*, l. 3, 16). The philosophical extension of the subject's political duty of obedience to a personal quest for a state of 'stableness' also appears in *Truth*: 'That thee is sent, receyve in buxumnesse [obedience]' (l. 15). Patterns and terminology that constitute Chaucer's most commonly expressed political ideas often appear in his discussions of moral, emotional and philosophical dilemmas.

The political ideal of common profit appears in the *Parliament of Fowls*. Chaucer's reworking of Cicero's *Dream of Scipio* near its beginning shows a vision of the celestial order and harmony of the spheres and connects this heaven to public service on earth: those who 'werke and wysse [direct themselves] / To commune profit' will come to that place of bliss.[14] To Cicero's vision of a heavenly destiny for public servants, Chaucer adds the complicating topic of love. There will be no harmonious afterlife for unruly people, such as breakers of the law and lechers. The portrayal of Nature similarly draws on a philosophical vision of cosmic order evident in the twelfth-century *Complaint of Nature* of Alain de Lille. The bird debate resembles the English Parliament, divided between the Lords (the birds of prey – warriors) and Commons (lower birds in the medieval hierarchy, worm or seed eaters and water birds). Though Nature, presiding as sovereign, represents Creation's rational design, the ruling-class bird-lovers are in conflict, and unlikely to fulfil her ordinance for them of mating and reproduction. Intriguingly the lower classes seem closer to serving common profit and carrying out the Creator's design. The common-ers, though mocked as vulgar by the noble birds and the author, are nevertheless permitted by Nature to express their views and their voices provide valid viewpoints in this poem's complex exploration of the conundrums of individual desire in relation to divine order and common profit.

Chaucer often depicts women with sympathy, respect and admira-tion, as wise counsellors, and at times as superior to men who oppress and exploit them (as in several of the legends of good women). Another group deemed inferior by birth, the common people, are often presented with the age-old prejudice that they are mindless, unstable, insensitive, noisy, easily swayed and readily roused to vio-lence and unrest. Yet, perhaps more strikingly, Chaucer introduces more positive images. Nero's people rise against his tyranny. In the 'Physician's Tale', a thousand-strong mass intervenes on the side of justice, having perceived where the guilt lay (ll. 260–71); the text presents them as wiser than the judge.[15] Two shrewd peasants, the wealthy Thomas from the 'Summoner's Tale'[16] and the poor widow from the 'Friar's Tale',[17] round on clerical conmen. To a wilful and tyrannical ruler, Walter in the 'Clerk's Tale', the people make a wise petition, skilfully and cautiously presented, that he marry and produce an heir: an instance of the neglect of his duty to serve common profit. Nevertheless, Chaucer later adds a passage, without parallel in his sources, expressing the traditional fear of the capacity of the people for disorder:

> O stormy peple! Unsad [unstable] and ever untrewe! [disloyal]
> Ay indiscreet [lacking judgement] and chaungynge as a fane!
> [weathervane]
> Delitynge evere in rumbul that is newe,
> For lyk the moone ay wexe ye and wane! ('Clerk's Tale', ll. 995–1001)

Similarly uneven, disparate images of the lower classes beset the 'Clerk's Tale'. Its lowly peasant Griselda (the most heroically *sad* and *trewe* of subjects) is shown as innately capable of being a perfect ruler, yet her abject submission is presented as admirable and her best and only response to tyrannical abuse of power. The tale's tyrant gets off lightly and is even presented as legitimately testing his wife, just as God tests the human soul. The tale's inconsistent presentation of class, together with the multiple readings offered at its close (ll. 1141–1212), suggests disquiet with its premise that obedience is sufficient solution to capricious tyranny, whether in marriage or politics.

The Clerk and Man of Law show victims of oppression, wives, whose submission eventually restores their secure position, respect and happiness. An analogous, though even more fairy-tale, solution to misused power concludes the 'Wife of Bath's Tale' and the 'Franklin's Tale'. In each, someone who has been granted power over another's normal rights (the Squire's power to deprive the Knight of his husbandly sexual rights and the hag's power to over-rule her upper-class husband) voluntarily cedes that superiority, and thereby restores harmony. Like political theories that depend on the ruler acting well, these two dénouements posit individual morality, rather than structural changes in society, for solving conflicts of interest. Chaucer boldly essays a discussion in the 'Franklin's Tale' (ll. 741–802) of whether lordship within the hierarchy of marriage can be replaced by friendship and equal readiness to obey. This secures Arveragus 'blisse' and 'solas' in his marriage, the passage concludes (l. 802) – but note the sudden shift verbally to the conventional focus on the husband's primacy. The daring exploration of more equal possibilities only goes so far and thereafter Chaucer's tale stages a fascinating crisis over what ensues if hierarchical assumptions are crossed: what if a notion of 'truth' and honour that applies to men (keeping one's word) is extended to a wife (for whom fidelity and honour, instead, inhere in keeping herself sexually entirely for her husband)?

A further crisis interrogates the implications of what were to happen should a mere professional, financially dependent on his fees and not in possession of land, choose to act like a member of the 'gentil' class (ll. 1607–22). The text asks its audience a question: who was the most 'fre' (l. 1622)? It is a word meaning 'generous' but also connotes possession of 'gentilesse', that key, virtually indefinable, socially superior identity and ethos. That a professional gives up a massive thousand pounds fee, in an aspirational impulse to rival the behaviour of the higher (land-possessing) class above him, curiously mingles admiration for the social myth of upper-class 'gentilesse' with a demonstration that the social divide that marks the 'gentils' as congenitally superior can dissolve.

The tale fits the Franklin, representative of an upwardly mobile class that historians label 'gentry', a class increasingly prominent in the later fourteenth century: land-owners, purchasing rather than inheriting estates, rising in wealth and (as his 'General Prologue' portraits accurately depict) frequently taking over local administrative positions. Such men were useful in Richard II's policies of strengthening regional networks centred on royal power. The Franklin, happily providing the hospitality of an old-world 'vavasour' (ll. 353, 360), anxious to instil *gentil* manners in his son, nonetheless typifies new men – like Chaucer himself – breaking into positions of bureaucracy and politics (both are members of parliament and JPs), imitating the ethos of the *gentil* class while negating the hierarchical barriers that traditionally preserved their economic and political positions. How apt that the tale ends on a question.

Another tale raising questions about social hegemony and myths that support it is the 'Wife of Bath's Tale'. The lower-class wife, whose skills saved her gently born but wilful, discourteous and woman-oppressing husband, is given a speech (ll. 1109–1206) disputing the assumption that birth creates a right to be called *gentil*. Though starting with blunt contempt – 'Swich arrogance is nat worth an hen'[18] – the speech is no call for democracy in the sense of structural political or economic changes based on a recognition of human equality. Its primary argument is that *gentils* should behave well. Only 'gentil dedes' give moral rights to the title (l. 1115). The idea that virtue was the true definition of *gentilesse* became a popular subject in the fourteenth century. Chaucer's *Gentilesse* elegantly reprises the arguments.[19] The religious elements that enter here, that Christ was a poor man and all Christians can be equal in moral worth, have a potential for leading to ideas of political equality, but these are never present. This is about morality, not politics or class, yet it parallels the growing sense that kingship carries obligations, as does *gentil* birth. By offering widening and increasingly moral senses of *gentil* (a change happening, too, in linguistic and semantic terms), the argument opens a way to respect and advancement based on ability and personal qualities rather than birth.

Further readiness to demolish automatic respect for the nobly born appears in the *Legend*'s several exposés of rulers who were far from admirable, exploiting and betraying noble and generous women who aided them. The 'Parson's Tale' expounds the standard doctrine that God ordained high and low degree and that envy and grumbling are sins, but, under the heading of Avarice, the main attack is on lords who, like wolves, abuse their position, extorting unjust and cruel fees

and taxes from their peasants.[20] Mentioning the belief that serfdom
originated in a curse for sin on Cain's descendants, the Parson concentrates on ethical, not political, aspects: sin itself is the true thral-
dom; a churl can be saved as readily as a lord; and '[e]very synful man
is a cherl to synne' (X. 760).

Society and social mobility

In practice, mobility and social mobility were everywhere in
Chaucer's England. People moved to where opportunities and higher
wages were; economic migrants moved to London where there were
opportunities for advancement (Chaucer's grandfather moved in this
way from East Anglia); many former serfs moved into wage-earning
positions; as incomes from land dropped, lords and middle-class people who rented estates (lawyers and merchants) diversified; commerce
flourished; the dramatic and terrifying events, natural and political,
of Chaucer's lifetime (the Black Death, the 1381 Rising, struggles
between the king and his opponents, ending in invasion, deposition
and Richard's death) made English society markedly insecure and subject to change and movement. Yet the post-Black Death population
drop (lowered by a third to half or more since the previous century), a
labour shortage and resulting higher incomes for many ordinary people and, especially, skilled artisans and professionals, brought increased
prosperity, security, comfort, consumerist aspirations and confidence.
Chaucer's Canterbury stories and choice of literally mobile and
socially diversified middle-ranking professions as story-tellers match
this turbulence. He eschews one widespread traditional model: that
of a social division into 'three estates' (knights, clergy and labourers),
popular with conservatives. This implied a static economy and class
structure, and omits groups such as artisans, merchants and professionals. In medieval theoretical models of society women were sometimes
categorized as a separate class and maritally: as virgin, widow or
wife, though real-life records like the Poll Tax documentation record
their regular participation in (typically household-based) businesses.
Chaucer's two female portraits depict well-to-do women, the Wife
(who fulfils also the Widow category) and Prioress (the Virgin), both
with important managerial roles, running a business and a convent.
   Starting with a manorial group (Knight, Squire, Yeoman), followed
by the Monk and Prioress, doubtless envisaged as of similar background (the Prioress fills the gap of the upper-class lady to match the
Knight), Chaucer's tales and portraits present examples of contemporary professions experiencing upward mobility: guildsmen, successful

artisans including millers and carpenters, merchants, lawyers. His descriptions accurately capture the lifestyle, tastes and possessions such groups were able to enjoy. Chaucer with brilliant topical sociological accuracy as well as satire paints aspirational lifestyle detail: the materialist values and canny profits of a trader playing with international exchange rates in the 'Shipman's Tale'; the entertaining that promotes business; the Merchant trading as all businessmen did (despite theoretical forbidding of interest) on credit and his necessary show of liquidity; the Franklin's fashionable fishponds and sauces; and the must-have fashions of the Guildsmen or Alison and Absolon in the 'Miller's Tale'.

Upper-class and aspirational mores appear in views and manners: the premium the Prioress places on table manners or Symkyn on a virgin bride (modern villagers were rejecting traditional peasant toleration of cohabitation unmarried till a child was conceived). Other details expose fears and hostility awakened by new peasant ambitions and confidence, and the events of 1381. Though the Reeve and Miller Symkyn have made money, Chaucer presents this as due to large-scale cheating. Both intimidate people. Symkyn's upward mobility, his and his wife's fashions and dominance in village society, his bold family game-plan of rising through the social classes (from churl to yeoman now and in the future upwards to who knows what heights?) are condemned by Chaucer's narration not just as vulgar but as sinful pride (I. 4313), and this justifies the students' ruthless punishment through violence and destroying the aspirational marriage prospects of his daughter. The 'Nun's Priest's Tale' dairywoman is admired for contentment with a lifestyle typical of peasants a generation or two earlier: her narrow cottage and diet low on white bread, fresh meat or fish, and alcohol. The tale mentions the 1381 leader Jack Straw and his rebels (VII. 3393–6) and the comic self-importance of the farmyard cock can be read as an allegory not only of Adam's Fall, through Pride, and of Fortune's power (the tale follows the Falls of famous men in the 'Monk's Tale'), but of the folly and sin of lower orders getting above themselves.

Chaucer's position in the political milieu

Chaucer himself illustrates social mobility: from a comfortably off family within the upper levels of the merchant elite which ruled London, he entered royal service. He became an 'esquire' but of a new sort, from employment as a royal servant, not because of gentle birth. Chaucer's grand-daughter Alice became Duchess of Suffolk. Chosen as a 'Knight of the Shire', MP, undoubtedly as a king's supporter, he experienced, and survived, the perils of the 1386 parliament when several royal supporters were executed. Speaking of unjust accusations against his heroine Constance, he recalls the pale face of one being led to execution when pleas for mercy have failed (II. 645–51). Being a king's man may have led to his resignation or dismissal from the post of Controller of Wool Customs and his move out of London to Kent for a time. Many of his friends were king's supporters; some were known supporters of Lollardy, which between 1385 and 1400 was increasingly regarded by authorities as dangerous, i.e., as both heretical and potentially politically destabilizing. Chaucer's Parson's portrait suggests that he is visualized, positively, as one of Wycliffe's 'poor priests', who imitated the supposed poverty of Christ and the Apostles and taught their parishioners a gospel-based faith. Chaucer's support for any of the various ideas associated with Lollardy has proved hard to ascertain, but his knowledge of it and engagement with the issues is clear.

Chaucer, born and dwelling for a long time in the City of London, a royal bureaucrat at Westminster and other palaces, lived amongst the important political figures and events of his age, geographically at an intersection of many contemporary spheres of influence, innovation and power: ecclesiastical, royal, commercial and intellectual. His wife was Lady in Waiting to Gaunt's second wife, Constance heiress of Castile: that may explain the praise of Constance's ruthless father, Pedro the Cruel ('Monk's Tale', ll. 2374–90). *The Book of the Duchess* is probably a memorial to Gaunt's first wife, Blanche (though its final puns on John, Lancaster and Richmond may also include a reference to his subsequent marriage to Constance and claim to the title 'kynge' of Castile) (ll. 1314–20). The *Legend of Good Women* compliments Queen Anne, but new lilies added to roses in the G rewriting may compliment Richard's second, French, bride (G. 161).

Chaucer apparently maintained good relations with both Richard II and John of Gaunt's family, despite periodic political differences between the two men. After Henry IV replaced Richard II, Chaucer's poem petitioning for a renewed annuity from the new regime (it was granted, though after a delay) ends with an address to Henry, naming three justifications for his kingship: his descent, his conquest (flatteringly compared with a glamorous invasion conveniently and gloriously in Britain's distant originary past, Trojan Prince Brutus's conquest), and 'eleccioun', a word in Middle English which was learned, abstract and Latinate, meaning 'choice' and conveying thus here the idea of a dignified approval by the people of Henry's takeover (it could also have a sense of a destined or astrologically favoured time). In reality, 1399–400 saw many still supporting Richard; many were exiled, silenced, deprived of office or killed – like Richard himself. It was a bloodthirsty, tense, ugly period, even by the standards of politics in Chaucer's lifetime.

The society and the personal milieus in which Chaucer lived were politically turbulent, contentious and often perilous. The *House of Fame*'s unedifying picture of petitioners at Fame's court competing for her favour, and the *Legend*'s statements about envy, lying, false accusations and flatterers at court (G. 326–40) paint a picture of political circles that might well have confirmed Chaucer in returning so often to imagery of the world as a place not ruled by just or wise order, but a government by unstable Fortune. *Fortune* begins:

> This wrecched worldes transmutacioun,
> As wele or wo, now povre [poor] and now honour,
> Withouten ordre or wys discrecioun [judgement]
> Governed is by Fortunes errour. (ll. 1–4)

Tellingly, the Envoy asks 'Princes' to petition for advancement for the author from his truest friend (King Richard? King Henry? When was *Fortune* written?). The general philosophical *sentence* that humans live in an unreliable world, and one of the only good outcomes is to discover who one's true friends are, turns out here also to serve a practical and personal situation, as Chaucer, the governmental civil servant, contrives to get into 'som beter estat': climb back up the ladder again. Nonetheless, perhaps more striking is his advice in *Truth* that the only solution is to step aside from the 'prees' (l. 1) and the 'climbing' (l. 3), be contented with what one has and '[u]nto this world leve now to be a thral' (l. 23).

Notes

1. Geoffrey Chaucer, 'The Squire's Tale', *The Canterbury Tales*, in *The Riverside Chaucer*, ed. Larry Benson (Oxford: Oxford University Press, 1988), pp. 169–77 (V. 19–27). All references to Chaucer's works are from *The Riverside Chaucer*.
2. Chaucer, *Lak of Stedfastnesse*, p. 654 (ll. 22–8).
3. Many of Chaucer's works exist in fragments and in different manuscript versions. They are either numbered or lettered to distinguish between them.
4. This is an allusion to the idea, popular with Richard, that rulers are set apart by birth.
5. Chaucer, *Legend of Good Women*, pp. 587–630 (G. 353–70).

6. Chaucer, 'The Monk's Tale', *The Canterbury Tales*, pp. 240–52.
7. Chaucer, 'The Manciple's Tale', *The Canterbury Tales*, pp. 282–6.
8. Chaucer, 'The Clerk's Tale', *The Canterbury Tales*, pp. 137–53.
9. Chaucer, 'The Knight's Tale', *The Canterbury Tales*, pp. 37–66 (ll. 3041–6).
10. It is a question Boethius asks and his *Consolation of Philosophy* offers the answer that those human aspirations and pleasures that are subject to transience and disappointment concern temporal matters which are worthless, compared with the life of the mind and spirit.
11. Chaucer, *The Complaint to Mars*, p. 643.
12. Chaucer, 'The Franklin's Tale', *The Canterbury Tales*, pp. 178–89.
13. Chaucer, *Troilus and Criseyde*, pp. 471–585.
14. Chaucer, *The Parliament of Fowls*, pp. 383–94 (ll. 74–5).
15. Chaucer, 'The Physician's Tale', *The Canterbury Tales*, pp. 190–3.
16. Chaucer, 'The Summoner's Tale', *The Canterbury Tales*, pp. 128–37 (ll. 1948–53; 2129–58).
17. Chaucer, 'The Friar's Tale', *The Canterbury Tales*, pp. 122–8 (III. 1618–23).
18. Chaucer, 'The Wife of Bath's Tale', *The Canterbury Tales*, pp. 105–22 (l. 1112).
19. Chaucer, *Gentilesse*, p. 654.
20. Chaucer, 'The Parson's Tale', *The Canterbury Tales*, pp. 287–328 (l. 765).

6

The Consolations and Conflicts of History: Chaucer's 'Monk's Tale'

Rob Gossedge

Chaucer's meditations on the recording, rewriting and understanding of history occur in the context of a struggle between the dominant sacred view of history as a providential, divinely superintended plan and an emergent secular historiography that sought its own internal logic of causation for the events of history. While the late medieval historiographical and epistemological struggles are visible in many of Chaucer's writings – and prominently in the tales of the classical past, *Troilus*, *Anelida* and the 'Knight's Tale' – nowhere in Chaucer's oeuvre is the conflict between sacred and secular models of history dramatized so directly as in the under-appreciated 'Monk's Tale'. Its self-conscious staging of divergent historiographical worldviews is most clearly demonstrated in the discord between the text's form and its speaker. As a series of tragic histories of great men (and a single great woman), it was inspired by Boccaccio's virulently democratic and anti-monarchist *De casibus virorum illustrium* (On the Fates of Illustrious Men, 1355–74), a title which serves as the incipit to the 'Monk's Tale' in many manuscripts. Yet its speaker is a member of the Benedictine order, that great repository and production factory of historical knowledge throughout the Middle Ages, but which so often viewed history, in Lee Patterson's words, 'as a desert place of exile, a chaos of random events, or, as in Boethius's view, a repetitive cycle of meaningless acts of rise and fall'.[1] Chaucer's 'Monk's Tale', then, draws on two distinct, but still interrelated, traditions. It reflects the contemporary, voguish and politically radical intellectualism of Chaucer's *trecento* colleagues in Italy, but is also firmly part of – and set against – a canonical historiographical tradition that sought to explain historical change as nothing more than the workings of fickle Fortune and her ever-present wheel.

Changing fortune: Boethius and Boccaccio

The very idea of Fortune, despite its ubiquity in historical writings, is profoundly unhistorical. Derived from Fortuna, the Roman good-luck goddess, Fortune became a symbol for life's capriciousness during the Christian *zeitgeist*. Though St Augustine found her incompatible with the Christian understanding of God's providence, her later prominence in medieval thought was a legacy of Boethius' sixth-century *De consolatione Philosophiæ* (The Consolation of Philosophy), wherein apparently random and often ruinous turns of Fortune's Wheel are interpreted as inevitable and providential. As Lady Philosophy teaches Boethius, in coming to understand how earthly fortunes can so quickly turn to misfortune, Christians can learn to shun the material world and better prepare themselves for the other world of eternal joy. Yet, as spiritually useful as it might be in terms of personal meditation, as a rhetorical device for explaining the vicissitudes of history Fortune's mutability is, to use Larry Scanlon's phrase, a 'threadbare narrative'.[2] As the putative origin of historical change, whether experienced as a community or, more often, an individual, she only exposes how little meaning change has: there is no logical purpose to historical action, and the otherwise tangible relationship between cause and effect – say, between a king's tyranny and that same king's overthrow – is always and insistently illusory. Instead, as Boethius's Lady Philosophy explains, speaking in the voice of Fortune, life becomes a game:

> This is our power, this is the game we always play. We turn our wheel on its flying course; we delight in changing the low to the high and the high to the low. Rise up, if you wish, but on this condition: don't consider yourself injured when you descend, as the rules of my game demand.[3]

As Scanlon has argued, 'like any metaphor which defines social experience as a game, this one has an aspect that is profoundly conservative'.[4] It was the conservatism at the heart of this game – the absolutely random, rather than the socially prescribed, contingency of material power – that made Fortune not only so appealing to the Church, but also maintained its immense popularity as a shaping, defining metaphor of aristocratic and royal existence.

As is well known, Chaucer's mature writings are greatly shaped by a Boethian outlook. He produced the first Middle English translation of the *Consolation* around 1380, and Boethian thought strongly influences many of Chaucer's most important works: it intellectually sophisticates his treatment of Boccaccio's *Teseida* in the 'Knight's Tale'; is the dominant philosophical model that underpins 'The Tale of Melibee' (which directly precedes the 'Monk's Tale' in Fragment VII of the *Canterbury Tales*); and is the central methodology for Chaucer's exploration of erotic desire in *Troilus and Criseyde*. The Boethian conception of Fortune is also apparent in several other tales, including those of the Franklin, Clerk and Nun's Priest; and it returns in the Parson's long sermon on the sin of pride, as well as Chaucer's late ballade, *Fortune*, on 'this wrechhed worldes transmutacioun'.[5] As vital as Boethius' *Consolation* is for Chaucer at theological, spiritual and individual levels, the 'Monk's Tale' empties Boethius' conception of history as a means of elucidating both ancient and modern history – and parodies those contemporary fourteenth-century historians who sought to explain historical change through such a metaphor. This parody is itself powerfully charged by the historical writings appearing in contemporary Italy, the most important of which was Boccaccio's *De casibus virorum illustrium*, a work that served as a model and major intertext for Chaucer's own 'Book of Falls'.

For Boccaccio, writing in democratic Florence in the 1350s, but within sight of the tyrannical rule of the despotic Viscontis in contemporary Milan, history was not a game. His *De casibus virorum illustrium* was a history of fallen rulers, both men and women, from Adam and Eve to the tyrants of contemporary Italy, ending with Walter, Duke of Athens and brief despot over the Florentines – that 'personal plague and blot on the name of Florence' – whose overthrow led to the establishment of the republic in 1343.[6] Borrowing the structure of Petrarch's *De viris illustribus* (On Great Men) begun in the 1330s and gathering 'Fortune, kingship, and the exemplum into a single, unrelenting focus', Boccaccio's *De casibus* was an excoriating attack on contemporary tyrants and the 'narrative alter ego' of Boethius' *Consolation*.[7] Far more widely read than the vernacular *Decameron* in Boccaccio's own century, the first version of the *De casibus* was completed in 1360, and the second version finished in around 1374. Boccaccio could find no patron worthy enough to dedicate the second version to, and so instead provides a list of great figures of his own day whom he considered unworthy of his greatest scholarly undertaking.[8]

In the *De casibus*, Boccaccio imbued the Boethian fall with a moral, political rigour. The preface describes how the great men of his own day had become 'so attracted to vice and debauchery' that they believe that they have 'put Fortune perpetually to sleep'. In their supposed security of place (thinking they have clamped 'with iron bands [...] their little empires to adamantine foundation'), they have given themselves over to oppressing their subjects 'with all their power'. The purpose of his work, Boccaccio writes, is to encourage virtue through contemplation of the fate of illustrious men of history:

> But you who hold sway over mighty empires, open your eyes and unplug your ears. And to ensure that a deadly sleep does not carry you off, stay wide awake, ignoring minor figures to consider kings: their tears, despositions, exiles, chains, imprisonments, tortures, execrations, deaths; and the shedding of blood, the broken bodies, scattered ashes; heirs driven across the world, royal plunderings, and kingdoms destroyed.[9]

Speaking directly to the governing classes in the dominant discourse of Latin, this is, as David Wallace writes, 'scholarly exemplification as a form of resistance to contemporary tyrannical rule'.[10]

The *De casibus* tradition in Chaucer

Chaucer never addresses the powerful with anything like Boccaccio's vitriol. More conservative in political outlook, and writing far from the democratic security of *trecento* Florence, Chaucer speaks to power far more obliquely. Critics, as so often with this text, have been sharply divided as to the extent of Chaucer's indebtedness – even knowledge – of Boccaccio's *De casibus*.[11] Equally contentious, even among those scholars who are in agreement that Chaucer was well acquainted with the *De casibus*, is Chaucer's ideological relationship to the Boccaccian literary-political project. Warren Ginsberg has argued that the 'Monk's Tale' is 'extremely reluctant to explore the possibilities of a confederation between politics and fiction' similar to that of the *De casibus*, whereas Richard Neuse has gone so far as to perceive in the Monk 'a perfect double or counterpart of Boccaccio'.[12] Donald Howard, meanwhile, located Chaucer firmly on the side of the tyrants: not only did he suggest that Chaucer's *Boece* was produced as a 'Mirror for Princes' for the young Richard II, he also, in his 1987 biography of the poet, related a highly speculative story of a meeting between Chaucer and Bernabò Visconti in 1378, in which the poet was a beneficiary of the despot's 'munificence', receiving copies of a number of Boccaccio's works.[13]

At the root of many of these, often irreconcilable, differences in critical opinions on the text's socio-literary origins and ideological thrust is the layered textual fabric of Chaucer's tale. As with all of the *Canterbury Tales*, the pilgrims are listening to one oral performance, while the reader attends to a very different literary document. In the 'Monk's Tale', however, the juxtaposition between what the fictional pilgrims hear and what the actual reader reads is radically different. At the literary level the tale is a highly sophisticated miniaturization and distillation of Boccaccio's *De casibus*. While it contains only seventeen, often extremely short 'biographies', compared to Boccaccio's fifty-six, far longer, 'lives', in the extent of its learning, and the expanse of its historical worldview, the 'Monk's Tale' imitates the intellectual encyclopaedic form of the *De casibus*. It is constructed from a great range of sources: Boethius provides the figure of Fortuna, Nicholas Trevet's commentary on the *Consolation* (c. 1300) supplies the definition of tragedy, and the *De casibus* provides the overall structure. Alongside these historiographical and philosophical models are the diverse sources for the individual tales, including Scripture, apocrypha, classical historians, Jean de Meun's *Roman de la rose* (The Romance of the Rose, c. 1285), Boccaccio's *De claris mulieribus* (On Famous Women, 1362), Dante's *Divina commedia* (The Divine Comedy, 1321) and Vincent of Beauvais' *Speculum Historiale* (The Mirror of History, 1260), together with contemporary hearsay and court gossip regarding the goings-on in far-away Italy.

Yet at the level of – fictional – oral performance, the Monk can only deliver a series of half-remembered, imprecisely told and misattributed miniature tales of fallen princes – of which, he declares, he has a hundred in his cell:

> Now herkeneth, if you liketh for to heere.
> But first I you biseeke in this mateere,
> Though I by ordre telle nat thise thynges,
> Be it of popes, emperours, or kynges,
> After hir ages, as men writen fynde,
> But tellen hem som bifore and som bihynde,
> As it now cometh unto my remembraunce,
> Have me excused of myn ignoraunce. (VII. 1983–90)

As either a mnemonic exercise or an example of oral storytelling, the 'Monk's Tale' is poor fare. Whereas the falls of the *De casibus* had been organized within a highly complex dream vision, the Monk rattles off his tragedies any which way he can. He begins with an apology for his storytelling abilities, and many critics, aligning themselves with the impatient pilgrims, have sighed with relief when the Knight puts a stop to the tales that follow.

Even Chaucer's most celebrated addition to his source material, the introduction of the term 'tragedy' into English, is itself subject to a repetitive, dulling presentation. The Monk first defines tragedy as:

> a certeyn storie,
> As olde bookes maken us memorie,
> Of hym that stood in greet prosperitee,
> And is yfallen out of heigh degree
> Into myserie, and endeth wrecchedly. (ll. 1973–7)

One of the 'olde bookes' the Monk refers to here is Chaucer's own *Boece*, in which he described tragedy in near-identical terms: 'tragedy is to seyn a dite of a prosperite for a tyme, that endeth in wrechidnesse.'[14] This definition was itself a modification of Nicholas Trevet's statement on tragedy in his well-known, early fourteenth-century commentary on Boethius: 'Tragedia est carmen de magnis iniquitatibus a prosperitate incipiens et in adversitate terminans' ('Tragedy is the song of great iniquities that begins in prosperity and ends in adversity').[15] In glossing tragedy in this way, Trevet had added a moral dimension (and sense of causality) to Boethius's understanding of the amoral, capricious workings of fortune, namely that princes fall because of their own iniquitous behaviour. Boccaccio's *De casibus* had powerfully focused on such princes' criminal activity. Chaucer, in both the *Boece* and the 'Monk's Tale', omits the phrase 'de magnis inquitatibus' from his translation, and thus tragedy takes on an amoral vein akin to Boethius's understanding of fickle Fortune. But before the Monk begins his tragedies, he repeats, with minor variation, his definition again:

> I wol biwaille in manere of tragedie
> The harm of hem that stoode in heigh degree,
> And fillen so, that ther nas no remedie
> To brynge hem out of hir adversitee.
> For certein, whan that Fortune list to flee,
> Ther may no man the cours of hire withholde;
> Lat no man truste on blynd prosperitee;
> Be war of thise ensamples, trewe and olde. (ll. 1991–8)

Whereas Boethius had fostered a spirit of *contemptus mundi* (contempt for the world) in order to encourage contemplation of eternal and spiritual joy and Boccaccio's '*historia*' had supplemented its account of Fortune's governance of this world with political invective and social complaint, implying that if rulers were to moderate their criminal behaviour then they might be saved from a tragic end, Chaucer's

Monk refuses to offer anything more than the stark lesson: 'Lat no man truste on blynd prosperitee'. The effect is to intensify – and limit – the meanings of the *De casibus*. Unlike Boethius, the Monk focuses only on this world, and offers no reference to spiritual values, and, unlike Boccaccio, he remains uninterested in social justice or progressive politics. Tragedy, in the Monk's hands, is little more than an exercise in reductivism – his repeated examples of tragedy are locked in a cycle of despair: there is 'no remedie' to adversity; no man can resist Fortune's trajectory.

Fortune's 'false wheel'

While a number of critics have seen the Monk's accounts of the fallen princes in similarly reductivist mode,[16] others have resisted readings of the tales as mechanistically adhering to the Monk's definition of tragedy.[17] Though undoubtedly a gloomy, if often sensationalist, series of tragedies, the stories themselves often seem to work against the Monk's prologue's stranglehold on the tragedies' *sentence*. Most seem determined by their own internal and independent logic, quite free from the hopeless and agency-free capriciousness of Fortune insisted upon in the Monk's prologue. All too often, real (or imagined) history appears as a spoke in Fortune's wheel, as the causes of so many great princes' falls are located in their own actions. Time and again, the Monk's tragic vignettes illustrate the emptiness of Fortune, and its associated concept of tragedy, as a metaphor for historical change.

The first two of the Monk's 'ensamples trewe and olde' are Lucifer and Adam. Fortune does not appear in either of these single-stanza falls: she, we are told in the Lucifer *casus*, 'may noon angel dere' (l. 2001); and Adam's expulsion from 'paradys' is located – vaguely – in his 'mysgovernauce' (l. 2012), a term that will link his fall to that of other 'kynges' of this text. Fortune is also absent from the following tale of Sampson, but is mentioned at the end of the tale of Hercules (l. 2136), Sampson's classical avatar. As the tragedies continue, however, Fortune steadily increases her hold on both the text and the protagonists' fates. She casts Nebuchadnezzar down (ll. 2189–90) and forsakes his son, Belshazzar (l. 2241); ends the reign of Zenobia (ll. 2347–9); raises up and then forsakes Pedro of Spain (l. 2376); brings Peter of Cyprus from sorrow to joy (ll. 2397–8); causes Ugolino to be imprisoned along with his children (ll. 2413–14); proves that, though Nero is strong, 'was she stronger' (l. 2521); elevates the pride of Antiochus so that he believes himself to be a rival to God (l. 2583); initially makes Alexander 'the heir of hir honour' (l. 2643), but also dictates the roll of life's dice ('thy sys Fortune hath turned into aas', l. 2661); is first Caesar's friend, and then his foe (l. 2723); and sends Croesus 'swich hap' that he forgets her role in governing his fate, which is always a mistake.

Entering the sequence a few tales in, Fortune begins as an abstract concept, but gradually becomes a character in her own right: she kisses Holofernes 'so likerously, and ladde hym up and doun / til that his heed was of, er that he wiste' (ll. 2557–8). By the Nero *casus* she has even begun to speak:

> By God! I am to nyce
> To sette a man that is fulfild of vice
> In heigh degree, and emperor hym calle.
> By God, out of his sete wol I hym trice;
> Whan he leest weneth, sonnest shal he falle. (ll. 2522–6)

Though she laughs at Nero's gruesome end, fickle Fortune also refuses to weep at the death of Alexander, the flower 'of knyghthod and of fredom' (ll. 2662, 2642). Fortune's 'false wheel' (l. 2446) is no mechanism to distinguish the fate of the innocent from the guilty. Alexander, Zenobia and Julius Caesar are all blameless in their accounts – as are, in this presentation, the more contemporary figures of Ugolino of Pisa and Peter of Cyprus. Hercules' and Sampson's only fault was that they trusted in their wives. And this anxiety over female 'maistree' is greatly expanded upon in the tale of Zenobia, the only woman to figure in her own *casus*. Though she commits no crime, and is described as without sin (ll. 2279–94), Fortune nonetheless 'made hire falle / To wrecchednesse and to mysaventure' (ll. 2349–50). She who was once helmed for battle, is now forced to wear a vitremyte, or female headdress; and instead of the victor's sceptre, she now carries a distaff for spinning wool. Fortune may be capricious, but she has a strangely misogynistic manner of arranging Zenobia's fall.

Though Fortune remains diligently indiscriminate in bringing rulers to their fate, there is, nonetheless, a certain set of sins and faults that the despotic rulers share, the most important of which are gluttony, luxuriousness, pride and, connected to it, the appropriation of God's majesty. Gluttony is a feature of several falls: Alexander is partial to 'wyn' (2644); Holofernes lies drunk at night (l. 2568); and Belshazzar throws lavish, even sacrilegious, feasts at which he eats and drinks from sacred vessels (ll. 2191–201). Luxury is apparent in the stanza on Bernabò, described as a 'God of delit' (l. 2400); and Nero is strongly associated with the sin of 'delicacy': he fishes in the Tiber with nets of spun gold, and wears robes embroidered with rubies, sapphires and pearls (ll. 2468–76). Pride, meanwhile, envelops many of the Monk's 'ensamples', including Croesus, Antiochus, and Holofernes, so 'pomp-ous in heigh presumpcioun' (l. 2555). Proud also are Nebuchadnezzar and Balshazzar. Father and son, and kings of Babylon, they both appropriate the worship due to God for their own kingly reigns. They set themselves up on 'myghty trone', surround themselves with 'precious tresor' and carry a 'glorious ceptre' (ll. 2143–44), but have forgotten that the 'glorie, and honour, regne, tresour, rente' that they hold is but a loan from God, who possesses the real 'domynacioun' (ll. 2210–11, 2219). Nebuchadnezzar may term himself 'kyng of kynges' (ll. 2167), but their projection of 'majestee' (which is also used of Antiochus and Pedro of Spain at lines 2576 and 2376) is an affront to the true King of Kings.

These four categories of sin, written across the spectrum of the Monk's seventeen tragedies, are each topical. Richard II, especially in the last few years of his reign, was explicitly associated with luxury, glut-tony, pride and, due to the 'elevated concept of quasi-divine royalty' that he cultivated, majesty, which had not previously been associated with English kings.[18] In the 'obituary' written by the Monk of Evesham, Richard appears as a concentration of all the Monk's many despots:

> Of average height, fair-haired, with a pale complexion and a rounded, feminine face… He was prodigious with gifts, extravagantly ostentation in his dress and pastimes, and unlucky as well as faint-hearted in for-eign warfare. Towards his servants he often displayed great anger; he was also puffed up with pride, consumed by avarice, much given to luxury, and fond of burning the candle at both ends, sometimes staying up half the night, and at other times right through until morning, drinking and indulging himself in other unmentionable ways.[19]

Even Richard's faint-heartedness is echoed in the sense of crippling fear that overcomes both Belshazzar (ll. 2204–5) and Nero (l. 2538). More importantly, Richard, like so many of the Monk's tragic figures, was overthrown by those close to him, and from 1397 Richard was accused of tyranny explicitly – precisely the same term to describe perhaps the worst of all the Monk's examples, Bernabò and Nero (ll. 2400, 2537).

Writing Richard's fall

While often dismissed as a crude apprentice piece reworked by a mature Chaucer to fit into *The Canterbury Tales*,[20] the 'Monk's Tale', then, seems far more likely (as David Wallace and Jane Zatta have argued) to have been produced within a society living under, or at least in sight of, the growing tyranny of Richard II and its ultimately allied cult of majesty.[21] Helen Phillips has gone so far as to suggest the text may have been finished in the very last years of Chaucer's life: that is, after the deposition, imprisonment and murder of Richard in 1399.[22] Moreover, the topicality of the Monk's tragedies is not only to be found in the adumbration of Ricardian tyranny buried within the *casi*, but can be seen in the very form of Richard's fall as it was recorded and explained in contemporary chronicles. Indeed, the histories of Adam of Usk and Thomas Walsingham seem to echo the very form of the *casus* that Chaucer relentlessly parodies in the 'Monk's Tale'.

According to Adam's report of his encounter with the deposed, imprisoned king in 1399, Richard himself placed his own overthrow within a tradition of *casus*-like falls:

> There and then the king discoursed sorrowfully in these words: 'My God!, a wonderful land is this, and a fickle; which hath exiled, slain, destroyed or ruined so many kings, rulers, and great men, and is ever tainted and toileth with strife and variance and envy;' and then he recounted the histories and names of sufferers from the earliest habitation of the kingdom. Perceiving then the trouble of his mind, and how that none of his own men, nor such as were wont to serve him, but strangers who were but spies upon him, were appointed to his service, and musing on his ancient and wonted glory and on the fickle fortune of the world, I departed thence much moved at heart.[23]

As an agent of the Lancastrian regime, Adam had been instructed to visit the king in order to assess his 'mood and bearing' by William Beauchamp. But he can respond only with sympathy – a sympathy that is two-fold: not only is he 'much moved at heart' at the king's distress, his chronicle also colludes in Richard's presentation of himself as a fallen prince within a tradition of ruined 'kings, rulers, and great men'.[24] Yet Adam, here positioned in his own chronicle as one of the 'strangers who were but spies upon' the king, had not always been a mere spectator to 'the fickle fortune of the world'. He had joined with Bolingbroke on his march from Bristol to Chester and, as a lawyer, had served on the commission to find legal grounds for the king's deposition. But now faced with the king in the midst of his fall, he is unable to comprehend what he sees outside the interpretive model of Fortune – despite having been an agent of that fall himself.

The Benedictine cleric Thomas Walsingham presents the most extensive account of the events of 1399. Walsingham was critical of the king throughout most of Richard's reign, and was unambiguous in chronicling how, from 1397, he brought ruin upon himself through his tyranny. And yet, when he comes to describe the deposition itself, Walsingham's account comes to resemble one of those vignettes of misfortune told by Chaucer's Monk:

> [in 1397] England seemed to be basking in peace and the future looked entirely favourable: the country had an impressive-looking king who had just married the daughter of the King of France and had thereby acquired not only great riches but a truce to last for thirty years, and it had more, as well as more talented, lords than any other kingdom could boast. It was at this time, however, that through the rashness, cunning, and pride of the king, the entire kingdom was suddenly and unexpectedly thrown into confusion.[25]

Here, though Walsingham is keen to stress the suddenness of Richard's fall, he still locates its causes in the king's own actions and behaviour. On the very eve of his downfall, however, Richard's demise is transformed into a result of divine intervention:

> While the king remained in Ireland attacking the Irish, imagining that he was achieving great things, God suddenly decided to humble his pride and bring succour to the people of England, who were now so miserably oppressed that they had lost all hope of deliverance and relief unless God were to reach forth and help them.[26]

While he had been careful to explain the political contexts and the personal motivations that brought about Bolingbroke's usurpation, faced with the deposition itself, Walsingham's narrative falls back on the familiar pattern of providential history. Only divine intervention can explain the traumatic magnificence and unexpectedness of Richard's fate.

Both Adam of Usk and Thomas Walsingham place Richard within a genre of fallen princes, wherein the image of fortune's fickleness obscures and veils the otherwise all-too-visible historical forces that brought about the revolution. With fortune – or God – as the dynamizing force of change, the actions of Bolingbroke, as well as such Lancastrian *apparatchik*s as Adam, are rendered negligible in terms of their ethical and political significance. For the Lancastrian historians keen to legitimize their *arriviste* position, Richard's capture, imprisonment and death was only another manifestation, another reproduction, of the same cycle of worldly misfortune that had been in motion since the very first fall of man. For them, Richard's story had already been written.

Reinventing the wheel: Chaucer's modern instances

Chaucer's 'Book of Falls' resists the overpowering appeal of Fortune as a metaphor for explaining historical change that so seduced the Lancastrian chroniclers – most potently as the Monk's final tales move inexorably closer to the contemporary English court. In early manuscripts, including the Hengwrt and Ellesmere, the 'Monk's Tale' concluded not with the Croesus *casus* that closes the tale in most later manuscripts (as well as the *Riverside Chaucer*), but with the so-called 'modern instances' of Ugolino of Pisa, Pedro the Cruel of Spain, Peter I of Cyprus and Bernabò Visconti of Milan.[27] At first glance, Chaucer's inclusion of the falls of four recent great men appears to be an exercise in political timidity: they seem geographically distant and sparse on detail. Yet, each was notorious in Chaucer's own day and the Monk's insistence on the role of Fortune in governing their fates relentlessly exposes Fortune's inadequacy as a historiographical metaphor.

The source of the Ugolino *casus*, the oldest of the modern instances, is taken from Dante's *Inferno*, as the Monk identifies (l. 2325). But Chaucer dramatically rewrites the story of monstrous cannibalism into one of pathos, in which Ugolino and his three children are unjustly imprisoned, and finally starved:

> His yonge sone, that thre yeer was of age,
> Unto hym seyde, 'Fader, why do ye wepe?
> Whanne wol the gayler bryngen oure potage?
> Is ther no morsel breed that ye do kepe?
> I am so hungry that I may nat slepe.
> Now wolde God that I myghte slepen evere!
> Thanne sholde nat hunger in my wombe crepe;
> Ther is no thyng, but breed, that me were levere.' (ll. 2431–8)

As Helen Cooper writes of this scene, 'the portrayal of innocence, however – and of positive virtue, in the children's offer to let their father eat their own flesh – makes the easy *moralitas* of the turning of the wheel of Fortune shockingly inadequate, even immoral'.[28] The tales of the other three modern instances are inadequate in quite different ways.

The *casus* of Pedro of Spain, King of Castile, is likely based on oral sources, perhaps even personal knowledge. Chaucer may have met Pedro in Spain in 1363; certainly Chaucer's wife, Phillipa, appears to have been attached to the household of Pedro's daughter, Constance, after she married John of Gaunt in 1371.[29] The Black

Prince had fought alongside him in his war against his half-brother, Enrique of Tratamare. A strong centralist, Pedro of Spain was known in a contemporary Spanish chronicle as 'Pedro the Cruel'.[30] None of these personal and political connections, however, have any impact on the two stanzas devoted to 'O noble, O worthy Petro, glorie of Spayne' (l. 2375). The tragedy of Peter of Cyprus is briefer still:

> They in thy bed han slayn thee by the morwe.
> O worthy Petro, kyng of Cipre, also,
> That Alisandre wan by heigh maistrie,
> Ful many an hethen wroghtestow ful wo,
> Of which thyne owene liges hadde envie,
> And for no thyng but for thy chivalrie
> Thus kan Fortune hir wheel governe and gye,
> And out of joye brynge men to sorwe. (ll. 2391–8)

Peter of Cyprus was also murdered in 1369. He too had connections with the English court: he visited England in 1363, and many Englishmen took part in his numerous expeditionary campaigns, including the young Henry Bolingbroke.[31] His most famous victory, though it achieved no lasting effect and ended with a hasty retreat after several days of looting, was the Alexandrine Crusade, mentioned both in this stanza and in the 'General Prologue', where it is listed as one of the many campaigns in which Chaucer's Knight had fought (I. 51). Though Peter was the most famous crusader of the fourteenth century, his history has little impact on his *casus*. Instead, he falls due to a mixture of misfortune and envy, whereas his actual death was more likely to have been motivated by 'resentment at his personal misconduct and his oppressive rule'.[32] Increasingly the tales draw attention to what they omit.

The final modern instance is that of Bernabò Visconti. His death in December 1385 was known initially as hearsay in court circles, and then in more established literary form. Froissart, for instance, included an account of the violent career and final deposition of Bernabò in the second volume of his *Chronicles* (completed in 1388). He relates how Bernabò and his brother Galeas had put their other brother to death, and how Bernabò heavily taxed the people and oppressed the whole region of Lombardy. He also remarks that his subjects abused him and praised his nephew, Gian Galeazzo, who eventually ambushed Bernabò, imprisoned him and finally murdered him. Froissart comments: 'News of this was soon spread abroad: some were pleased at it, others vexed; for sir Bernabò had in his time done so many acts of cruelty, and without reason, that few pitied him, saying, he had well deserved it'.[33] Yet Chaucer's stanza says nothing of this:

> Off Melan grete Barnabo Viscounte,
> God of delit, and scourge of Lumbardye,
> Why sholde I nat thyn infortune acounte,
> Sith in estaat thow cloumbe were so hye?
> Thy brother's sone, that was thy double allye,
> For he thy nevew was, and sone-in-lawe,
> Withinne his prisoun made thee to dye, –
> By why, ne how, noot I that thou were slawe. (ll. 2399–406)

Chaucer had known Bernabò personally as he had been despatched to Milan in 1378 to enlist the tyrant's assistance in England's ongoing continental wars. Bernabò was also connected to Chaucer's circle in other ways: Violata, Bernabò's niece, married Chaucer's first patron, Lionel, Duke of Clarence; and Bernabò's daughter Caterina had been offered in marriage to Richard II following the death of Anne of Bohemia.[34] Though Bernabò was dead and Chaucer's diplomatic career was long over by the late 1390s, the spectre of the despotic Visconti was still alive in the English court on the eve of Richard's own demise. Richard II and Charles VI, as part of their truce of 1396, planned an Anglo-French expedition against Bernabò's usurper.[35] While the English had been no friend of this latest Visconti, whom they regarded as an ally of France, when Richard put the Milanese proposal to parliament in January 1397, the common wanted no part in it, nor did the nobles, probably including Bolingbroke, who soon entered (ultimately unsuccessful) negotiations to marry Lucia Visconti, Gian Galeazzo's cousin. By 1398, Richard was making overtures to Bernabò's murderer.[36]

For William Rossiter, 'the entire stanza [on Bernabò] gives the impression of being an afterthought or a late addition',[37] yet it can be read as the epicentre of Chaucer's entire historiographical project. Though it does not mention Fortune by name, it is the most extreme form of the Monk's type of *casus*: it recounts nothing of his life or the causes of his death; misfortune and treachery are alone the agents of his fall. That the Monk admits in the last line to not knowing how or why Bernabò was killed calls to attention the self-conscious limitedness of Fortune as a means to interpret history. While David Wallace has written that the Monk's final words on Bernabò 'accentuate only his incapacity to prevent the memory of Bernabo from draining away through the cracks of history at the moment of his death', there is another form of oblivion conjured up here: the oblivion of the old-style means of writing history.[38]

Conclusion

Of course, the 'Monk's Tale' is not history *per se* – but a fictive web that holds together historiographical, scriptural, lay and ecclesiastic material in an interrogative series of juxtapositions that together form Chaucer's most complex and revisionist engagement with the late medieval practices of writing history. Metatextual and highly allusive though it is, the 'Monk's Tale' is no mere academic study of changing historiographical models, but a text that speaks powerfully of (and to) the age in which it was written. Whether written in the years preceding Richard's downfall, or in its immediate aftermath, what is certain is that this is a tale about the possibilities of writing history under the pressure of those very historical forces that monastic authors so often tried to elide.

Notes

1. Lee Patterson, *Chaucer and the Subject of History* (Madison, WI: University of Wisconsin Press, 1991), p. 87.
2. Larry Scanlon, *Narrative, Authority, and Power: The Medieval Exemplum and the Chaucerian Tradition* (Cambridge: Cambridge University Press, 1994), p. 126.
3. Boethius, *The Consolation of Philosophy*, trans. Scott Goins and Barbara H. Wyman (San Francisco, CA: Ignatius Press, 2012), p. 36.
4. Scanlon, *Narrative, Authority, and Power*, p. 124.
5. Chaucer, 'Fortune', in *The Riverside Chaucer*, ed. Larry Benson, 3rd edn (Cambridge: Cambridge University Press, 1988), pp. 652–3 (l. 1).
6. Giovanni Boccaccio, *The Fates of Illustrious Men*, trans. Louis Brewer Hall (New York: Frederick Ungar, 1965), p. 227.
7. Scanlon, *Narrative, Authority, and Power*, 121; Richard Firth Green, *Poets and Princepleasers: Literature and the English Court in the Late Middle Ages* (Toronto, Buffalo; London: University of Toronto Press, 1980), p. 145.
8. Henry Angsar Kelly, *Chaucerian Tragedy* (Cambridge: Brewer, 1997), p. 29.
9. Boccaccio, *The Fates of Illustrious Men*, pp. 1, 242.
10. David Wallace, *Chaucerian Polity: Absolute Lineages and Associational Forms in England* (Stanford, CA: Stanford University Press, 1997), p. 305.
11. Cf. Mike Pincombe, 'English Renaissance Tragedy: Theories and Antecedents', in *The Cambridge Companion to English Renaissance Tragedy*, ed. Emma Smith, Garrett A. Sullivan Jr (Cambridge: Cambridge University Press, 2010), pp. 3–16 (4); Piero Boitani, 'The Monk's Tale: Dante and Boccaccio', *Medium Ævum* 45 (1976), 50–69 (69); Wallace, *Chaucerian Polity*, p. 311.

12. Warren Ginsberg, *Chaucer's Italian Tradition* (Ann Arbor, MI: University of Michigan Press, 2002), p. 238; Richard Neuse, 'The Monk's *De Casibus*: The Boccaccio case reopened', in *The 'Decameron' and the 'Canterbury Tales': New Essays on an Old Question*, ed. Leonard Michael Koff and Brenda Deen Schildgen (Cranbury, NJ: Associated University Presses, 2002), pp. 247–77 (p. 255).
13. Donald Howard, *Chaucer: His Life, His Works, His World* (New York: Dutton, 1987), 229–30.
14. Chaucer, *Boece, Riverside Chaucer*, 2.2, gloss to l. 70.
15. Nicholas Trevet, cited in Henry Angsar Kelly, *Ideas and Forms of Tragedy from Aristotle to the Middle Ages* (Cambridge: Cambridge University Press, 1993), p. 128.
16. Scanlon, *Narrative, Power, and Authority*, p. 215; Trever Whittock, *A Reading of the 'Canterbury Tales'* (Cambridge: Cambridge University Press, 1968), p. 218.
17. Derek Pearsall, *The Canterbury Tales* (London: Allen and Unwin, 1985), p. 280; Michaela Paasche Grudin, *Chaucer and the Politics of Discourse* (Columbia, SC: University of South Carolina Press, 1996), p. 138.
18. Helen Phillips, *An Introduction to the Canterbury Tales: Reading, Fiction, Context* (London: Macmillan, 2000), p. 185.
19. *Vita Ricardi Secundi*, in *Chronicles of the Revolution: 1397-1400: the Reign of Richard II*, ed. and trans. Chris Given-Wilson (Manchester: Manchester University Press, 1993), pp. 241–2 (p. 242).
20. Pearsall, *The Canterbury Tales*, p. 280.
21. Jane Zatta, 'Chaucer's Monk: a mighty hunter before the Lord', *Chaucer Review* 29.2 (1994), 111–33; Wallace, *Chaucerian Polity*, p. 300.
22. Phillips, *An Introduction to the Canterbury Tales*, p. 185.
23. Adam of Usk, *Chronicon*, in *Chronicles of the Revolution*, pp. 157–61 (p. 161).
24. Cf. David Wallace, *Chaucerian Polity*, pp. 335–6.
25. Thomas Walsingham, *Annales Ricardi Secundi*, in *Chronicles of the Revolution*, pp. 70–7 (p. 71).
26. Walsingham, *Annales Ricardi Secundi*, pp. 115–25 (p. 115).
27. Walter Skeat, *The Evolution of the Canterbury Tales* (London: Kegan Paul, Trench, Trübner, 1907), pp. 7–29.
28. Helen Cooper, *The Structure of the Canterbury Tales* (London: Duckworth, 1983), p. 178.
29. Derek Brewer, *The World of Chaucer* [1978] (Cambridge: Brewer, 2000), p. 91.
30. Clara Estow, *Pedro the Cruel of Castille, 1350-1369* (Leiden: Brill, 1995).
31. H. C. Luke, 'Visitors from the east to the Plantagenet and Lancastrian kings', *The Nineteenth Century* 108 (1930), 760–9; Derek Pearsall, 'Chivalry', in *A Companion to Chaucer*, ed. Peter Brown (Oxford: Blackwell, 2000), pp. 57–74 (p. 60).
32. F. W. Robinson, *The Poetical Works of Chaucer* (Cambridge: Cambridge University Press, 1933), p. 856.

33. Froissart, *Chronicles of England, France and the Adjoining Countries*, trans. Thomas Johnes [1803–1810], 2 vols (London: William Smith, 1839), II.31–2.
34. Wallace, 'Italy', in *A Companion to Chaucer*, pp. 218–34 (pp. 219–20).
35. Christopher Phillpotts, 'The fate of the truce of Paris, 1396-1415', *Journal of Medieval History* 24.1 (1998), 61–80.
36. Jonathan Sumption, *The Hundred Years War* (London: Faber and Faber, 2009), vol. 3, *Divided Houses*, pp. 784, 845; Given-Wilson, *Chronicles*, p. 26.
37. William T. Rossiter, *Chaucer and Petrarch* (Cambridge: Brewer, 2010), p. 62.
38. Wallace, *Chaucerian Polity*, p. 329.

7

Authors and Readers in Chaucer's *House of Fame*

Lewis Beer

Introduction

Geoffrey Chaucer's *House of Fame* (c. 1378) is a dream-vision poem in three books. In the first book, the dreamer/narrator ('Geffrey') finds himself in the Temple of Venus, which is made of glass and has the story of Virgil's *Aeneid* depicted on its walls. In the second book, the dreamer ventures outside into a desert and is picked up by a talking eagle, who takes Geffrey to the House of Fame. In the third book, Geffrey explores the House of Fame itself: he sees many famous authors standing on pillars and watches as the goddess Fame distributes good, bad and indifferent reputations to nine groups of suitors. Finally, Geffrey is taken to see another edifice, variously referred to by critics as the House of Rumour or House of Tidings, in which hordes of people run around telling, embellishing and falsifying stories. The poem ends abruptly when a 'man of gret auctorite' appears and the rumour-mongers flock towards him. Several aspects of Chaucer's poem, including the eagle and the invocations to each book, are borrowed from or heavily influenced by Dante Alighieri's *Commedia* (c. 1321). In the *Commedia*, the narrator travels through Hell, Purgatory and Paradise before finally seeing God. The poem is divided into three sections, or *cantiche* (singular: *cantica*), commonly known as the *Inferno*, the *Purgatorio* and the *Paradiso*. The *Commedia* is, among other things, an allegory of the Christian soul's progress from sin through repentance and penance to salvation.

Chaucer's use of Dante in the *House of Fame* has been the subject of intense scholarly debate since the nineteenth century. In recent decades, it has become almost axiomatic among Chaucer scholars that the *House of Fame* is 'a literary statement about the unreliability of literary statements', to use Sheila Delany's oft-cited formulation.[1]

In such readings, Chaucer is usually seen as having responded to Dante's visionary, prophetic masterpiece with wry scepticism. Where Dante is confident and authoritative in forging a path from earth to heaven via poetry, Chaucer has little or no confidence in his power to write 'truly' about past, present or future. If Dante locates his poem's authority in its divine subject matter, divine purpose and divine effects, Chaucer locates whatever authority he may have in his insistent denial of authority; he plays down the significance of his own writing and has little conviction of the effect that his poem might have on its audience.[2] In the last few years, however, several critics have argued that the *House of Fame* not only wrests interpretative authority out of the hands of the author, but also places that authority firmly in the hands of the reader. Sarah Powrie argues that Chaucer, '[r]ecognising that fame is contingent upon an interpreting audience, [...] invites his reader's interpretation and invests the reader with hermeneutical authority, so as to initiate the literary afterlife of his text'.[3] According to this reading, Chaucer's poem emerges as an extended tribute to its own readers, identifying them as the most crucial participants in the writing process, and as the producers of textual meaning(s).

This essay, however, argues that the *House of Fame* places far less faith in its readers' authority than such critics have suggested. The whole poem is a meditation on the ways in which all of us try, but fail, to exert authorial control over our lives and reputations, and interpretative control over the lives and reputations of others. We are, all of us, both misinterpreted (as authors) and misinterpreting (as readers) virtually all of the time. To illustrate this argument, the essay begins by contrasting Dante's addresses to his readers in the *Commedia* with Chaucer's at the start of the *House of Fame*, then discusses the development of the author/reader dynamic in the course of the latter poem, before concluding with a detailed comparison between the ending of the *House of Fame* and one of Dante's addresses to the reader in the *Paradiso*. By framing the essay in this way, and by suggesting a Dantean parallel which has not been previously noted, I aim to clarify the distinction between Dante's and Chaucer's attitudes – as writers and readers – to the work of 'making meaning' out of allegorical texts.

Chaucer's anti-Dantean address to the reader

The reader is addressed directly seven times in each *cantica* of the *Commedia*. These addresses serve different functions in different contexts. Sometimes Dante attempts to dispel our disbelief by claiming to share it, as in the *Inferno*:

> If now, reader, you are slow to believe
> what I say, that will be no marvel,
> for I, who saw it, hardly allow it.[4]

Sometimes he appeals to our imagination to reinforce the truth of his vision;[5] sometimes he swears by the truth of his account in a manner which asks us to take for granted its veracity;[6] and sometimes, all but admitting that his poem does not describe a literal journey, he nevertheless insists that it is true:

> Sharpen here, reader, your eyes to the truth,
> for the veil is now surely so fine
> that passing within is easy. (*Purg.* 8.19–21)

For all their diversity, one thing Dante's addresses to the reader share is an intention to make his story seem credible and authoritative, whether on the literal or allegorical level. In these moments, Dante positions us as the 'lettore' [reader], and himself as our 'autore' [author]; in short, he establishes his *authority*.

At the same time, just as importantly, Dante exhorts us to interpret as we read, to recreate his experiences in our own minds and to apply his lofty prophecies to our own lives. Erich Auerbach emphasizes the reader's dependence on the author in this dynamic, arguing that Dante's reader 'is not his equal [...] he may not argue with him on a level of equality, he must "take it or leave it"'. Dante figures the reader as 'a disciple [...] not expected to discuss or to judge, but to follow; using his own forces, but the way Dante orders him to do'.[7] Building on these ideas, William Franke suggests a more active interpretative role for Dante's readers:

> It is their acts of interpretation of themselves, as they confront the inter-
> pretive challenges presented by the poem, that will be decisive for the
> readers' lives and even for their afterlives. Sin and salvation in Dante's
> afterlife stem from how one interprets oneself, and the reading of the
> poem can be crucial to determining the outcome of this drama.[8]

Dante thus displays a high degree of faith, not only in his own authority as a divinely inspired poet-prophet, but also in our capacity to receive his poem-prophecy in accordance with his instructions. For Dante and his readers, the stakes could not be any higher: nothing less than the fate of our souls will be determined by the way in which we, as interpreters, locate ourselves in relation to this author's authority. He demands a kind of deference from us, but importantly, not passivity. We affirm Dante's authority most of all when we work hard to interpret his salvific vision, when we make the story of his conversion our own.

The opening of the *House of Fame* also works hard to establish the dynamic between reader and author, but whereas Dante emphasizes his authority as writer and encourages us to believe in and engage seriously with his poetic account, through the exercise of our imaginations and our critical faculties, Chaucer both adopts (as author) and recommends (to his readers) a stance of benign, uncritical passivity. The first three lines set the tone:

> God turne us every drem to goode!
> For hyt is wonder, be the roode,
> To my wyt, what causeth swevenes.[9]

For over fifty lines, the poem's narrator delineates the various possible types and causes of dreams, leaving the Dantean conception of dreams as spiritual prophecies until the very end of this long opening sentence:

> Or yf the soule of propre kinde,
> Be so parfit, as men fynde,
> That yt forwot that ys to come,
> And that hyt warneth alle and some
> Of everych of her aventures
> Be avisions or be figures,
> But that oure flessh ne hath no myght
> To understonde hyt aryght,
> For hyt is warned too derkly. (ll. 43–51)

The apparent loftiness of this definition is diluted by the more mundane causes – physiological, dietary, erotic – that precede it, and is then deflated by the defeatism of the line immediately following: 'But why the cause is, noght wot I' (l. 52). The passage ends by repeating the poem's first line almost verbatim, as well as the second line's reference to the Cross: the narrator prays 'that the holy roode / Turne us every drem to goode!' (ll. 57–8). This author denies his own ability to categorize – let alone explain – his dream, deferring to the authority of 'grete clerkys' (l. 53), and ultimately to God, to 'turne [this] drem to goode'. That action of 'turning' the dream relates not only to the author's (potential) function as explicator of his own vision, but also to our activity as readers.

From the outset, the *House of Fame* works to question the 'parfitness' of the human soul, and its capacity to receive, transmit or interpret sacred prophecies. The phrase 'hyt warneth alle and some' (l. 46), used to describe the activity of this allegedly 'parfit' soul, could refer either to the warnings issued by the prophet's inspired soul to his presumably enthralled readers ('alle and some'), or to the prophetic warnings issued by the soul of every person ('alle and some') to him/herself. As we saw above, these two meanings are interdependent in Dante's poetry, where the reader must respond actively to Dante's inspired verses by, as it were, inspiring themselves and 'turning' the *Commedia* to their own 'goode'. Chaucer's narrator leaves both these activities to God: regardless of whether his soul has delivered a true prophecy to him in this dream, or whether his readers' souls can make effective use of it, the emphasis falls on the obscurity of the received vision and the weakness of the interpreting flesh.

If the opening passage of the *House of Fame* constitutes an implicit address to the reader, who is included in the 'us' of lines 1 and 58 and the 'our' of line 49, the invocation that follows establishes that reader's position more explicitly, though in the third person. After praying to the god of sleep for the strength to 'telle aryght' (l. 79) his dream, the narrator then makes two further prayers regarding the fate of his audience. First, 'he that mover ys of al' (l. 81) is exhorted to bring joy of various kinds to those who hear the poem and 'take hit wel and scorne hyt noght' (l. 91); then 'Jesus God' (l. 97) is asked to bring down every possible misfortune, culminating in death, upon any reader or listener who 'thorgh envye, / Dispit, or jape, or vilanye, / Mysdeme hyt' (ll. 95–7). Such envious misinterpreters are condemned to the fate of Croesus, '[t]hat high upon a gebet dyde' (l. 106), in his case as a result of having misinterpreted his *own* dream, rather than someone else's. As in the long opening passage discussed above, the distinction between author and reader is blurred: to misread 'Geffrey' is in a sense to misread ourselves. We might conclude that a great deal is at stake in this business of interpretation, and that a heavy responsibility is placed upon us to 'turn this dream to good' as we read it.

However, the timorous passivity advocated by 'God turne us every drem to goode!' still applies here. As Jacqueline Miller observes, the narrator 'outlines only the barest, vaguest instructions to evoke proper judgment and acceptance', while going into far more detail about the various ways in which we might *mis*-judge his poem.[10] On the positive side, as readers of the poem, we need to 'take hit wel' (l. 91). Aside from that, this passage is a litany of proscriptions, fixated on the idea that any response that does otherwise than 'take hit wel' will stem from and expose our own inner corruption. Even in what little positive instruction we do get, that word 'take' seems open to multiple interpretations. To 'take', in Chaucer's English as much as in our own, can mean proactively to seize something, passively to receive it, or to 'understand' it. Although this last sense may seem the most relevant in the present context, there remains a question as to how we are to understand this dream: by actively interpreting and making something out of it, thus *turning* it into something else, or by passively receiving it and taking it as it is? So many threats hang over us if we 'mysdeme' Geffrey's vision, and we are told so insistently that our judgements will only rebound upon us, that just as Croesus should have listened to and accepted his daughter's correct interpretation of his dream without challenging it, so we might end up feeling that we, Geffrey's auditors, should simply 'take it' and like it.

This mock-curse is, I think, one of the funniest passages in Chaucer, but I disagree with Katherine Terrell when she says that it is 'humorous in its absolute futility' because Geffrey's readers 'will make of his poem what they will, regardless'.[11] While the blessing and the curse are not to be taken seriously, and are futile in the sense that they will not take effect, the substance of this joke lies more in the comic excess of the invocation. In his opening sentence, the narrator spent altogether too much time enumerating dream-types and dream-causes about which he then had nothing to say; now, in his invocation, he expends far too much energy forestalling spiteful interpretations of a vision which, as we might already have anticipated by now, will be thoroughly inoffensive and inconsequential. The *honi soit qui mal y pense* sentiment is endearingly misplaced, because there is no 'mal' to be found in (or read into) this poem.[12] The interpretative approach Geffrey recommends to us – 'take hit wel' – is a projection of his own receptive authorial stance, and the result is (or at least is supposed to be) a kind of non-vicious cycle in which the narrator reports his benign, inconsequential dream and we take it well, thus affirming its benign inconsequentiality. The contrast with Dante's scathingly polemical epic, and with the *Commedia*'s confrontational, exhortatory attitude to its readers, is stark. In a sense, Chaucer's readers have more freedom of interpretation than Dante's, but in another sense this freedom is rendered hollow by the deliberate insignificance of this vision. Again and again, the *House of Fame* will fail to tell us what we need (or want) to know, will fail to give us the raw materials out of which an interpretation could be fashioned, and so will prompt us to respond to its somewhat insecure authorial silence with a similarly insecure interpretative silence. To be misunderstood and to misunderstand are the pitfalls we and Geffrey must strive to avoid, even at the cost of succumbing to defeatism.

Books 1 and 2: re-reading, re-writing and running away

At the start of his dream, in the Temple of Venus, Geffrey finds himself reading the story of Virgil's *Aeneid*, which is engraved on the walls. What he reads is not precisely the *Aeneid* itself, however, but a translation of it, and one that seems ambiguously composed of words and pictures – on the basis of Geffrey's redaction, it is sometimes hard to tell. When Geffrey reaches the story of Aeneas' doomed love affair with Dido, things get even more complicated. This episode, the bulk of which occupies just one of the twelve books in the *Aeneid*, balloons into an extended digression on Aeneas' treachery in abandoning his lover and on the faithlessness of men in general. Geffrey brings in alternative perspectives on this story from Ovid's *Metamorphoses* and *Heroides*, and finally urges us to '[r]ead Virgile in Eneydos, / Or the Epistle of Ovyde' (ll. 378–9) if we want to know more, emphasizing the plurality of perspectives that are on offer. He also seems to contribute some of his own material to Dido's laments, confusingly taking credit for one of her speeches while also attributing it to his dream: 'In suche wordes gan to pleyne / Dydo of hir grete peyne, / As me mette redely – / Noon other auctour alegge I' (ll. 311–4). Is Geffrey the 'auctour' in the sense that he wrote this passage himself, or merely in the sense that this was his dream and he is reporting it?

Dido's (and Geffrey's) laments in this passage focus primarily on problems of interpretation. For one thing, there is the difficulty of interpreting other people, such as Aeneas: as the narrator says, 'There may be under godlyhed / Kevered many a shrewed vice' (ll. 274–5), and the lesson he draws from Dido's 'nyce lest' (l. 287) (her misguided, misinterpreting love of Aeneas) is that 'he that fully knoweth th'erbe / May saufly ley hyt to his yë' (ll. 290–1). Geffrey introduces this as 'a proverbe' (l. 289), a piece of received wisdom for which he cannot take credit, and which is all the more credible for that. Dido misreads Aeneas, trusting in her own interpretative capacities, when she would have done better to heed the proverbial wisdom about men's hypocrisy, '[f]or this', as Geffrey observes, 'shal every woman fynde' (l. 279). Not only does Dido's reliance on her own faculties expose her to betrayal by the mis-construed Aeneas, but this betrayal then turns her own actions into a text to be 'red and songe / Over

al thys lond, on every tonge' (ll. 347–8). Dido blames 'wikke Fame'
(l. 349) for this negative publicity, complaining that 'O, soth ys, every
thing ys wyst / Though hit be kevered with the myst' (ll. 351–2). This
hard-won proverbial wisdom seems, at first glance, to suggest that her
public shaming simply involves the revelation of truths she would
rather conceal, but Geffrey's sympathy for Dido, and his insistence
that Aeneas, not she, was at fault here, undermine any sense that she
deserves the shame that will now be heaped upon her. Dido herself
goes on to complain that 'though I myghte duren ever' (l. 353), people
will always speak of her in the same way:

> I shal thus juged be:
> 'Loo, ryght as she hath don, now she
> Wol doo eft-sones, hardely';
> Thus seyth the peple prively.
> But that is doon, nis nat to done. (ll. 357–61)

Her only crime has been to misinterpret Aeneas; however, not only
will this act be made to reflect badly on her, but it will also be
perpetuated throughout the rest of her life, to the point where this
'shameful' affair will cancel out and replace anything she does from
now on. Her complaint 'avayleth hir not a stre' (l. 363), because it has
no effect on what 'seyth the peple prively'. These private, independent readings of Dido, influenced by the broadcasts of 'wikke Fame',
produce a uniformly wrong consensus.

Dido emerges as a thoroughly disillusioned reader and writer, inca-
pable of deciphering Aeneas-the-text or of controlling the broadcast
and reception of her own life story. Geffrey himself, after sympathiz-
ing angrily with Dido's plight, retreats into citations of other 'auc-
toritees' – '[a]s men may ofte in bokes rede' (l. 385), 'as the story telleth
us' (l. 406), 'as the book us tellis' (l. 426) – that illustrate the injustice
of men's behaviour towards women, before at last returning to his
original text, the *Aeneid*, to provide a belated and bathetic contrasting
view of Aeneas' abandonment of Dido:

> But to excusen Eneas
> Fullyche of al his grete trespas,
> The book seyth Mercurie, sauns fayle,
> Bad hym goo into Itayle. (ll. 427–30)

The narrator offers no further comment on this excuse, but returns
to describing what he saw in the Temple of Venus. His impassioned
expansion of the Dido story peters out with an acknowledgement

that what we have been presented with here are several competing 'takes' on a mythical incident, no single one of which has a secure relation to the truth. As Miller puts it,

> The wavering and ambivalence that characterise the narrator's efforts to assume full authorial rights over the text also restrain and betray that effort; and they indicate that such a position is as untenable as subservience to an outside source seems to be.[13]

It is in this disempowered state that Geffrey then leaves the temple and finds himself in a terrifyingly barren desert. Just as he prayed to God at the start of the poem, amid his uncertainty about how to read dreams and how to control his readers' interpretations of his own dream, so now he responds to the authorial and interpretative confusions of the Temple of Venus with a prayer to Christ: 'Fro fantome and illusion / Me save!' (ll. 493–4). For all the vehemence of his diatribes during the temple episode, this narrator does not occupy any stable or consistent position with regard to the texts he reads, re-reads, pits against each other and contributes to. Unable to defer to or mount a strong challenge against these authorities, he runs away and panics. The experience is not generative or empowering for this reader – rather, it results in mere emptiness, and a knee-jerk appeal to a higher power that far transcends the literary authorities which Geffrey has been grappling with.

Such a degraded view of the reading experience is perpetuated in Geffrey's dialogue with the eagle. The eagle explains that Jove has sent him to carry Geffrey out of his own house for a while:

> For when thy labour doon al ys,
> And hast mad alle thy rekenynges,
> In stede of reste and newe thynges
> Thou goost hom to thy hous anoon,
> And, also domb as any stoon,
> Thou sittest at another booke
> Tyl fully daswed is thy looke. (ll. 652–8)

Not only does the eagle equate Geffrey's bureaucratic drudgery with his recreational reading of the classics – the *Aeneid* is just 'another booke' – but he also undermines any notion that engaging with such texts is conducive to the dreamer's own creativity. As we have already seen in the opening and throughout Book 1, the vast array of available texts and authorities simply renders Geffrey 'daswed' [dazed]. Although the eagle-borne journey is ostensibly supposed to rectify this problem by showing Geffrey new and exciting things, the dreamer's responses to the eagle's breathless enthusiasm seem similarly 'daswed'. When prompted, he approves of what the eagle tells him about how sounds travel to the House of Fame, but with a perfunctory 'Yis' (l. 864) and a certain amount of bet-hedging: the eagle's theory is, Geffrey concedes, 'A good persuasion' and 'lyk to be' true (ll. 872–3). Later, the eagle offers to show Geffrey the stars, so that he can supplement his book-learning with first-hand experience. Geffrey politely refuses the offer:

> I leve as wel, so God me spede,
> Hem that write of this matere,
> As though I knew her places here;
> And eke they shynen here so bryghte,
> Hyt shulde shenden al my syghte
> To loke on hem. (ll. 1012–17)

The phrase 'as though' serves to acknowledge the possible gap between what the books tell Geffrey and what the reality is 'here', even as Geffrey insists that this gap does not trouble him. Again, his readerly timidity is framed by an appeal to God and motivated by fear about his own weak capacities.

At the beginning of the *House of Fame*, Chaucer's narrator exemplifies and recommends – indeed, comically demands – an attitude of non-committal receptivity in the face of the myriad texts that populate our world. Books 1 and 2 offer a fuller exploration of the risks involved in generating and/or engaging with texts. Geffrey's anxieties are still comical, but seem reasonable enough in a world where texts like the *Aeneid* and people like Dido can be so open to attack from all quarters. To return to the proverb that should have warned Dido not to trust Aeneas, 'he that fully knoweth th'erbe / May saufly ley hyt to his yë' (ll. 290–1) – but who can ever know anything or anyone 'fully'? Geffrey knows enough about the competing versions of Dido's story to know that 'full' knowledge of what really happened is inaccessible. To judge from what we have read so far, it may *never* be safe to lay the herb against one's eye, to put one's whole trust in another person, to confront the full truth even on those rare occasions when it is made available to us, or to do any more than Geffrey does: observe without investigating and record without passing definitive comment. In some ways, he is like the House of Fame itself, passively receiving the surfaces of earthly life. On the other hand, Fame's manipulation of this material provides a telling contrast with Geffrey's own literary practice.

Book 3: self-sufficiency and self-authorization

The suitors who approach the goddess Fame naively seek to control the reception and interpretation of their actions by the rest of the world. The moral of this passage, in which Fame gives deserved fame, blame or obscurity to some, and undeserved fame, blame or obscurity to others, is that nothing we do or say can have any predictable effect on our subsequent reputations. People are walking texts, forever trying, with varying degrees of sincerity, to compose and project a certain image of themselves as good, bad or invisible; but the way they are perceived is ultimately determined, not by their own efforts, but by a mindless, capricious quasi-deity. At first, Geffrey's only response is to scratch his head (l. 1702) when he sees the suitors who have done good deeds but wish to remain unknown. If this head-scratching gesture seems a clear indication of puzzlement, it is rendered more ambiguous by Geffrey's later claim that he already knew '[t]hat somme folk han desired fame / Diversly' (ll. 1899–900), and that these 'tydynges' (l. 1894) are not the 'wonder thynges' (l. 1893) he was promised by the eagle. It is characteristic of this poem to figure indifference as an appropriate response to a revelatory vision, especially since this part of the vision reiterates an idea that the poem has already articulated several times. Fame's suitors indeed tell us nothing new, though they clarify the universal application of what the *House of Fame* has said so far about texts and human relationships.

Accordingly, when Geffrey is asked by a stranger whether he has come here in pursuit of fame, his response could apply to his identity as a writer or simply as a human being, or both:

> I cam noght hider, graunt mercy,
> For no such cause, by my hed!
> Sufficeth me, as I were ded,
> That no wight have my name in honde.
> I wot myself best how y stonde;
> For what I drye, or what I thynke,
> I wil myselven al hyt drynke,
> Certeyn, for the more part,
> As fer forth as I kan myn art. (ll. 1874–82)

Geffrey resembles most of all those obscurity-craving do-gooders who prompted him to scratch his head earlier, but unlike them he refuses even to say whether his actions are good or bad. In fact, he says nothing whatsoever about actions: his name, how he 'stands', his experiences, his thoughts, his proficiency in his own art, these are the things by which he defines himself, and to which no one else must be allowed access. No one should have his name 'in honde'; he is the only one who knows his own 'standing' or condition; he will 'drynke' his thoughts and experiences for himself, at least to the extent that he knows his own art – an extent which, presumably, only he can measure. This is an extraordinary statement of self-sufficiency, but coming as it does after the depressing pageant of fame-seekers it also carries the same anxious, defensive tone that pervaded the earlier parts of the poem. Geffrey's vehemence on this point, reinforced by oaths like 'by my hed' and 'as I were ded', stems from his terror of what might happen to him if others did get their hands on his name, or if his thoughts and experiences were served up for others to 'drynke'. What is most interesting here is that this attitude of self-containment is identified as a key requirement of his 'art'. It is fundamental to his poetic practice that he reveals nothing of his own perspective, drinking it all down for himself and leaving us too with, as it were, nothing to drink but our own thoughts.

When he is taken to the tumultuous House of Tidings, where he does his best '[m]e for to pleyen and for to lere, / And eke a tydynge for to here' (ll. 2133–5), and when he finally does receive the tiding he was hoping for, Geffrey declares that it

> shal not now be told for me –
> For hit no nede is, redely;
> Folk can synge hit bet than I;
> For al mot out, other late or rathe,
> Alle the sheves in the lathe – (ll. 2136–40)

It is important to notice the conflicting self-justifications in these lines. Geffrey will keep this tiding to himself because '[f]olk can synge hit bet than I', but also because 'al mot out'; on the one hand, he is not capable of doing justice to this piece of news, but on the other hand there is no 'nede' to do justice to it, indeed no question of doing so, because one way or another it will 'out'. The 'al mot out' proverb recalls Dido's lament, 'O, soth ys, every thing ys wyst / Though hit be kevered with the myst' (ll. 351–2). There Dido was complaining that Fame would broadcast her betrayal to the rest of the world, and that not only would this news 'out', but it would also be interpreted unfavourably and then perpetuated in that distorted form for all time. When Geffrey echoes this sentiment at the end of the poem, he has just seen the 'lesyng and [the] sad soth sawe' (l. 2089) mingling together and flying out of the window: 'Thus saugh I fals and soth compouned / Togeder fle for oo tydynge' (ll. 2108–9). Certainly, 'every thing ys wyst' and 'al mot

out', but according to this vision what is thus exposed and known is
an indistinguishable medley of truth and lies. The 'folk' who can sing
the tiding better than Geffrey will also falsify it, and even if they do
not, Fame will when she gets her hands on it. The veracity of texts
is compromised at every stage – composition, distribution, reception,
interpretation, modification – and Geffrey's response is to abstain from
the whole process. His account of the Houses of Fame and Tidings is
fixated on surfaces and details, and he refuses to editorialize except,
paradoxically, in his very refusal to editorialize.

By this point in the poem, Chaucer has captured, to perfection, a
sense of total disillusionment with the activities of authors and readers. And yet, here he is, still writing – and here we are, still reading.
The poem's final lines address this troubling contradiction:

> I herde a gret noyse withalle
> In a corner of the halle,
> Ther men of love-tydynges tolde,
> And I gan thiderward beholde;
> For I saugh rennynge every wight
> As fast as that they hadden myght,
> And everych cried, 'What thing is that?'
> And somme sayde, 'I not never what.'
> And when they were alle on an hepe,
> Tho behynde begunne up lepe,
> And clamben up on other faste,
> And up the nose and yën kaste,
> And troden faste on others heles,
> And stampen, as men doon aftir eles.
> Atte laste y saugh a man,
> Which that I [nevene] nat ne kan;
> But he semed for to be
> A man of gret auctorite. (ll. 2141–58)

Compare this ending to one of Dante's addresses to the reader in the
Paradiso. Rising into the sphere of Mercury, that part of heaven where
blessed souls go whose service to God was marred by their desire for
fame, Dante addresses the reader as he describes the way the souls
thronged to him:

> As in a fishpond tranquil and pure
> the fish approach what comes from outside,
> if they deem it to be their food,
> so saw I more than a thousand splendours
> drawing towards us, and from each we heard:

'Behold one who will increase our loves!' [...]
Think, reader, how deprived you would feel,
how anxious to know more,
if what begins here did not proceed,
and you will see by your example
how much I desired to hear from them their condition.
(*Paradiso*. 5.100–5, 109–13; my italics)

Dante's assumption that, in failing to complete his poem, he would leave us in anguished yearning to hear the rest of it is characteristic of his self-authorizing addresses to his readers, while Chaucer's deliberate failure to end the *House of Fame* places him in ironic contrast to his more self-confident, more authoritative Italian predecessor. Helen Cooper suggests that Dante himself could be the 'man of gret auctorite' at the end of Chaucer's poem: Dante, the

> 'seeming authority' who had claimed to make the judgements of Fame into the judgements of God, is left by the argument of Chaucer's 'Dante in Inglissh' with nothing left that he can say.[14]

The 'one who will increase our [heavenly] loves' appears instead '[t]her men of [secular] love-tydynges tolde', and the 'thousand splendours' Dante sees flying towards him are echoed and parodied by the 'Wynged wondres' Geffrey saw 'faste fleen, / Twenty thousand in a route' (ll. 2118–19) a little earlier in his vision. Throughout the *Commedia*, Dante is greeted with admiring wonder by the dead souls. In the *Purgatorio*, one soul asks another, 'Who is that? (*Purg.* 14.1), to which the other responds, 'I do not know who he is…you ask him' (ll. 4–5). In the *House of Fame*, the rumour-mongers' reactions to the appearance of the 'man of gret auctorite' clearly parody Dante's reception in the afterlife: 'everyche cried: "What thing is that?" / And some sayde: "I not never what"' (ll. 2147–8).

The key question to ask about Chaucer's 'man of gret auctorite' may not after all be 'Who is he?', especially since Geffrey himself claims not to be able to 'nevene' him. Grappling with the unknown quantity of the stranger's identity, while not a complete waste of time, may only lead us into deeper confusion in the end. Instead, we might ask *why* this man 'semed' to be of 'gret auctorite'. The fishpond episode from the *Paradiso* gives us a clue to the answer. Just as Dante accumulates more authority every time he addresses his readers (making us believe in his vision, making us interpret it), so in his encounter with blessed souls he simultaneously increases his authority from the other side, as it were, thanks to the crowd of 'splendours' seeking to 'increase their loves' through him. His authority comes from the way he writes his own reception by enthralled, dependent audiences – in this case, by the fictional dead souls and by the real-life readers. Just so, the *House of Fame's* 'man of gret auctorite' *seems* to warrant that label purely by virtue of his reception. It is because so many people are clamouring to see and hear him, despite their total ignorance as to his status or identity, that he appears to possess authority; it is in that crowd of readers that his authority resides. There, the poem is saying, is an author for you, and there are his readers. The former is unidentifiable – pure seeming without substance. The latter constitute a mindless, grasping, self-defeating 'hepe'. If we have understood what the poem has been doing until now, we will be inclined to do precisely what the empty space after line 2158 obliges us to do: leave it empty, and walk away from the now silent text.[15]

Notes

1. Sheila Delany, *Chaucer's 'House of Fame': The Poetics of Skeptical Fideism* (Chicago, IL: University of Chicago Press, 1972), p. 108.

2. For an overview of pre-1995 criticism on the *House of Fame*, see A. J. Minnis, V. J. Scattergood and J. J. Smith (eds), *Oxford Guides to Chaucer: The Shorter Poems* (Oxford: Clarendon Press, 1995), pp. 161–251. On Chaucer's relation to Dante, see William Franke, '"Enditynges of worldly vanitees": truth and poetry in Chaucer as compared with Dante', *Chaucer Review*, 34 (1999); 87–106, Glenn A. Steinberg, 'Chaucer in the field of cultural production: humanism, Dante, and the *House of Fame*', *Chaucer Review*, 35 (2000), 182–203; and Karen Elizabeth Gross, 'Chaucer's silent Italy', *Studies in Philology*, 109 (2012), 19–44.

3. Sarah Powrie, 'Alan of Lille's *Anticlaudianus* as intertext in Chaucer's *House of Fame*', *Chaucer Review*, 44 (2010), 246–67. Cf. Katherine Terrell, 'Reallocation of hermeneutic authority in Chaucer's *House of Fame*', *Chaucer Review*, 31 (1997), 279–90 and William Quinn, 'Chaucer's recital presence in the *House of Fame* and the embodiment of authority', *Chaucer Review*, 43 (2008), 171–96.

4. *The Divine Comedy of Dante Alighieri: Inferno*, Vol. 1, trans. Robert M. Durling (Oxford: Oxford University Press, 1996), 25.46–8. All further references to the *Inferno* are to this edition and are given parenthetically in the body of the text.

5. 'Remember, reader, if ever in the mountains a fog caught you [...] and your imagination will easily come to see [...]' (17.1–2, 7–9). *The Divine Comedy of Dante Alighieri: Purgatorio*, Vol. 2 (Oxford: Oxford University Press, 2003). All further references to the *Purgatorio* are to this edition and are given parenthetically in the body of the text.

6. 'So may I return, reader, to that devout triumph on whose account I ever weep for my sins [...] I saw [...]' (22.106–8, 110). *The Divine Comedy of Dante Alighieri: Paradiso*, Vol. 3 (Oxford: Oxford University Press, 2011). All further references to the *Paradiso* are to this edition and are given parenthetically in the body of the text.

7. Erich Auerbach, 'Dante's addresses to the reader', *Romance Philology*, 7 (1953–4), 268–79 (p. 276).

8. William Franke, 'Dante's *Inferno* as poetic revelation of prophetic truth', *Philosophy and Literature*, 33 (2009), 252–66 (p. 254).

9. Chaucer, *The House of Fame*, in *The Riverside Chaucer*, ed. Larry D. Benson (Oxford: Oxford University Press, 1987), ll. 1–3. All further references are to this edition and are given parenthetically in the body of the text.

10. Jacqueline T. Miller, 'The writing on the wall: authority and authorship in Chaucer's *House of Fame*', *Chaucer Review*, 17 (1982), 95–115 (p. 104).

11. Terrell, 'Reallocation of hermeneutic authority', p. 289.

12. Cf. Marion Turner's argument that the *House of Fame* is 'fundamentally engaged with the troubled discursive environment of contemporary London', and with the 'chaotic textual anxieties' of this time and place. *Chaucerian Conflict: Languages of Antagonism in Late Fourteenth-Century London* (Oxford: Clarendon Press, 2006), p. 17.

13. J. T. Miller, 'The writing on the wall', p. 108.

14. Helen Cooper, 'The four last things in Dante and Chaucer: Ugolino in the house of rumour', *New Medieval Literatures*, 3 (2000), 39–66 (p. 66).

15. Cf. T. S. Miller who, despite affirming Chaucer's concerns about the dangers of misreading, argues that he ultimately 'strives to keep us conscious along with him that, whatever great work he may read or whatever great work he may produce, something more remains to be read, and something more remains to be written'. 'Writing Dreams to Good: Reading as Writing and Writing as Reading in Chaucer's Dream Visions', *Style*, 45 (2011), 528–48 (p. 544). For similarly generative but more religiously inflected readings of the silence at the end of the *House of Fame*, see J. T. Miller, 'The writing on the wall', p. 112 and David Lyle Jeffrey, 'Sacred and secular scripture: authority and interpretation in *The House of Fame*', *Chaucer and Scriptural Tradition*, ed. David Lyle Jeffrey (Ottowa: University of Ottawa Press, 1984), pp. 207–28 (p. 228).

8

Tie Knots and Slip Knots: Sexual Difference and Memory in Chaucer's *Troilus and Criseyde*

Ruth Evans

Andreas Huyssen observed in 2000 that 'one of the most surprising cultural and political phenomena of recent years has been the emergence of memory as a key concern in Western societies'.[1] Surprising, because, as Huyssen argues, the turn to what he calls 'present pasts' – those pasts that are kept alive in the present through memorial practices, of which Holocaust memory is the pre-eminent example – is not only at odds with twentieth-century modernity's privileging of 'present futures' but also strongly opposed to 'the categories of space, maps, geographies, borders, trade routes, migrations, displacements, and diasporas [that are privileged] in [...] postcolonial and cultural studies'.[2] Seeking to account for the remarkable rise of memory culture since the 1980s, Huyssen locates it in a variety of historical phenomena, including 'the broadening debate about the Holocaust, [...] genocidal politics in Rwanda, Bosnia, and Kosovo', national memories, consumer culture, archival technologies, 'our deep anxiety about the speed of change and the ever shrinking horizons of time and space', and the deployment of memory as a synonym for justice.[3] Concomitantly, over the past thirty or so years, there has been a spate of books and articles on memory and memory practices in the Middle Ages, by scholars of very different stripes. One might well ask of this body of medieval scholarship, as Huyssen does of transnational postmodernity, 'Why memory? Why now?' What is just as striking about this body of work is the relative absence of any attention to the question of memory and gender.[4] My concern in this essay is to explore the interlacing of memory, sex and gender in Chaucer's tragic romance *Troilus and Criseyde* by focusing on the deployment of the image of the knot. The poem's knots of love are also nodes of memory: sites to which remembrance is inextricably hitched, but which become tragically untied.

Memory in *Troilus and Criseyde*

One of the central themes of *Troilus and Criseyde* is memory: the poem explores different ways of, and motives for, remembering; it commemorates the supposedly historical figure of Criseyde; it records Troilus's painful haunting by her memory after she has left Troy; it laments Criseyde's scandalous forgetting of Troilus's love for her, yet struggles not to condemn her for it; and it transmits the historical memory of the English 'nation' that is preserved in the medieval Troy narratives and in contemporary English re-appropriations of Trojan history, simultaneously constituting itself as a rewriting, in textual form, of just such a historical memory.[5] The poem also conducts – but does not resolve – an elaborate conversation between the competing claims of memory and history that pulls between two poles of Greek thought, that is, between the cosmological and the eschatological: between a notion of memory that is oriented towards history and a memory that is taken out of time, that is separate from history.[6] The poem exploits the medieval Christianization of memory and alludes to the monastic tradition of trained memory, but it also powerfully proposes that memory makes ethical demands on us that history does not.[7] For late fourteenth-century readers, as for readers today, the poem functions as a *lieu de mémoire* (memory place), a narrative that gathers up different, and even incommensurate, temporalities and (hi) stories as part of the collective memory of the English nation: it is less 'history' than memorial topology, by which I mean that memories have different shapes from histories.[8]

Memory is not only a major theme of Chaucer's text; it explicitly orders the responsible reception of its meaning. In the narrator's opening injunction to the lovers in its audience, the poem argues for an ethical and affective understanding of remembrance, one that joins the individual to the community through an experience of shared suffering:

> If any drop of pyte in yow be,
> Remembreth yow on passed hevynesse
> That ye han felt, and on the adversite
> Of othere folk.[9]

To recollect one's own personal unhappiness in love and that experienced by others is to avoid condemning Troilus for placing all his faith in Criseyde and thus to put oneself in the right frame of mind for understanding Troilus's story. What the text seems to mean by this ethical injunction to remember 'passed hevynesse' is something close to Jacques Derrida's idea of hospitality as an act that is not 'governed by a duty' but which is 'graciously offered beyond debt and economy, offered to the other, a hospitality invented for the singularity of the new arrival, of the unexpected visitor'.[10] Chaucer's poem not only conceptualizes its readers as offering hospitality to Troilus, but also offers itself as just such a singular 'new arrival' or 'unexpected visitor': the poem demands that readers draw on their own memories of love in order to show it hospitality. Acts of memory also shape our ethical responses to the text by requiring that we too remember what it was like to be unhappy in love (as the poem's medieval audience is enjoined to do), not so that we can affect a spurious sense of kinship with the medieval past but in order to keep open our responsibility towards that past.

Also ethical is the narrator's attempt to 're-memory' Criseyde by probing the differing claims of history, literature and cultural memory as disciplinary *technai* for narrating a past of romantic, sexual love, and for imagining its present and future.[11] Yet *Troilus and Criseyde* is striking in its insistence that Criseyde has a weak memory and that Troilus has an agonizingly retentive one. The poem is a tragedy in part because Troilus cannot forget Criseyde, but Criseyde appears all too easily to forget Troilus. In Book 5, once Criseyde has left Troy for the Greek camp and the lovers are forcibly and brutally separated, Troilus revisits on horseback Criseyde's empty palace and all the places in Troy where their love affair had unfurled, poignantly investing these places with his memories of her, as if fixing them in his mind, just as the medieval rhetoricians recommended that one visualize objects in specific architectural emplacements (so-called memory-palaces), the better to recall them:

> every thyng com hym to remembraunce
> As he rood forby places of the town
> In which he whilom hadde al his pleasaunce. (5.563–5)[12]

Criseyde, by contrast, '[w]ith wommen fewe, among the Grekis stronge' (5.688), all too rapidly capitulates to Diomede's sexual advances. Troilus slips out of her memory to such an extent that in one letter that she writes to him – and by this point it is clear that she has no intention of returning to Troy – she rebukes him for the 'unreste' (5.1604) he displays in his letters to her: 'Nor other thyng nys

in your remembraunce, / As thynketh me, but only youre pleasaunce.'
(5.1607–8). She makes his memory of his delight in her a source of
disapprobation: Troilus, she claims, thinks only of his pleasure, and not
of her plight.

In *Troilus and Criseyde*, the narrator's interventions sometimes
serve to reinforce a traditionally misogynist view of Criseyde: like all
women, she is 'slydynge of corage' (5.825). As a result, it is all too easy
to read Troilus's obsessive fidelity to Criseyde and Criseyde's faithless
amnesia as divided along a familiar medieval gendered binary: women
are fickle and men are loyal. But I want to resist this reading, just as
Chaucer later resisted it in one of his (in)famous retractions. In the
G-version of the Prologue to *The Legend of Good Women*, the God of
Love rebukes Chaucer for writing *Troilus and Criseyde*:

> Hast thow nat mad in Englysh ek the bok
> How that Crisseyde Troylus forsok,
> In shewynge how that wemen han don mis? (G. 264–6).

Chaucer, Cupid claims, has done a disservice to love in presenting
Criseyde as faithless. Yet is there a gender difference in medieval
memory practices? Forgetfulness was seen in the Middle Ages as a
marker of the fallen condition of all humankind. In what sense, then,
was the work of memorization in the Middle Ages gendered? I turn
first to a consideration of the gendering of memory in the medieval
arts of memory.

Can't get you out of my mind: every man in his humour

In the extensive late medieval literature on artificial memory, references to gender and sexual difference are rare. When they appear,
they are largely incidental. The lack of reference to women in these
treatises is in part due to the monastic and scholastic origins of the
artes memoriae.[13] Women do not figure in them because they are neither practitioners of the arts of memory nor threats to men's work of
memorization. Yet the treatises do discuss the effect of the humours
on mnemonic storage and retention. Given the widespread medieval
understanding, derived from Galen, of the body's complexion as composed variably of four humours, which formed the basis of gender
difference in the Middle Ages, is there a somatic basis for the different
attitudes to remembrance of Troilus and Criseyde? Let me say right
away that the medieval *artes memoriae* do not see the body as the only
determinant of the ability to retain and recall memorial impressions.

Memory is seen above all as something that can be trained – but certain humoral predispositions affect that training process.

Medieval memory-writers follow Aristotle in agreeing that memory is imprinted corporeally but without any material trace. Drawing on a widespread metaphor for memory – that of wax receiving an impression – Aristotle claims in the *De anima* that we receive 'the form of sensible objects without the matter, just as wax receives the impression of a signet ring without the iron or the gold'.[14] A signet ring leaves *signa*, impressions, but not traces of its material substance. The memory treatises amplify this by arguing that the humours variously assist or impede the fixing of impressions in natural memory. Some people are naturally disposed to remember and some to forget; for example, as Albertus Magnus argues in his late thirteenth-century *Commentary* on Aristotle's treatise *On Memory and Recollection*, 'infants' and 'the decrepit' are liable to forgetfulness.[15] According to the early thirteenth-century Bolognese rhetorician Boncompagno da Signa, the 'sanguine are said to remember well on account of the disposition and moderation of this humor [blood], which is of an amicable and refined nature'.[16] Phlegmatics, however, he continues, 'do not remember in this way [that is, well], because phlegm is the most compact and viscous humor'.[17] Thomas Aquinas agrees: 'Minds that are too moist or in flux do not retain [...] *signa* or impressions, and this is the case of either children or old people.'[18] Albertus Magnus likewise remarks that '[a] mental image does not remain in the soul in certain people, as for example in the excessively moist'.[19] Cholerics, on the other hand, in Boncompagno's words, 'on account of the ferocity and mutability of the humor, easily increase their knowledge and quickly commit to memory', yet 'are unable to retain, because what comes suddenly, recedes suddenly, and what is in constant motion cannot remain in place'.[20] None of these writers, I should say, specifically mentions the humoral differences between men (hot and dry) and women (cold and moist), because – I suspect – the treatises are not intended for female readers.

Melancholia is the humoral category that occasions most discussion, because, as Boncompagno observes, it is 'the name of an illness [something temporary] as well as the name of a humor [something essential, fixed]'.[21] Those of a melancholic disposition have difficulty acquiring knowledge because melancholy is a 'hard humor [that] is of the earth', but on the other hand they preserve their memories because 'what is imprinted into a substance with solidity and hardness is not moved with ease'.[22] Those suffering from the illness of *melancholia*, however, even if they are not naturally of a melancholic disposition,

'easily acquire knowledge and are able to remember it admirably'.[23] If
for Freud it is 'hysterics that suffer mainly from reminiscences', in the
Middle Ages it is melancholics that do so. For Albertus Magnus, the
best temperament for remembering is 'dry-hot melancholy, the intellectual, the inspired melancholy'.[24] Troilus, who is not naturally melancholic but whose traumatic response to Criseyde's absence causes
him to suffer acutely from 'melancolie', at least on three occasions in
Book 5 (5.1646, 1216, 622), is therefore predisposed to be painfully
memorious. Criseyde, however, being a woman and therefore cold
and moist – that is, phlegmatic – is humorally predisposed not to have
a good memory.

There is one instance in Boncompagno da Signa's treatise on
memory that refers directly to female forgetfulness. In a passage that
argues that 'offensive acts […] cling more fervently to the memory',
Boncompagno remarks that '[w]omen, of course, remember those
who beat them and afflict them through mistreatment, and forget
those others who cherish and honor them'.[25] Yet I resist the idea
that Boncompagno has written Criseyde's epitaph – or indeed that
he offers Troilus a humoral get-out. Chaucer's poem offers anything
but this reductive view of the relationship between sexual difference
and remembrance. Criseyde's apparent forgetfulness in love, just like
Troilus's fidelity to her memory, is not determined by her humoral
make-up, but neither is Criseyde a calculatedly strategic forgetter.
I want to turn now to the poem's deployment of one particular trope
of memory, that of the knot – a figure that can refer in the late Middle
Ages both to memory and love – to explore the gendered meanings
of love and memory in *Troilus and Criseyde*.

The knots of memory: love-knots in *Troilus and Criseyde*

The dominant tropes for memory in the Middle Ages are the wax
tablet and the treasury or storehouse.[26] However, in a long list of
objects that serve to supplement what he calls 'the weakness of natural memory', Boncompagno da Signa includes not only 'all books
that have been written' and 'all inscriptions on wax tablets', but also
'epitaphs, all paintings, images and sculptures; all crosses, of stone, iron,
or wood set up at the intersections of two, three, or four roads; […]
the marks and points on knucklebones, varieties of colors, *memorial
knots*'.[27] This list is a remarkable reminder of the extent to which
medieval culture was, in Carruthers's words, 'fundamentally memorial'.[28] 'Memorial knots' – tied in a girdle or tipet, for example – are
common in both secular and monastic culture.[29] *Troilus and Criseyde*

is concerned with what Megan Murton describes as 'the religious subtext' of Boethius's *Consolation of Philosophy*, and it takes very seriously the Boethian idea of a quasi-divine bond of love, as expressed in Troilus's hymn in Book 3, in which he prays to 'Love, that knetteth lawe of compaignie, / And couples doth in vertu for to dwelle', petitioning Love to '[b]ynd this acord'.[30] Love, for Troilus, not only knits together human society and human lovers, but is also capable of binding himself and Criseyde ['this acord'] in a passionate, sexual relationship. In Chaucer's poem, sex, sexuality and gender form knots that for Troilus cannot be easily untangled, in part because he sees them as formed by the binding power of that same love that maintains order and harmony in the cosmos.

At the height of their relationship in Book 3, Troilus describes being captivated by Criseyde as if he were caught in a net that binds him so tightly to her that it cannot be undone by the virtue or physical charms of any other lady:

> The goodlihede or beaute which that kynde
> In any other lady hadde yset
> Kan nought the montance of a knotte unbynde
> Aboute his herte of al Criseydes net;
> He was so narwe ymasked and yknet,
> That it undon on any manere side,
> That nyl naught ben for aught that may bitide. (3.1730–6)

Criseyde is here figured as a hunter that has spread her net over Troilus's 'herte' and captured it so securely that he is unable to free himself from a single one of its knots. Playing with the courtly convention of feudal bondage to the lady and with the Boethian conceit of love as the 'holy bond of thynges' (3.1261), in Troilus's words of fervent gratitude before the consummation, and as the divine principle which impels Love 'with his bond' to 'cerclen hertes alle and faste bynde / That from his bond no wight the wey out wiste' (3.1766–8) in Troilus's hymn to Love, the poem proposes that Troilus is completely and utterly bound, both by Criseyde and to Criseyde. The love-knots by which Troilus feels himself bound to her are also mnemonic: he cannot undo a single knot of his love for her or of her claims on his memory.

Although Troilus is willingly captured (3.1728–9), medieval audiences might have heard darker undertones here. The image of Troilus toiling in the confines of Criseyde's memorial net of love, so enmeshed that he is unable in any way to free himself, might also suggest that there are unpleasurable aspects of the experience of being emotionally bound to another person. There is also an echo of Ovid's tale of the blacksmith Vulcan, who forged an artfully invisible bronze net to trap his wife Venus and her lover Mars in their bed.[31] The image of Criseyde casting her net over Troilus thus recalls Vulcan's public shaming of the lovers Mars and Venus, helplessly caught *in flagrante delicto* in his delicate web, ironically recalling Criseyde's concern for her honour at the beginning of the affair with Troilus in Book 2 and anticipating her later regret and shame that her name will 'rolled […] ben on many a tonge' (5.1061).

Given its placing in the mid-point of the poem, the image of Criseyde's all-powerful reticularity – her net-like substance – identifies her with Vulcan and brings to mind deception and subterfuge – Vulcan's as much as Venus's – and thus also foreshadows Criseyde's eventual adulterous liaison with the Greek Diomede, a liaison where, ironically, she will be the snared rather than the ensnarer. The net metaphor is echoed in the narrator's reference to Diomede's calculated plan to seduce Criseyde, where he plots

> [w]ith al the sleghte and al that evere he kan,
> How he may best, with shortest taryinge,
> Into his net Criseyde's herte brynge. (5.773–5)

The irony of Diomede planning to capture Criseyde's heart in his net, where she had previously captured Troilus in her net, are not lost on the reader, who is led to ponder the shifting valences of power, gender, love and memory that are invoked by this repeated image, in which Criseyde is figured as both the trapper and the trapped.

A further irony is raised by Pandarus's earlier remark to Criseyde in Book 2 that she has been lucky enough to 'han swich oon ykaught withouten net!' (2.583). For Pandarus, Criseyde is artless; she is not in any way responsible for ensnaring Troilus, and she has no need to resort to Vulcanian subterfuge. Troilus also uses the net image in the consummation scene of Book 3, where he refers to Criseyde's eyes as 'nettes':

> O eyen clere,
> It weren ye that wrought me swich wo,
> Ye humble nettes of my lady deere! (3.1353–5)

Criseyde's reticular gaze may be disarmingly 'humble' (modest), but Troilus is not only captivated by her eyes but also wounded by them. The image is a commonplace of courtly fictions, with their insistence that visual stimulation is necessary to Eros and that amorous looking is 'an extension of the flesh', a corporeal, sexual act.[32] Troilus also acknowledges that he cannot interpret Criseyde's intentions and yet is unable to relinquish their hold over him:

> Though there be mercy written in youre cheere,
> God woot, the text ful harde is, soth, to fynde!
> How koude ye withouten bond me bynde? (3.1355–8)

For Troilus, Criseyde has magically bound herself to him by an invisible bond, one that he is in awe of but also finds perplexing. Yet the later image in Book 3 of Criseyde ensnaring Troilus in her net inculpates her, making it seem as if she desires, as Vulcan does of Venus, not only to catch him but also to catch him out. The ambiguous image of the net resurfaces with pejorative connotations in Book 4, when Criseyde assures Troilus that she will return to Troy within ten days, because she has worked out how she can catch her traitorous father Calchas 'withouten net' (4.1371), by appealing to his 'coveytise' (4.1369), the implication being that she will not have to try very hard. He will be easily caught by her wiles. Multiple ironies accumulate in the knots of the poem, forcing the reader to question each of the characters' investment in, and responsibility towards, sexual love, and to ask: what is the origin of the compulsion to repeat that characterizes Troilus's traumatic remembrance of Criseyde, and what is the origin of Criseyde's oblivion of the ties that bind her to Troilus?

Re-memorying Criseyde

Exiled from Troy to the Greek camp in Book 5, Criseyde, like Troilus, suffers from the burden of memory. At first she spends her time apart from him 'al his goodly wordes recordynge' (5.718) (as the etymology of 'recording' reminds us, recollection names the process of summoning up what has been learnt by heart, what is imprinted in the heart as well as in the memory), setting her sorrowful heart on fire '[t]horough remembraunce of that she gan desire' (5.721). She laments her inability to predict the future:

> On tyme ypassed wel remembred me.
> And present tyme ek koud ich wel ise,
> But future tyme, er I was in the snare,
> Koude I nat sen; that causeth now my care. (5.748–9)

Her words ironically recall those of Boncompagno da Signa: 'Memory is a glorious and wonderful gift of nature, by which we recall the past, comprehend the present, and *contemplate the future through its similarities with the past*.[33] Her misfortune is her failure to anticipate her future. It is also, as she acknowledges, a failure of memory. She is unable to complete Boncompagno's temporal sequence that would allow her to 'contemplate the future through its similarities with the past'. But Criseyde's future was unpredictable. The image of the snare recalls not only the knots of memory and love but also the net of political intrigue that makes Criseyde a pawn in the war between Troy and Greece. Memory may be, in Boncompagno's words, 'a glorious and wonderful gift of nature', but Boncompagno's vision of an individual's calm ability to recall and anticipate past, present and future – just like Troilus's vision of the indissoluble bonds of love – takes no account of the unpredictability of human, sexual love that is, ironically, played out against the backdrop of a war that is caused by human, sexual love, but violently dissimilar from its amorous cause.

When Criseyde promises to herself in Book 5 that she will escape from the Greek camp and elope with Troilus, the narrator ruefully comments that only two months from thence she was

> ful fer fro that entencioun!
> For bothe Troilus and Troie town
> Shal knotteles throughout hire herte slide;
> For she wol take a purpos for t'abide. (5.767–70)

The image of Troilus and Troy sliding 'knotless' out of her heart as she decides to stay in Greece is a cruelly ironic reworking of the knot metaphor that Troilus uses in Book 3 to describe the closeness of his bond with her. The knots of love and memory bind Troilus tightly to Criseyde but they do not prevent Criseyde from playing fast and loose with her man. Her memory of her love for Troilus and for her birthplace 'slide' from her heart (or so the narrator tells us), just as she is 'slydynge of corage' (5.825). In a further irony, as Jessica Rosenfeld observes, '[h]er knotless string will metamorphose once again to become Diomede's "hook and lyne"'.[34] Criseyde's tie knots become slipknots, and then they become the means by which another man will reel her in. Troilus, on the other hand, cannot put her out of his mind.

Why is it that the ties of affect appear to mean so little for Criseyde? Rosenfeld argues that 'Criseyde's betrayal is born not out of her fickle femininity, nor necessarily out of political pragmatism, but out of a desire to keep her worldly felicity stable, a refusal to accept the "perhaps" at the heart of her and Troilus' friendship and love affair'.[35] Rosenfeld is right to contest a misogynist reading of

Criseyde's betrayal, but she may not be entirely right to see Criseyde as hoping for stability. I would argue that Criseyde is not even offered the possibility of remembering, of having an active role in the memory-work of the poem. Troilus, by contrast, is offered this possibility. Immediately after Troilus has replayed his memories of the absent Criseyde by visiting each place in Troy that is sacred to their affair, he tells the God of Love in Book 5 that the suffering he has caused him is worthy of being preserved for posterity:

> O blisful lord Cupide,
> Whan I the proces have in my memorie
> How thow me hast wereyed on every syde,
> Men myght a book make of it, lik a storie. (5.582–5)

This extraordinary *mise-en-abîme* moment – which is not found in any of Chaucer's sources – takes place neither completely inside nor outside the narrative. It anticipates Troilus's final ascension, in the poem's epilogue, to the eighth sphere, from where he looks down and judges the poem's events from a Christian vantage point. But here he is still firmly in pagan Troy. His observation that 'men' might turn his experience into a book, 'lik a storie', could be read as a bitter comment on the gap between the intimate experience of grief and the detached writing of that experience by those who have not suffered. But it is not clear that Troilus is bitter here. What is striking is his claim that he must first consign the 'proces' ('an orderly narrative') of his tragic history to his 'memorie' before anyone can write his 'storie'. Like Latin *storia*, the Middle English word preserves the double sense of 'story' that is inherent in Latin *storia*: something that can be both made up and true. From the present of the narrative Troilus looks back to his past and forward to his future commemoration in Chaucer's poem. Criseyde is not given a similar opportunity to re-memory herself, to intervene in her own future.

Courtly love and sexuation

I want to argue that the striking differences in Troilus's and Criseyde's attitudes to memory are the result of the logic of courtly love and its models of sexuation. Although the poem is at pains not to represent Criseyde as the archetypal lady of troubadour poetry, Troilus nevertheless persists in seeing her not as she is, but as a dream, thus conferring on her the courtly lady's 'uncanny, monstrous character' – precisely the figure that is capable of transferring her love to Diomede.[36]

When Troilus is waiting and watching pathetically for Criseyde to return to Troy, he assures Pandarus that he can at last see her in the distance: 'Have here my trouthe, I se hire! Yond she is!' (5.1158). But his eyes are playing tricks on him, as Pandarus's blunt reply makes plain: 'That I see yond nys but a fare-carte' (5.1162). This is not simply a case of misrecognition, nor of the projection of desire: it is symptomatic of Troilus's distorted, anamorphic representation of Criseyde. She is not the object of his desire; rather, what is Object-like in her is what causes his desire, as Žižek explains about the figure of the lady in courtly love:

> The Object can be perceived only when viewed from aside, in a partial, distorted form [...] the Object is attainable only by way of an incessant postponement, as its absent point-of-reference.[37]

One of the narrator's functions is to keep trying to turn the image – that is, Criseyde, as a distorted object – into the plane of the viewer so that it takes on its rightful appearance, to try to stop the Object being perceived in a partial, distorted form, as Troilus persists in seeing her. The narrator does not want to set up Criseyde as the impossible Thing. He wants the audience to see her straight on,[38] but this proves impossible.

Chaucer's poem imagines Criseyde as a memory place, in the sense that in so far as Troilus attaches memory to her she can never represent a truth (of Woman, of love) but can only be a representation of a representation. In the words of Pierre Nora, the great French historian of memory, 'all *lieux de mémoire* are [...] objects *en abîme*, which is to say, objects containing representations of themselves (hence implying an infinite regress)'.[39] The 'truth' of Criseyde's betrayal is not fully present either in the narrator's ostensibly authoritative account or in the characters' subjective recollection of events. This is an important reminder to us that there is no truth of Criseyde. Rather, Criseyde as Woman functions as a limit: she refuses generalization or universalization.

The meaning of Jacques Lacan's provocative assertion that '*La femme n'existe pas*' [Woman – with a capital W – does not exist] is that femininity escapes any attempt at a rigorous, autonomous definition. Femininity is not a contradiction to masculinity but an exception. We are used to thinking about sex in terms of the binary (as Joan Copjec puts it) 'sex is substance/sex is signification'.[40] That is, biology and culture. But for Lacan sexual difference is not reducible to biology or cultural construction, because sex is a real, not a symbolic, difference.

Rather, our sexed being, as Lacan puts it, 'results from a logical exigency in speech'.[41] Every time we try to define man and woman
qua sexed beings we run up against this 'logical exigency', this place
where language falls into contradiction with itself, as Copjec comments: 'Sex serves no other function than to limit reason, to remove
the subject from the realm of possible experience or pure understanding'.[42] Lacan calls it 'ab-sex-sense'. To understand gender as a historically contingent, variable construction is not at all the same thing as
to understand that sex names a radical impasse of language, a place
where meaning cannot be completed, where sense falters, where we
no longer have any knowledge of the subject.

There are two important implications here. First, as Copjec
observes, 'sex, in opposing itself to sense, is also by definition opposed
to relation, to communication'.[43] Sexual complementarity is an illusion:[44] masculine and feminine subjects cannot complete each other.
Criseyde can never be Troilus's 'al hool' [wholly] just as Troilus cannot be wholly hers. This is what Lacan means by his other scandalous
assertion that there is no sexual relation.[45] Two do not become one.
Two halves do not become a harmonious whole. Masculine and feminine subjects do not relate to what their partners relate to in them:
each enjoys the other in different ways, and each experiences different
anxieties in relation to love.[46] In Book 5, when Troilus is pining for
the absent Criseyde, he describes her as 'she that of his herte berth
the keye' (5.460–1). The allusion is to the key of remembrance that
unlocks the treasury of the memory: Troilus's heart is figured here
not only as the seat of love but as a repository of precious memories
to which only Criseyde has the password. It is a poignant image of
Troilus's single-minded love but also of the melancholic anxiety that
her absence occasions: her possession of the key symbolically deprives
him of his phallic function. The second implication of the statement
that 'there is no sexual relation' is that if we cannot ever fully know
the sexed subject, then we will never get to the bottom of why
Criseyde betrays Troilus. But we can focus instead on how Chaucer's
extraordinary poem stages the radical unknowability of sex. Troilus's
traumatic inability to unbind 'the montance of a knotte / Aboute his
herte of al Criseydes net', the memory of Troilus and Troy that slides
'knotteles' through Criseyde's heart, their starkly different experiences
dramatize that unknowability: a failure of love, but not Criseyde's – or
Troilus's – failure.

Notes

1. Andreas Huyssen, 'Present pasts: media, politics, Amnesia', *Public Culture*, 12.1 (2000), 21–38 (p. 21).
2. Huyssen, 'Present pasts', p. 21.
3. Huyssen, 'Present pasts', pp. 22, 23, 33, and 37.
4. Notable exceptions are Fradenburg, 'Voice Memorial', Elisabeth Van Houts, *Memory and Gender in Medieval Europe, 900-1200* (Toronto: University of Toronto Press, 1999), and, more recently, Margaret Cotter-Lynch and Brad Herzog, *Reading Memory and Identity in the Texts of Medieval European Holy Women* (Basingstoke: Palgrave, 2012); Elizabeth Cox, Liz Herbert McAvoy and Roberta Magnani (eds), *Reconsidering Gender, Time and Memory in Medieval Culture* (Woodbridge: Boydell & Brewer, 2015).
5. See Sylvia Federico, *New Troy: Fantasies of Empire in the Late Middle Ages*, Medieval Cultures 36 (Minneapolis and London: Minnesota University Press, 2003).
6. Jacques Le Goff, *History and Memory*, trans, Steven Rendall and Elizabeth Claman (New York: Columbia University Press, 1992), p. 68.
7. On the different moral responsibilities of Troilus and of Criseyde, see J. Allan Mitchell, 'Love and ethics to come in *Troilus and Criseyde*', in *Ethics and Eventfulness in Middle English Literature, The New Middle Ages* (New York: Palgrave, 2009), pp. 27–46.
8. On *lieux de mémoire*, see Pierre Nora, 'From *lieux de mémoire* to Realms of Memory', Pierre Nora *et al.* (eds), *Realms of Memory: The Construction of the French Past*, Vol. 1: *Conflicts and Divisions*, European Perspectives: A Series in Social Thought and Cultural Criticism (New York: Columbia University Press, 1996), pp. xv–xxiv.
9. Geoffrey Chaucer, *Troilus and Criseyde: A New Edition of 'The Book of Troilus'*, ed. B. A. Windeatt (London: Longman, 1990), 1.23–6. All further references are to this edition and are given parenthetically in the text.
10. Jacques Derrida, *Of Hospitality: Anne Dufourmantelle Invites Jacques Derrida to Respond*, trans. Rachel Bowlby, Cultural Memory in the Present, eds Mieke Bal and Hent de Vries (Stanford, CA: Stanford University Press, 2003), p. 83.
11. The term 're-memory' attempts to yoke together the competing claims of individual recollection and historical memory, a dynamic that I see as central to the narrator's project in *Troilus and Criseyde*, where the narrator presents his memory of Criseyde as one in which he is personally invested but which is in tension with the historical (and largely misogynist) tradition of the memory of Criseyde. For use of the term, see Toni Morrison, *Beloved* (New York: Knopf, 1987), p. 43.
12. See Ruth Evans, 'Memory's history and the history of Criseyde: Chaucer's *Troilus*', *Revista Canaria de Estudios Ingleses*, 47 (2003), 87–99, 92.

13. On the monastic origins of the craft of memory, see Mary Carruthers, *The Craft of Thought: Meditation, Rhetoric, and the Making of Images 400-1200*, Cambridge Studies in Medieval Literature 34 (Cambridge: Cambridge University Press, 1998), p. 2.
14. Aristotle, *De anima, Aristotle: On the Soul, Parva Naturalia, On Breath*, trans. W.S. Hett, Loeb Classical Library 288 (Cambridge, MA: Harvard University Press, 1986), 2.12.424a.
15. Albertus Magnus, *Commentary* on Aristotle, *On Memory and Recollection*, trans. Jan M. Ziolkowski, in *The Medieval Craft of Memory*, eds. Carruthers and Ziolkowski, pp. 118–52 (pp. 132–3).
16. Boncompagno da Signa, *On Memory*, p. 107.
17. Boncompagno da Signa, *On Memory*, p. 107.
18. Janet Coleman, *Ancient and Medieval Memories: Studies in the Reconstruction of the Past* (Cambridge: Cambridge University Press, 1992), p. 449.
19. Albertus Magnus, *Commentary*, p. 133.
20. Boncompagno da Signa, *On Memory*, p. 107.
21. Boncompagno da Signa, *On Memory*, p. 107.
22. Boncompagno da Signa, *On Memory*, p. 107.
23. Boncompagno da Signa, *On Memory*, p. 107.
24. Frances A. Yates's much earlier book *The Art of Memory* (London: Routledge and Kegan Paul, 1966), p. 80. See also Coleman, *Ancient and Medieval Memories*, p. 418.
25. Boncompagno da Signa, *On Memory*, p. 115.
26. Carruthers, *Book of Memory*, pp. 16–45.
27. Boncompagno da Signa, *On Memory*, p. 111. Emphasis mine.
28. Carruthers, *Book of Memory*, p. 8.
29. See Chaucer, 'General Prologue', A. 196–7; Marie de France, *Guigemar*; and Thomas Usk, *The Testament of Love*, ed. R. Allen Shoaf (1998), 2.1286.
30. See Megan Murton, 'Praying with Boethius in *Troilus and Criseyde*', *The Chaucer Review*, 49.3 (2015), 294–319 (p. 294).
31. Ovid, *Metamorphoses*, trans. David Raeburn (London: Penguin, 2004), 4.167–89.
32. Suzannah Biernoff, *Sight and Embodiment in the Middle Ages: Ocular Desires* (Basingstoke: Palgrave Macmillan, 2002), p. 58.
33. Boncompagno da Signa, *On Memory*, p. 105; emphasis mine. See also Coleman, *Ancient and Medieval Memories*, p. 537.
34. Jessica Rosenfeld, *Ethics and Enjoyment in Late Medieval Poetry: Love after Aristotle*, Cambridge Studies in Medieval Literature (Cambridge: Cambridge University Press, 2011), p. 157.
35. Rosenfeld, *Ethics and Enjoyment*, p. 156.
36. Slavoj Žižek, 'From courtly love to *The Crying Game*,' *New Left Review*, 202 (1993), 95–108 (p. 96).
37. Žižek, 'From courtly love to *The Crying Game*,' p. 96.
38. Cf. Carolyn Dinshaw, *Chaucer's Sexual Poetics* (Madison, WI: University of Wisconsin Press, 1989), p. 39.

39. Pierre Nora, 'General introduction: between memory and history,' *Realms of Memory: The Construction of the French Past*, trans. Arthur Goldhammer, eds. Pierre Nora *et al*, 3 vols, Volume 1: *Conflicts and Divisions*, European Perspectives: A Series in Social Thought and Cultural Criticism (New York: Columbia University Press, 1996), pp. 1–20 (p. 16).

40. Joan Copjec, 'Sex and the euthanasia of reason,' in *Supposing the Subject*, ed. Joan Copjec (London: Verso, 1994), pp. 16–44 (p. 17).

41. Jacques Lacan, *The Seminar of Jacques Lacan, Book XX. On Feminine Sexuality, The Limits of Love and Knowledge, 1972-1973 (Encore)*, ed. Jacques-Alain Miller, trans. Bruce Fink (New York: Norton, 1999), p. 10.

42. Copjec, 'Sex and the euthanasia of reason,' p. 21.

43. Copjec, 'Sex and the euthanasia of reason,' p. 21.

44. Suzanne Barnard, 'Introduction', in Suzanne Barnard and Bruce Fink (eds), *Reading Seminar XX: Lacan's Major Work on Love, Knowledge, and Feminine Sexuality* (New York: SUNY Press, 2002), pp. 1–20 (p. 9).

45. Lacan, *The Seminar of Jacques Lacan, Book XX*, pp. 56–7.

46. See Renata Salecl, 'Love anxieties', in *Reading Seminar XX*, eds Barnard and Fink, pp. 93–7 (p. 93).

9

Chaucer and the Poetics of Gold

Valerie Allen

Aureate Chaucer

In a well-known comment, poet John Lydgate celebrates the beauty that his contemporary Geoffrey Chaucer brought to the 'Rude speche' of the English language of the time. He was the first, says Lydgate, to distil '[t]he golde dewe dropes of speche and eloquence/ Into our tunge thurgh his excellence'.[1] Poet William Dunbar similarly speaks of Chaucer's 'fresch anamalit termes celicall' that 'coud illumynit haue full brycht' the poem that Dunbar was writing.[2] From this and similar contemporary accolades, Chaucer is credited with developing a literary English that enshrines the rhetorical riches of his classical predecessors. Performing such poetic adornment himself with the term 'aureat' (from Latin *aureatus*, 'decorated with gold'), Lydgate gives us a critical terminology for a distinctive style of late medieval English poetry that was highly descriptive and used (or coined) words deriving from Latin (or Romance) languages. 'Aureate', 'enamelled', 'golden' and 'illumined' became for these fifteenth-century poets key terms to describe this vernacular poetic that was seen to begin with Chaucer.[3]

It is worth considering for a moment the Latin literary tradition to which these writers had access and that shaped their assessment of Chaucer. Michael Roberts describes the late antique period of Latin literature (fourth to sixth centuries AD) as using a 'jewelled style', by which he means a style of writing that, beyond simply using a vocabulary laden with terms invoking colour and brightness, is characterized by heavy reliance on mastery of metrical form and on rhetorical devices such as antithesis, repetition and synecdoche to ornament the language.[4] Compared to the plainness of the earlier Roman literature, the florid nature of this late antique/early medieval literature often seemed to classicists to so over-ornament the verbal part that it compromised the integrity of the artistic whole. That jewelled style, however, is highly prized by medieval poets writing in Latin, and if their poetic testimonials are to be believed, Lydgate, Dunbar and their peers believed Chaucer to have brought something of that linguistic vividness to English poetry, thereby aligning the vernacular literature with the rich legacy of the Latin tradition.[5]

A 'jewelled' style characterizes the poet as a worker of gold and precious gems. This is a long-established analogy at least dating from Late Latin poetry, which carries through to late Middle English poetry, most explicitly in the shape of *Pearl*'s poet-narrator as a *jueler*.[6] Apart from its classical roots, the metaphor is also found in the Germanic literary tradition, for example in *Beowulf* (ll. 867b–874a), where the king's *scop* is said to have forged tales with the same skill that workers smithy metal. Such a metaphor places the poet's work closer to the manual than the cerebral, to craft more than art. Indeed, in fifteenth-century English, the term that best associates the poet with such wordsmithing is 'maker'.[7] Bending and stretching his language into elegant shapes, the maker adorns his golden lines with jewels of rhetoric.

The obvious question arises as to how Chaucer and these makers achieved stylistic effects in English that were distinctively Latin, especially since writers of this period were acutely aware of the different shapes that the two languages assumed. As an illustration of that difference, consider the ablative absolute, a Latin construction that uses a minimal number of words for a subordinate clause but when translated literally into English seems disconnected from the sense of the main sentence. Geoffrey of Vinsauf, writer of the treatise *Poetria Nova* in the early thirteenth century, categorizes the ablative absolute as an elegant brevity device.[8] The translator of the Middle English Bible, however, in discussing his 'Englishing' method, counsels sacrificing the deftness of the construction for the sake of clarity by using a wordier verbal phrase:

> In translating into English, manie resolucions moun make the sentence open, as an ablatif case absolute may be resoluid into these thre wordis, with couenable verbe, *the while, for if*, as gramariens seyn; as thus, *the maistir redinge, I stonde*, mai be resoluid thus, *while the maistir redith, I* stonde [...] and this wole, in manie placis, make the sentence open, where to Englisshe it aftir the word, wolde be derk and douteful.[9]

[With reference to translations into English, many expansions make
the statement clear, for example when an ablative absolute construction is expanded into these three terms, with the appropriate verb, *the
while, for* [and] *if*, as grammarians say; for example, 'the master reading, I stand' can be expanded into 'while the master reads, I stand'.
Doing this in a number of instances will make the statement clear
rather than translating it literally, which renders the passage vague and
ambiguous.]

What is compressed in Latin is in English dilated and ironed out into
straightness. English is wordier and structurally plainer than Latin. Not
lending itself as readily to the same stylistic effects, English, or what
Dunbar calls 'oure rude langage', requires additional work to compete
in elegance with Latin.[10] One way was to use or invent mannered,
polysyllabic English words with Latin or Romance roots, and Lydgate
in particular frequently did so. Indeed, this is the usual meaning of the
term aureation. Yet, as Christopher Cannon notes:

> The line between English and French is not crossed continually in
> Chaucer because he was the 'Father of English Poetry' but because to
> write English in the fourteenth century was to cross this line.[11]

It is notable that Chaucer held no remarkable record as a linguistic
innovator (certainly not by Lydgate's standards), and the stream of
French borrowings into English had already peaked and waned by the
time Chaucer composed.

Chaucer's 'Blingo'

Using a 'blinguistic' enumeration, this essay will examine how
Chaucer bejewelled the English language in order to broaden
the understanding of aureation beyond word-coinages by keeping a tally of his references in one form or another to gold, noble
metals and jewels. It will then draw out the connections between
Chaucerian poetics and the properties of bright gold that make it a
deep and ancient measure of beauty. The intention is to establish in
what ways Chaucer's poetry behaves like gold and why. A cursory
consideration of such terms using a concordance search yielded the
following results. The numbers are only approximate – not least
because a number of references are semantically equivocal – but the
figures do give a general sense of the ratios of occurrence among
the texts.[12]

Chaucer's 'Blingo'	*Canterbury Tales*	Other	Total
Combined references to: adamant, alabaster, beryl, carbuncle, coral, crystal, diamond, emerald, ivory, jasper, jet, marble, pearl, ruby, sapphire, and the generic terms of gems, jewels, perry and stones	44 12 – 'Knight's Tale' 7 – 'Monk's Tale'	36 9 – *Legend of Good Women* 8 – *Troilus and Criseyde* 8 – *House of Fame*	80
Brass	10 6 – 'Squire's Tale' (horse of brass)	4	14
Copper	6 All from 'Canon Yeoman's Tale'	1	7
Silver (noun and adjective)	32	1	33
Gold (Including nouns, adjectives and compounds: *golden*; *gold-bete*; *gold-hewen*; *goldlees*; *gold-smithrie*; *gold-tressed*. *Gilt* is excluded.)	92 19 – 'Knight's Tale' 10 – 'Canon Yeoman's Tale' 9 – 'Pardoner's Tale' 8 – 'Shipman's Tale' 7 – 'General Prologue'	41 11 – *House of Fame* 11 – *Legend of Good Women* 10 – *Troilus and Criseyde*	133

Some general observations can be made from the above data. Among the *Canterbury Tales*, that of the Knight stands out for sheer sumptuousness of description. That the preponderance of argentine allusion should occur in the *Canterbury Tales* indicates silver's connection to the mercantile world of the poem, where the word regularly refers to money and arms or clothing accessories, with the most frequent occurrences (17 in all) clustering in the 'Canon Yeoman's Prologue' and 'Tale', a story about an alchemical con job. References to gold are barely outnumbered by those to all other noble metals, and precious and semi-precious gemstones combined. Gold gives Chaucer expressive possibilities that other minerals cannot offer.

Gold and poetics

A naturally occurring element, gold has distinct properties that make it the desideratum of jewellers. Its foremost characteristics, to scientists of the time, were its ductility and density, or more colloquially, its pliability and heaviness. Encyclopaedist John Trevisa describes the metal in this way:

> Þan among metalle noÞing is so sadde in substaunce ne more nesshe, and Þerefore, Þogh it be in fyre, it wastiÞ nouȝt in smokyng and vapoures noiÞer leseth his weyghte, and it is nouȝt wastede in fyre; but onelyche if it melteÞ wiÞ strengthe of heete, Þanne ȝif any filthe is Þerynne or hoore, it is yclenede Þerof, and Þerefore golde [is] Þe more pure and shynyng. Amonge metalle noÞing streccheth more wiÞ hamour werke Þan golde for it streccheÞ so Þat bytwene Þe anfelde and Þe hamour withoute brekyng and rendyng of parties it streccheÞ into golde foyle. And among metalle is noÞing fairer in syght Þanne golde, and Þerfore among peyntours golde is chief and fairest in syght, and so it hiȝteÞ colour and shappe of colour and oÞere metalle.[13]

> [So among metals none is so heavy in substance or so soft, and thus even though it be placed in fire, it does not dissipate in smoke and vapour nor does it lose its weight, and it is not diminished in fire. Only if it melts in high temperatures does any dirt or impurity mixed in with it burned off from it, and thereby the gold becomes even purer and shinier. Among metals nothing is more pliable under the hammer than gold for it is so ductile that it stretches between the hammer and anvil into gold foil without breaking or tearing into bits. And among metals nothing is fairer to look at and thus it is the most preferred by painters and most beautiful, and so it beautifies colours, the forms of colours, and other metals.]

Bright and beautiful, gold, considered from the elemental angle, is best characterized as ductile and dense (Trevisa's 'nesshe' and 'sadde'). These qualities arise out of gold's singular composition, in which 'the packing together of many parts in a small space or place causes the weight (pondus)', as philosopher Albertus Magnus notes in his treatise on minerals.[14] Other metals, in contrast, contain internal pockets of air that make them combustible. Gold's parts are harmonized in a 'close union' (connexio), also called 'an agreement' (fœdus) or 'a gluing together of related things' (collam germanorum).[15]

Given the personalities that these metals acquire, one might say that gold has integrity and loves itself. Representing a kind of ideal being, this metal perfectly assimilates difference within. Its density arises from all its parts being packed together into a small space because they match perfectly. Small wonder, then, that its ability to undergo the ordeal of fire has long stood as an image of the virtue of endurance.[16] The metal is an archetype for the real thing. By analogy, poetry idealizes reality. As poet Philip Sidney would later observe in the sixteenth century, 'nature delivers a brazen world, the poet a golden'.[17] The observation points to another long-standing metaphor of poetry as alchemy, transmuting the base metal of reality into the gold of art.

Gold's ductility and density map neatly onto what medieval poetry theorists identify as the two chief strategies for adornment of poetic language: amplification (stretching and extending), and abbreviation (compacting and compressing). The one treatise that we do know Chaucer had some familiarity with, Vinsauf's *Poetria Nova*, presents amplification and abbreviation as the soul of ornamentation:

> Formula materiae, quasi quaedam formula cerae,
> Primitus est tactus duri: si sedula cura
> Igniat ingenium, subito mollescit ad ignem
> Ingenii sequiturque manum quocumque vocarit,
> Ductilis ad quicquid. Hominis manus interioris
> Ducit ut amplificet vel curtet.[18]

[The material to be moulded, like the moulding of wax, is at first hard to the touch. If intense concentration enkindle native ability, the material is soon made pliant by the mind's fire, and submits to the hand in whatever way it requires, malleable to any form. The hand of the mind controls it, either to amplify or curtail.]

Note the analogy in Vinsauf's words between the smith, plying metal in the fire, and the poet who bends poetic lines into wondrous metrical shapes, stretching or compacting the words as prosody and meaning demand.

One of the standard devices of amplification was description; in Vinsauf's scheme, it is the seventh of eight strategies.[19] The generic term for vivid description in classical Greek oratory was *enargia*, referring to the linguistic 'capacity to visualize a scene', and a set-piece description was often referred to as *ekphrasis*.[20] Entering first the Roman and then medieval rhetorical treatises, these terms were variously translated by a wide network of terms including *effictio*, *notatio*, *explicatio* and *descriptio*. Invoking objects, people or scenes, *descriptio* (along with its associated terms) was the lifeblood of medieval narrative structure. To recognize its importance, look no further than Chaucer's 'General Prologue', which constitutes in near entirety a series of standalone *descriptiones*. Poetic descriptive passages have a palpable design upon the listener or reader, for poets note only what is worth hyperbolizing, their purpose being not simply to identify by name but to describe with effect. Descriptive technique can be varied in multiple ways, for example, through lists, as when Chaucer spends a stanza cataloguing various types of tree in the *Parliament of Fowls* (ll. 176–82). Despite identifying *descriptio* as an amplificatory device, Vinsauf also categorizes it as a figure of thought and general stylistic ornament.[21] Indeed, for medieval poetry, elaborate description comes close to being an aspect of the narrative itself.

Amplification often seems preferred over abbreviation in medieval poetics and one of the reasons for this, as we saw with the discussion of the ablative absolute above, is that elisions and omissions supportable in Latin do not work in the vernacular. Brevity formulae nonetheless populate Chaucer's poetry, often occurring within amplificatory passages of description: 'But shortly for to speken of this thyng' and 'But it were al to longe for to devyse' ('Knight's Tale', ll. 985, 994); 'And, shortly of this thing to pace' (*House of Fame*, l. 239). Just as descriptive elaborations function as general devices of ornamentation in medieval poetics, so do verbal syncopations such as *articulus* (omission of conjunctions), *occupatio* (announcement of omitted material) and *diminutio* (understatement).[22] Chaucer is a master of ironic implication, saying one thing but meaning another. Thus, with reference to the Monk's theories concerning his rule, Chaucer the narrator remarks, 'And I seyde his opinion was good' ('General Prologue', l. 183). Whole sermons of castigation compact themselves into seven words of seeming praise. Just as language expands to describe what the poet wants to emphasize, so gold bends and stretches into the artistic design of the jeweller; and just as language contracts into pointed understatement or irony, so gold's 'atoms' densify into solidity, leaving no space within for alloy or admixture.

Beautiful gold

Chaucer's many poetic references to gold describe it in terms of brightness, a characteristic of gold noted by Trevisa (above). *Shene* and *brighte* accompany the word repeatedly to make pairs or triplets of metrical feet. From the Canterbury poem alone we find: 'gold ful sheene'; 'brighte as any gold'; 'as the gold it shoon'; 'shynynge as gold so fyn'; 'gold that brighte shoon'; 'shoon as the burned gold with stremes brighte'; and 'that shineth as the gold'. And, if references to (gold) florins be allowed: 'the floryns been so faire and brighte'; and 'the beautee of thise floryns newe and brighte'.[23] This preoccupation with brightness raises the question of beauty because *claritas*, translated variously as 'lustre', 'clarity', 'brightness' and 'radiance', is one of the primary qualities of beauty as expounded by medieval philosophers. *Claritas* relies on an epistemology – even a theology – of light, for beauty is an attribute of divinity. The importance of light derives from Neoplatonist thought, especially as represented by the third-century philosopher Plotinus and fifth-/sixth-century theologian Pseudo-Dionysius the Areopagite, for whom light emits energy, and thus diffuses itself and is radiant.[24] Like light, beauty is self-evident (note the verb *videre* in the word 'evident'). It is not something one needs to be persuaded about, in the same way that no one argues that two and two equal four – they just do and either you see it or you do not. The *quod erat demonstrandum* of a mathematical proof shows that it has reached a point when inferences are no longer needed and the truth of the proposition proclaims itself. In the same way, radiant beauty is deictic. It shows itself as an objective reality, and the only proper response is, 'Yes, I see'. This radiance facilitates an appreciation of proportion, of how the parts of the whole connect with each other.[25]

Summarizing received wisdom on the subject, Thomas Aquinas delineates three conditions for beauty:

> Nam ad pulchritudinem tria requiruntur: primo quidem integritas sive perfectio, quae enim diminuta sunt, hoc ipso turpia sunt. Et debita proportio sive consonantia. Et iterum claritas, unde quae habent colorem nitidum, pulchra esse dicuntur.[26]
>
> > [Beauty requires three conditions: the first is integrity (*integritas*) or perfection, for those things that are defective are consequently ugly. The second is proportion (*proportio*) or harmony. And the last is radiance (*claritas*), thus things that have bright colour are said to be beautiful.]

What is beautiful will thus be a totality, well proportioned and radiant, implying both reflective quality and saturated hue. When these conditions are applied to gold, the purer the gold the brighter it is, for it does not tarnish in the presence of air or moisture, and the purest gold is the yellowest, so in this way gold's colour and brightness do entail each other. Thus, in the 'Knight's Tale', King Lycurgus wears a bearskin with claws 'yelewe and brighte as any gold' (l. 2141). Chaucer does once refer to red-gold, in describing Thopas's shield of 'gold so reed', perhaps because gold turns red when annealed.[27] Redness thus refers to the metal's refinement rather than the presence of an alloy such as copper, which turns gold pink.

Beyond being a characteristic of *claritas*, hence of beauty, 'colour' (whether Middle English *colour* or Latin *color*) is a key term that connects aesthetics to language because it is a technical term for rhetorical adornment. When the Franklin refers to the *colours of rethoryk*, he refers to the stylistic devices discussed by Vinsauf (among others) and inherited from Latin treatises, thereby invoking a literary tradition with which Chaucer is well acquainted, despite the Franklin's demurral.[28] An associated technical term that descends from classical rhetoric is 'flowers' (Middle English *floures*, Latin *flores*).[29] Chaucer's fascination with them is ubiquitous – see, for instance, the prologue to the *Legend of Good Women*. Enamelling the narrative, flowers also reflexively allude to poetry itself as an act of beautification.

The virtues of gold and jewels

So far, the relationship between gold and jewels on the one hand, and Chaucer's style and poetics on the other, has been figurative: poetic language behaves like gold, and gold is a deep metaphor for poetry. But both poetic language and gold (as well as jewels) have special influences that can best be called virtues, in the old, quasi-magical sense of the word. These precious substances, extracted from the earth, possess mineral virtue, properties unique to each kind of substance and which can protect or heal its wearer.[30] In like fashion, metrical form bestows a kind of incantatory power upon language to make poetry spellbinding. Through metrical constriction and rhetorical adornment, the English vernacular – notorious at the time for being unstable and fleeting – 'gemmifies' to gain the durability and self-motion or agency of a mineral substance.[31] The very act of making such metrically controlled poetry mineralizes language and bestows special linguistic virtues upon the words. Used as we are today to the prosodic freedoms of modern poetry, which often creates its own metrical rules rather than fitting into predetermined shapes, we require an extra imaginative effort to appreciate how intrinsic Chaucer's metrical forms such as rime royal and the ballade are to the beauty of the verse, how poetic form itself is meaningful, and how lines so crafted can be thought of as a linguistic jewel.

In this mineral poetic, the textual and the material merge, for words acquire spatial dimension, becoming precious objects in themselves rather than mere bearers of concepts whose concreteness extends no further than a certain kind of conventionalized vocal noise or a scratch on a page. Nowhere does the materiality of language so make its presence felt as in the medieval art of manuscript illumination. Consider, for example, the book that Valerian in the 'Second Nun's Tale' reads, written in letters of gold.[32] Medieval illuminators created such lettering not with metallic paint but with foil of real gold, pressed into the page, as the metal stretches out to wrap around these words that amplify and magnify their subject. Never lying entirely flat, a page embellished with the gold leaf will leave the foil slightly raised, as if it were a golden dewdrop on the page. Given that the gold of illuminated pages is made of the actual metal and that other colours themselves often derive from stone (ground lapis lazuli, for example, giving an intense blue), these mineralized pages possess *virtus* of their own, acting upon the reader. It is in this quite literal sense that Lydgate prays for 'aureate licoure' to enter his pen in order to write golden letters on the page in praise of St Margarete.[33] As the linguistic and the sculptural merge, poetry works its fascinating charm.

Gold assayed

Just as often as he celebrates gold's brilliance, Chaucer registers its purity: words such as 'riche', 'brend', 'ful fyn', 'burned' and 'pured' litter his lines. In one sense, little hangs on the distinction because purity and brilliance entail each other: the finer the gold, the fewer alloys it contains, hence the yellower and brighter it will be. Yet the difference matters, for whereas brilliance is visible, purity can only be ascertained through assay. With gold's purity, Chaucer shifts attention towards another deep characteristic of beauty: integrity. If Chaucer makes beauty visible by gilding language, he also tests it for probity. The word 'assay' (as noun and adjective) occurs in Chaucer's works more often than silver does, and the object most often assayed is not coin but that which best embodies beauty: woman.[34] The Clerk makes this point forcibly, leaning heavily on the woman/coin analogy:

> But o word, lordynges, herkneth er I go:
> It were ful hard to fynde now-a-dayes
> In al a toun Grisildis thre or two;
> For if that they were put to swiche assayes,
> The gold of hem hath now so badde alayes
> With bras, that thogh the coyne be fair at ye,
> It wolde rather brest a-two than plye. ('Clerk's Tale', ll. 1163–9)

[But listen to one more word, gentlemen, before I finish. It would be very hard nowadays to find two or three women like Griselde in the town. For if they were put to the test in the same way, the gold of which they are made is now so badly alloyed with brass that although the coin be fair to look at, it would sooner break in two than bend.]

'Not all that glisters is gold' is a proverb that Chaucer uses at least twice in his works ('Canon Yeoman's Tale', ll. 962–3; *House of Fame*, l. 272) – three times if we count this paraphrase. What is beautiful should be self-evidently so, yet the poet exhibits enough mistrust in shiny surfaces to suggest that in another aspect beauty only emerges over time and under duress and that without that probative process it remains unascertainable. For all its self-evident luminosity, Chaucer suggests, beauty has to be interpreted.

In one particular poem, his investments in aureate language, poetic form and womanly beauty converge. The *Complaint to his Purse* is composed in a fixed metrical form that originated in French poetry and song: the ballade. It traditionally comprised three stanzas sharing the same metrical form and set of rhymes, a refrain concluding each stanza, and often an envoy using the same rhymes. Chaucer combines this form with another that seems to have been largely of his own devising (rime royal) where the stanzas are composed of seven decasyllabic lines deploying three rhymes in the following scheme: ababbcc. Adapted to the exigencies of the ballade, the rhyme scheme of the *Complaint* is ababbcC ababbcC ababbcC, where C denotes the refrain. Although he includes an envoy, its different rhyme scheme distinguishes it from the rest of the poem: ddeed.[35] Distributing only three rhymes across twenty-one lines, Chaucer has his work cut out for him in varying his lexicon because English offers fewer end-rhyme options than does French, the language for which the ballade was invented. Before we consider anything about its content, this jewelled verse is already intricately faceted. The demands of metrical form and rhyme placement provide the reason for the polysyllabification of French loan words in English ('eleccioun' and 'supplicacioun' in the envoy).

The poem's basic conceit is the double addressee of the lover's complaint: a woman and a purse. Both are 'light': the purse by its emptiness, the woman by her fickleness. In this way, the word reverses the poetics of luminosity: instead of indexing the principle of *claritas*, light now denotes the negatives of poverty and wantonness. By the time the word does properly denote radiance (l. 15), the reader can appreciate the triple pun. The refrain urges the beloved to become 'hevy': the purse by being filled with gold, the woman by carrying his child.[36] Medieval romance heroines traditionally have blonde hair, which allows Chaucer to equivocate between golden tresses and coins:

> Or see your colour lyk the sonne bryght
> That of yelownesse hadde never pere [peer/equal]. (ll. 10–11)

The impact of double meaning is felt from the opening line: 'To yow, my purse, and to noon other wight'. This supplies an eye-rhyme (as distinct from phonic rhyme) between weight and 'wight' (creature).[37] Between the poem's rhymes, repetitions, variations and *double entendre*, words grow as dense as gold, obliged to perform the referential labour of three or four words at a time. The golden dewdrops of Chaucer's language are assayed through the stressful conditions imposed by the ballade's form. Verbal density arises from words being constrained within the slim frame of metre. Brevity makes language contract, suggesting that, at least in this instance, poetic beauty must do much more than fill up a large space and wear lots of verbal bling. Chaucer develops rhetorical abbreviation from a device for elegant shorthand into a semantic density in which no word is simply what it seems, and where meanings glimmer in the depths, requiring hermeneutic effort to achieve 'clarity'.

It would be easy to mistake this hermeneutic play for the model of the *integumentum*, where the literal sense functions as an outer shell that contains an inner kernel of meaning. This is a model that Chaucer himself uses when he closes his 'Nun's Priest's Tale' by exhorting his hearers to take the fruit of meaning and leave to one side the husk ('chaf') (l. 3443). The *Complaint's* virtuosity, however, lies less in any tension between exterior and interior than in a linguistic surface that, like a mosaic, must be viewed from varying angles of reflection as the play of light reveals different facets of meaning. Indeed, rhetorical devices such as opposition place words at angles to each other as if they were reflecting light variously.[38] Hermeneutic effort lies less in excavation than in synthesizing disparate aspects of meaning into a whole.

Conclusion

As early as classical Rome, the Latin poet Horace noted how an over-preoccupation with adornment could disrupt the aesthetic balance between invention and style. What he refers to as the 'purple patch', if overindulged, makes description swamp narrative. Virtuoso descriptions so take on a life of their own that they become self-standing, as compositional units frame themselves into 'self-defined artistic units' that take precedence at the cost of the whole poem.[39] Miniaturization occurs as the effect of ornamental intensification and concentration. A ballade can be thought of as just such a patch of purple, like a jewel cut away from its rocky matrix, as through the fourteenth century the form became fixed and independent of its tangled roots in dance and troubadour song. Attracted as Chaucer is by sumptuous description, he finds in poetic form the power to transform 'rude' English into golden dewdrops of language. The *Complaint* is characterized by a semantic density that is achieved through metrical constraints, such as narrowly distributed rhyme schemes, and through witty conceits that play on linguistic polysemy. As poetic 'conceit' gradually develops into 'symbol', poetry increasingly loosens its hold on the outer form of fixed metrical shapes, such as the ballade, coming to depend more on symbolic content for its poetic force.[40] Chaucer, however, invests in poetry that is still in touch with its metrical form, where the conceit preserves and enhances its relation with poetic structure even as it foregrounds its polysemous playfulness. Intriguingly, the *Complaint*, dating from some point after October 1399, was very possibly Chaucer's last word on the matter of poetics.

Notes

1. The lines occur in the *Life of Our Lady*, ed. J. Lauritis, R. Klinefelter and V. Gallagher (Pittsburg, CA: Duquesne University Press, 1961), l. 1633.
2. *The Golden Targe*, ll. 257–8, in *William Dunbar: The Complete Works*, ed. John Conlee (Kalamazoo, MI: Medieval Institute Publications, 2004). For detailed consideration of the enamelling process as metaphor for poetry, see Lois A. Ebin, *Illuminator, Makar, Vates: Visions of Poetry in the Fifteenth Century* (Lincoln, NE: University of Nebraska Press, 1988), pp. 78–90.
3. Ebin, *Illuminator*, pp. 19–48; and Robert J. Meyer-Lee, 'The Emergence of the Literary in John Lydgate's *Life of our Lady*', *JEGP* 109.3 (2010), 322–48 (324). Also Seth Lerer, *Chaucer and His Readers: Imagining the Author in Late-Medieval England* (Princeton, NJ: Princeton University Press, 1993), pp. 22–56; and P.M. Kean, *Chaucer and the Making of English Poetry, Volume II: The Art of Narrative* (London: Routledge & Kegan Paul, 1972), pp. 210–39.
4. Michael Roberts, *The Jeweled Style: Poetry and Poetics in Late Antiquity* (Ithaca, NY: Cornell University Press, 1989), pp. 1–37.
5. See, for example, Baudri of Bourgeuil's *Adelae Comitissae; and* Valerie Allen, 'Ekphrasis and the object', in *The Art of Vision*, eds Andrew Johnson and Maggie Rouse (Athens, OH: Ohio University Press, 2015), pp. 23–55.

6. *Pearl*, ed. Sarah Stanbury (Kalamazoo, MI: Medieval Institute Publications, 2001), ll. 241–300. For the late-antique analogy between poet and jeweller, see Roberts, *The Jeweled Style*, pp. 13, 55.

7. Ebin, *Illuminator*, pp. 198–9. See Isidore's distinction between art (*ars*) and craft (*artificium*), in which the latter consists in moving the hands, the former in being free of such labour. Wladyslaw Tatarkiewicz, *History of Aesthetics, Vol. II: Medieval Aesthetics* (The Hague and Paris: Mouton, 1970), p. 89. Such distinctions between different kinds of production date back to Plato and Aristotle and are widely invoked and elaborated upon.

8. *Poetria Nova*, ll. 695–6. Latin text in Edmond Faral, *Les Arts poétiques du XIIᵉ et du XIIIᵉ siècle: recherches et documents sur la technique littéraire du moyen âge* (Paris: Champion, 1924), p. 218. Translation from the *Poetria nova of Geoffrey of Vinsauf*, trans. Margaret F. Nims, Mediaeval Sources in Translation 6 (Toronto: Pontifical Institute of Mediaeval Studies, 1967), p. 40.

9. *The Holy Bible Containing The Old and New Testaments, With the Apocryphal Books, in the Earliest English Versions made from the Latin Vulgate by John Wycliffe and his Followers*, Vol I, ed. Josiah Forshall and Frederic Madden (Oxford: Oxford University Press, 1850), p. 57.

10. Dunbar, *The Golden Targe*, l. 266.

11. Christopher Cannon, *The Making of Chaucer's English: A Study of Words* (Cambridge: Cambridge University Press, 1998), pp. 75–6.

12. *A Glossarial Concordance to the Riverside Chaucer*, ed. Larry D. Benson (New York: Garland, 1993). Poems of disputed authorship and translations (*Boece* and the *Romaunt of the Rose*) were excluded, along with the *Treatise on the Astrolabe*.

13. John Trevisa, *On the Properties of Things: John Trevisa's Translation of Bartholomaeus Anglicus De proprietatibus rerum: A Critical Text*, ed. M. C. Seymour *et al.* 3 vols (Oxford: Clarendon Press, 1975–1988), pp. 828:25–829:4.

14. Albertus Magnus, *Book of Minerals*, trans. Dorothy Wyckoff (Oxford: Clarendon Press, 1967), IV:vii, p. 228. The Latin comes from A. Borgnet (ed.), *Opera omnia* (Paris, 1890–1899), 5:92. http://arts.uwaterloo.ca/~albertus/index.html, last accessed 11 March 2015. Gold, which has a density of 19.3 relative to water's density of 1, is mixed to perfection: Wyckoff, p. 226 (editorial notes). For fuller discussion of gold's mineral nature, see Valerie Allen, 'Mineral virtue', in Jeffrey Jerome Cohen (ed.), *Animal, Mineral, Vegetable: Ethics and Objects* (Washington, DC: Oliphaunt Books, 2012), pp. 123–52.

15. Albertus, *Book of Minerals*, IV:vii, pp. 228–9; Borgnet (ed.), *Opera omnia*, 5:92.

16. I Peter 1.7. Despite gold's incorruptibility, it remains a soft metal, *pace* Lerer, *Chaucer and his Readers*, pp. 186–7.

17. From Sidney's *Defence of Poetrie*, cited by Clark Hulse, 'Tudor Aesthetics', in Arthur F. Kinney (ed.), *The Cambridge Companion to English Literature,*

1500–1600 (Cambridge: Cambridge University Press, 2000), pp. 29–63 (p. 56).

18. Vinsauf, *Poetria nova*, ll. 213–18 ; Faral, *Arts poétiques*, p. 203 ; Nims, pp. 23–4. For discussion of the devices, see Faral, *Arts poétiques*, pp. 61–85; also Ernst Robert Curtius, *European Literature and the Latin Middle Ages*, trans. Willard R. Trask, Bollingen Series 36 (Princeton, NJ: Princeton University Press, 1953, repr. 1990), pp. 487–94.

19. Vinsauf, *Poetria nova*, ll. 554–62; Faral, p. 214; Nims, p. 36.

20. Ruth Webb, *Ekphrasis, Imagination and Persuasion in Ancient Rhetorical Theory and Practice* (Farnham: Ashgate, 2009), pp. 8, 105.

21. Vinsauf, *Poetria nova*, ll. 1238–40; Faral, p. 235; Nims, p. 61.

22. Vinsauf, *Poetria nova*, ll. 1122–3, 1159–62, 1236–7; Faral, pp. 232, 233, 235; Nims, pp. 57, 58, 60–1.

23. 'General Prologue', l. 160; 'Knight's Tale', l. 2141; 'Miller's Tale', l. 3314; 'Wife of Bath's Tale', l. 304; 'Clerk's Tale', l. 1117; 'Franklin's Tale', l. 1247; 'Canon Yeoman's Tale', l. 962; 'Pardoner's Tale', ll. 774, 839.

24. Tatarkiewicz, *History of Aesthetics*, p. 29.

25. Tatarkiewicz, *History of Aesthetics*, p. 30: '[B]eauty is defined as *consonantia et claritas* […] that is, as harmony and light, or proportion and brilliance. In the history of aesthetics few expressions have found such lasting acceptance as this. Thrown out rather casually by the Pseudo-Dionysius, it was to become one of the basic ideas of aesthetics, especially in the High Middle Ages.'

26. St. Thomas Aquinas, *Summa Theologica* Ia Q.39, A.8, ad 1. *Corpus Thomisticum*, ed. Enrique Alarcón (Fundación Tomás de Aquino: 2000–13). Accessed 14 March 2015. http://www.corpusthomisticum.org/. Also Tatarkiewicz, *History of Aesthetics*, p. 261.

27. 'Sir Thopas', l. 869. For other examples, *MED red* [adj.] 1f. Albertus says that gold has a colour that is 'yellow or reddish' (*citrinus vel subrubeus*). *Book of Minerals,* Bk III, tractatus 2, ch 3 (p. 191); Borgnet (ed.), *Opera omnia*, 5:77b.

28. 'Franklin's Tale', ll. 716–27. For the meaning of *color* in classical Roman oratory, see Matthew B. Roller, 'Color', in Thomas O. Sloane (ed.), *Encyclopedia of Rhetoric* (New York: Oxford University Press, 2001), pp. 115–19. In the Middle Ages, *color* referred as a general term for rhetorical figures: Richard A. Lanham, *A Handlist of Rhetorical Terms*, 2nd edn (Berkeley, Los Angles and Oxford: University of California Press, 1991), pp. 36–7.

29. Roberts, *The Jeweled Style*, p. 49.

30. Allen, 'Mineral Virtue', pp. 134–8. See *OED virtue* (n.) II. 8–10.

31. For the unstable status of English, see Valerie Allen, 'The Shape of the Vernacular', *Envoi*, 9 (2000), 1–16 (5—6).

32. *SNT* 202, 210. In *Purgatorio* xi.79–84, Dante refers to such illuminated texts as pages that smile.

33. Kean, *Chaucer and the Making of English Poetry*, p. 231.

34. In the same set of texts (see footnote 13), 50 total occurrences, of which 12 occur in 'Clerk's Tale', 11 in *Troilus and Criseyde*, 6 each in the 'Tale of Melibee' and *The Legend of Good Women*, the remaining 15 scattered throughout various works, in none of which does the word appear more than 3 times. *Boece*, which was excluded from this tally, contains 8 references.

35. I have focused on the most metrically dense part of the poem and therefore not taken the envoy into consideration. For a more complete interpretation that takes into account the poem's envoy and political dimension, see Meyer-Lee. Lerer's comments about Lydgate's supplication in his own poetry for *restauracioun* (restoration/re-aureation) are also apposite here. *Chaucer and His Readers*, pp. 37–8.

36. Although the *OED* gives the fifteenth century as the earliest attested meaning of 'pregnant' for the word 'heavy', the connection is bound to be much earlier. Latin *gravis* means both heavy and pregnant as does Insular French *gref*. *OED* heavy (adj.) 3. http://www.anglo-norman.net/cgi-bin/form-s1 for Old French.

37. See *MED wight* (n.) 1, meaning 'creature' and *MED weght* (n.1), meaning 'weight', which lists *wight* as an alternative recorded spelling. The orthography of Middle English was less standardized than modern English.

38. Compare Arthur Mizener arguing for Criseyde's static character, which emerges under changing conditions rather than the character changing under different conditions. 'Character and Action in the Case of Criseyde', *PMLA*, 54 (1939), 65–81. Roberts, *The Jeweled Style*, pp. 70–91 for pieces set at angles for faceted effects. Since medieval stones were polished as cabochon but not faceted, it is to the mosaic that we must look for the multiple refractions now associated with cut jewels.

39. Roberts, *Jeweled Style*, p. 37, 57 for miniaturization.

40. Hulse, 'Tudor Aesthetics', p. 57: 'Poetry's effect derives from the internal mimetic nature of the language, not from external incidentals such as whether or not it rhymes'.

Part III
Religious Texts and Contexts

10

The Torment of the Cross: Perspectives on the Crucifixion in Medieval Lyric and Drama

Beatrice Fannon

The Crucifixion is the central event in salvific history and pro-vides the focal point for much of the literature of the Middle Ages. The following essay looks in some detail at a variety of thirteenth- and fourteenth-century religious lyrics which take aspects of the Crucifixion for their subject, and then, after discussing the treatment of the Crucifixion in a number of the Corpus Christi cycle plays, explores the sacrificial and sacramental vision of the Eucharist offered in the Croxton *Play of the Sacrament*.

The theology of the Cross

The roots of the theological significance of the Crucifixion are found in the Bible. For instance, Isaiah's prophecy in the Old Testament fore-tells the torment that awaited the Messiah:

> Despised, and the most abject of men, a man of sorrows, and acquainted with infirmity: and his look was as it were hidden and despised, where-upon we esteemed him not. Surely he hath borne our infirmities and carried our sorrows: and we have thought him as it were a leper, and as one struck by God and afflicted. But he was wounded for our iniquities, he was bruised for our sins: the chastisement of our peace was upon him, and by his bruises we are healed. (Isaiah 53: 3–5)

Isaiah's prophecy succinctly articulates the theology of the Redemption that was later expressed by Saint Paul in his First Letter to the Corinthians: 'that Christ died for our sins' in order to atone for the sins of mankind.[1] In the Second Letter to the Philippians,

Paul further elucidates the complex theological idea of the relationship between the Incarnation (God becoming flesh) and the shame
of the Crucifixion in the divine plan of Salvation, writing how
Christ,

> emptied himself, taking the form of a servant, being made in the likeness
> of men, and in habit found as a man. He humbled himself, becoming
> obedient unto death, even to the death of the cross. (Philippians 2: 6–8)

Paul describes how God by these two significant acts of love – by
becoming man, and, still more incompatibly with His divinity, by
accepting a criminal's death – accomplishes the Redemption. The
sacrifice of the Crucifixion, however, according to Catholic theology, is at once an historical event and one that is outside time. At
the Consecration of the Mass, the self-same sacrifice of the cross is
performed at the altar, when the bread and wine are transubstantiated
into the Body and Blood of Christ. Accordingly, the experience of
Christians at the Consecration is profound: they stand grieving at the
foot of the cross with Mary and Saint John (John 19: 25), but with the
awareness that they are responsible for Christ's death because of their
sins. Importantly, the Eucharist is at once a sacrament and a sacrifice,[2]
an act of atonement and a vehicle for grace.

The development of liturgical practices and the iconography
associated with the cross can be traced back to the finding of the
True Cross by Saint Helena, the mother of Emperor Constantine, in
the fourth century, which also coincided with the end of the persecution of Christians and the establishment of Christianity as the
official religion of the Roman Empire.[3] In addition, the Crusades
have been pinpointed as a catalyst for stimulating religious devotion
to the Passion, 'awakening […] a deeper realisation of all the sacred
memories represented by Calvary and the Holy Sepulchre'.[4] The
related iconographic imagery of the 'Man of Sorrows' (also known
as the *Imago Pietas*, the Image of Pity) springs from the Isaiah passage
quoted earlier: a tradition that developed in the thirteenth century,
depicting Christ, dejected and despised, displaying His wounds.
Eamon Duffy observes that 'the devotional ubiquity of the Image
of Pity in late medieval England testifies to its ability to console as
well as to frighten and disturb'.[5] The most iconographically striking
image, however, is the crucifix, the crucified Christ suspended on the
cross. It is a familiar image, though, paradoxically, its very familiarity
can mean that its centrality to medieval literature and culture is easily
overlooked.

Medieval lyrics

Medieval lyrics offer a range of moving reflections on the Crucifixion
and often convey a very intimate, intensely emotional vision of man's
communication with the divine. Some are derived from liturgical
sources, such as the fourteenth-century 'Popule meus quid feci tibi?'
('O my people, what have I done to you?')[6] taken from the *Impropria*
or the Reproaches from the Old Testament prophet Micah (6: 3),
which are traditionally sung on Good Friday. Other lyrics dwell on
the theological reasons for the Crucifixion and vary from an acknowledgement of mankind's collective responsibility for the event,[7] to a
more personal awareness of guilt. For instance, the thirteenth-century
lyric 'When I Think on Jesus' Death' describes a strong emotional
engagement with the Crucifixion, as well as prompting the correct
religious response:

when y þenke on ihesu ded	When I think on Jesus' death
min herte ouerwerpes,	My heart collapses
mi soule is won so is þe led	My soul is as heavy as lead
for mi fole werkes.	Because of my foul deeds.
ful wo is þat ilke mon	Exceedingly woeful is that same man
þat ihesu ded ne þenkes on,	That does not think on Jesus' death,
what he soffrede so sore.	How he suffered so grievously.
for my synnes y wil wete,	I will weep for my sins
ant alle y wyle hem for-lete	And I will forsake them all
nou & euermore. (ll. 11–20)[8]	Now and evermore.

Importantly, the events of the Crucifixion are portrayed as being per-
tinent to every man and to all time; Christ died for the speaker's own
'fole werkes' (l. 14). The lyric emphasizes the sorrow caused by meditat-
ing on Jesus' death, but this brings about a change of heart in the sinful
man, enabling him to reform his life in the hope of achieving salvation.
This stimulus to devotion is made more effective in other fourteenth-
century lyrics, as Christ becomes the speaker and addresses the reader
directly. In a similar way to the *Imago Pietas*, He draws attention to His
own wounds to emphasize the pain and humiliation that He suffered
for the sins of the viewer/reader, providing a more intimate call to
devotion while underscoring the sense of individual culpability.[9]

   In Saint John's Gospel, Christ speaks to His mother from the cross
and this speech act provides a starting point for a number of lyrics. In
the thirteenth-century lyric 'A Dialogue between Our Lady and Jesus
on the Cross', Mary complains of her own grief, while her son tries
to explain to her the reasons for His death:

'Moder, nou I may þe seye,
Betere is þat ich one deye,
Þen alle monkun to helle go.'
'Sone, I se þi bodi I-swonge,
Þine honde, þine fet, þi bodi I-
stounge;
Hit nis no wonder þey me be wo.'

'Mother, now I may say to you
It is better that I alone die
Than all mankind go to hell.'
'Son, I see your body scourged
Your hands, your feet, your body
pierced
It is no wonder they make me
sorrowful.'

'Moder, if ich þe dourste telle,
If ich ne deye þou gost to helle;
I þolie deþ for monnes sake.'
'Sone, þou me bi-hest so milde;
I-comen hit is of monnes kuinde
Þat ich sike and serewe make.'

'Mother, if I durst tell you,
If I do not die, you will go to hell;
I suffer death for man's sake.'
'Son, you command me so meekly;
It is because of mankind's nature
That I sigh and make moan.'

'Moder, merci, let me deye
And adam out of helle beye,
And monkun þat is forlore.'
'Sone, wat sal me þe stounde?
Þine pinen me bringeþ to þe
grounde,
Let me dey þe bifore.' (ll. 19–36)[10]

'Mother, please, let me die
And Adam redeem out of hell,
And mankind that is lost.'
'Son, what, shall you pain me?
Your suffering brings me to the
ground,
Let me die before you.'

The lyric emphasizes the bloody spectacle of Christ's wounds, often noted as a feature of medieval iconography of the Crucifixion,[11] and connects Christ's agony with Mary's pain in observing the spectacle. While Christ's words are focused on the theological rationale for His death, Mary's response is grounded in the emotions of the grieving mother; she expresses a desire to die with her son, rather than beholding His Passion. Mary's seeming theological ignorance here contrasts with the more traditional view of her as the perfect Christian who has been granted special knowledge of divine things because she has been a privileged witness to the Incarnation. In the lyric, Mary's wish to die before Christ, though perhaps a very natural response for a mother, is a somewhat dubious reaction in her case as it suggests that she has given in to despair, whereas the Crucifixion, though painful, heralds the hope of salvation. Indeed, in this and other similar lyrics Christ gently rebukes His mother and explains why His death is needful. This trope of one of Christ's disciples opposing the events of the Crucifixion is found in a biblical passage from Matthew. It is Peter, however, who is reprimanded, not Mary:

From that time Jesus began to shew to his disciples, that he must go to Jerusalem, and suffer many things from the ancients and scribes and chief priests, and be put to death, and the third day rise again. And Peter taking him, began to rebuke him, saying: Lord, be it far from thee, this shall not be unto thee. Who turning, said to Peter: Go behind me, Satan, thou art a scandal unto me: because thou savourest not the things that are of God, but the things that are of men. (Matthew 16: 21–3)

While in the Bible Christ's words prioritize the 'things that are of God', Mary's concern in the lyric is very much grounded in the 'things that are of men'. Importantly, the lyric demonstrates an interest in exploring the human element of Mary's feelings, rather than considering how this clashes with the theology of salvation. This disjunction between popular literary genres and orthodox theology draws attention to the dangers of reading religiously themed medieval texts as a straightforward rendering of Christian theology, rather than recognizing their function as stimulating affective piety through their examination of human responses to divine and seemingly incomprehensible events.

Developing from the debates set at the foot of the Cross, a number of lyrics move the dialogue between mother and son to the cradle. In the fourteenth-century 'Dialogue between the B[lessed] V[irgin] and her Child', an anonymous speaker relates the wonder of 'A maiden child rokking' (l. 4).[12] The intimate scene of the Virgin mother lulling her son to sleep is marred only because she is not singing to Him. The child rebukes her for this oversight:

'Sing nov, moder,' seide þat child,   'Sing now, mother,' said that child
'Wat me sal be-falle   'What shall befall me
Here after wan i cum to eld –   Hereafter when I come to old age –
So don modres alle.   So do all mothers.

Ich a moder treuly   I know a mother truly
Þat kan hire credel kepe   That is able to care for her cradle
Is wone to lullen louely   Is accustomed to soothe lovingly
& singgen hire child o slepe.   And sing her child to sleep.

Suete moder, fair & fre,   Sweet mother, fair and noble
Siþen þat it is so,   Since that it is so,
I preye þe þat þu lulle me   I pray you that you soothe me
& sing sum-wat þer-to'. (ll. 9–20)   And sing something thereto'.

Mary is at a loss to sing of events that might befall her child in His old age, because, as she tells Him: 'Wist I neuere ȝet more of þe/ But gabrieles gretingge' (ll. 23–4). However, she goes on to sing what she does know of the child: of the Annunciation (ll. 25–36), of Christ's

Davidic descent (ll. 37–40), of Elizabeth's conception of Saint John the Baptist (ll. 41–4), of Christ's birth 'On midwinter nith' (l. 50), and of the angelic message that the shepherds received (ll. 53–6). This is the extent of her divine knowledge, but her song is of things past, not of those future events of which the Christ-child has asked her to sing. Instead, the child chimes in, singing to His mother of what will come to pass and the great suffering which awaits Him:

'Moder,' seide þat suete þing,	'Mother,' said that sweet thing,
'To singen I sal þe lere	'I shall teach you to sing
Wat me fallet to suffring,	What suffering falls to me
& don wil i am here. (ll. 61–4)	And to do while I am here.'

He sings of the Circumcision (ll. 65–8), the Epiphany (ll. 69–72), the Presentation and the prophecy of Simeon (ll. 73–6), His teaching at the temple at the age of twelve (ll. 77–80), His ministry (ll. 85–8), His baptism and the attendant Trinitarian revelation (ll. 89–92), His temptation in the desert (ll. 93–6), and the gathering of the disciples (ll. 97–100). He then relates how the prophecy of Simeon (Luke 2: 35) will be fulfilled, how the 'Sarpe swerde of simeon/ Perse sal þin herte' (ll. 117–18), that is, the great pain that Mary will experience seeing her child on the cross:

Samfuly for i sal deyʒe,	For shamefully I shall die
Hangende on þe rode,	Hanging on the cross,
For mannis ransoun sal i peyʒe	I shall pay for man's ransom
Myn owen herte blode (ll. 121–4)	With my own heart's blood.

Mary is distressed at hearing that she has borne a child only for Him to suffer a shameful death. Christ then reassures her of the Resurrection (ll. 129–32), Ascension (ll. 132–3), Pentecost (ll. 133–4), Assumption (ll. 137–40), and His Second Coming (ll. 141–2). The lyric closes as it began, with the speaker relating that this is what he heard 'Als I lay þis ʒolis-day [Christmas Day]' (l. 147). Transferring the location of the dialogue from Calvary to the cradle increases the pathos of Mary's pain, and allows for an intimate exploration of a mother's grief as Mary is made aware of the impending doom of her new-born son. The lyric not only provides an intimate dramatization of the sorrow of Mary, but also attempts to explain the theology of salvation by transposing the events of the Crucifixion onto those of the nativity in order to emphasize the association between the Incarnation and the Crucifixion, an important connection for understanding the sacrament of the Eucharist.

Corpus Christi cycle plays

The feast of Corpus Christi, celebrated on the Thursday following Trinity Sunday, was first instituted in 1246 (though not fully adopted until the early fourteenth century) for the purpose of the adoration of the Eucharist. In various towns in England, the feast was celebrated with a procession of the Blessed Sacrament accompanied by a series of plays, the so-called Corpus Christi cycles, retelling salvific history from Creation to the Last Judgement and which were performed by the craft guilds. The Crucifixion, as one would expect, forms the devotional centrepiece of the cycles and as such draws out the theological connection between the Eucharist and the Crucifixion. David Bevington remarks that

> All the English cycles give major prominence to the story of Christ's Passion and Resurrection. As the drama of man's salvation reaches its climax, the action grows more intense and the playing area becomes more crowded with characters.[13]

Bevington's observation draws attention to the plays' exploitation of the dramatic possibilities of the Passion narrative. However, just as there are sometimes tensions between theology and the didactic purpose of the lyric, so the Corpus Christi plays add non-canonical material to biblical texts in order to help elucidate aspects of the Bible which perhaps seem obscure or silent on certain issues. While, for example, the N-Town Passion Play is generally quite faithful to the Gospel accounts, the plays in the Towneley Passion (comprising the 'Conspiracy and Capture', the 'Buffeting', the 'Scourging', the 'Crucifixion', 'The Play of the Dice' and 'The Hanging of Judas') add other elements to increase dramatic tension. For instance, Christ's silence while He is questioned in the Gospels[14] is further emphasized by the additional lengthy dialogues given to His interrogators (the chief priests and Pilate) in the plays. This contrast is also highlighted in the York 'Crucifixion', which juxtaposes the action and loquacity of the soldiers with Christ's passiveness and silence. The soldiers take delight in increasing Christ's suffering: the holes in the cross have been bored in the wrong place and so Christ's body is stretched into position using ropes (ll. 145–6);[15] and the soldiers deliberately jolt the cross to increase His pain when dropping it into the mortise (ll. 224). When Christ does speak, His words echo the Gospel narrative: 'My Fadir […] / Forgiffis thes men that dois me pine./ What they wirke wotte they nought (ll. 259–61). The play seems less interested in drawing out, as the lyrics had done, the theological reasons for the

Crucifixion, and more concerned with the dramatic potential offered by the Passion of emphasizing the torment of the cross. The play's vivid visual cruelty testifies to its affective nature and much of the Corpus Christi drama is aimed at moving the audience's emotions as well as reinforcing their understanding.

Some of the additions in the Towneley cycle act as an interpretive gloss on parts of the Gospels. For instance, the biblical Pilate is a difficult figure to read, especially regarding how much guilt he accrues in the Crucifixion. In John's Gospel, Christ is handed over to him to be judged, yet Pilate is unwilling to condemn Him and announces that he can 'find no cause in him' (John 18: 38). Christ advises Pilate: 'Thou shouldst not have any power against me, unless it were given thee from above. Therefore, he that hath delivered me to thee, hath the greater sin' (John 19: 11). After these words, Pilate seeks to release Jesus (John 19: 12), even going so far as to offer to free Him in accordance with the Jewish custom of releasing a prisoner on the Passover. This attempt is thwarted by the Jewish chief priests and elders, who instruct the mob to demand the release of Barabbas, a notorious brigand. In Matthew's Gospel, Pilate symbolically washes his hands to indicate that he will accept no part in the Crucifixion (Matthew 27: 24). This does not, however, appear to absolve him from guilt. In the *Summa Theologica*, Thomas Aquinas discusses the culpability of the various figures in the events of the Crucifixion:

> Judas betrayed Christ from greed, the Jews from envy, and Pilate from worldly fear, for he stood in fear of Caesar; and these accordingly are held guilty.[16]

According to Aquinas, Pilate's guilt is certain, but it is of a different ilk from that of the Jews and Judas. The Corpus Christi cycles, like Aquinas, are more definite in apportioning blame to Pilate, but offer a different reason. In the opening monologue of the Towneley 'Conspiracy and Capture' play, Pilate identifies himself as a dissembler:

> For I am he that may
> Make or mar a man,
> Myself if I it say,
> As men of cowrte now can:
> Supporte a man today,
> To-morn agans hym than.
> On both parties thus I play,
> And fenys me to ordan
> The right;

> Bot all fals indytars,
> Questmangers and iurers,
> And all thise fals outrydars
> Ar welcom to my sight. (ll. 27–39)[17]

Pilate's admission implies that the false witnesses – mentioned in the Gospels – who condemn Jesus are in league with Pilate. Furthermore, his monologue in the 'Scourging' more explicitly indicates that he dissembles friendship to Christ:

>   I am full of sotelty,
> Falshed, gyll, and trechery; (ll. 10–11)
> [...] I shall fownde to be his freynd vtward, in certayn,
> And shew hym fare cowntenance and wordys
> of vanyté;
> Bot or this day at nyght on crosse shall he be slayn.
> Thus agans hym in my hart I bere great enmyté
> Full sore. (ll. 31–5)[18]

The play thus reads Pilate's desperate attempts to free Christ in the Gospel as a pretence, while he secretly conspires with the chief priests to ensure that Christ is crucified. Thus, Pilate's crime, rather than being committed out of fear as indicated by Aquinas, becomes a deliberate, villainous act, as blameworthy as the actions of Caiaphas and Annas.

The Towneley cycle also seeks to provide a more concrete motive for Judas' betrayal of Christ. Because Judas betrays Christ in exchange for thirty pieces of silver in the Gospel, he has always been understood to have been avaricious. However, the 'Conspiracy and Capture' play identifies Judas' betrayal as stemming from an episode that occurs just before the events of the Passion.[19] In the Gospel, the disciples become angry because Christ has allowed a woman (traditionally identified as Mary Magdalene) to pour ointment over Him, which, they say, could have been sold to provide alms for the poor. Christ's response glosses the act as telegraphing his death and burial: 'she in pouring this ointment upon my body, hath done it for my burial' (Matthew 26: 11). The verses immediately following this event detail Judas' betrayal and so it is perhaps not surprising that the 'Conspiracy and Capture' assumes that Judas particularly objects to wasting the perfume, not on account of the poor, but because it could be sold for profit:

> For, certys, I had not seyn
> None oyntment half so fyne;

> Therat my hart had teyn,
> Sich tresoure for to tyne.
> I sayd it was worthy to sell
> Thre hundreth pens in oure present,
> For to parte poorew men emell;
> Bot will ye se whereby I ment?
> The tent parte euer withme went;
> And if iii hundreth be right told,
> The tent parte is euen thryrty. (ll. 290–303)

Judas admits to being a thief who has been helping himself to monies donated to the embryonic Church. His list of crimes mount up in the unfinished play 'The Hanging of Judas', which consists of a long monologue; here, Judas is also guilty of the crimes of Oedipus:

> Waryd and cursyd I have beyn ay.
> I slew my father and syn bylay
> My moder der,
> And falsly aftur I can betray
> Myn awn mayster. (ll. 2–6)[20]

Judas, therefore, commits patricide, incest, and suicide as well as being a thief and betraying the Son of God. Judas' mother laments the doomed birth of her son, and so, rather than following the Gospel narrative, the play seems instead to echo Christ's words: 'Woe to that man by whom the son of man shall be betrayed. It were better for him, if that man had not been born' (Mark 14: 21).

As the Corpus Christi cycle plays formed part of a dramatic procession led by the consecrated Host, they effectively offer a gloss for the Eucharistic procession: that is, they retell the events that find their ultimate expression in the sacrifice of the Eucharist. The plays, however, also seek to ensure that a distinction is made between the displaying of the Eucharist and the dramatic staging of biblical events. The Towneley cycle does this by drawing attention to its own theatricality. In the 'Scourging', Pilate identifies himself as a '*mali actoris*' (l. 13), which is both a legal term referring to a prosecutor and an 'actor/player'. Such self-conscious references to theatrical production highlight the artificiality of the plays and so make an important and vital distinction between the ritual procession of the Corpus Christi in its sacramental form of the Eucharist and the representation of Christ in the drama: Christ in the drama is only an actor; in the sacrament of the Eucharist Christ is Himself truly present.

Croxton *Play of the Sacrament*

While the Corpus Christi plays act as a gloss for understanding the Eucharist, the Croxton *Play of the Sacrament* instead dramatizes the doctrine of the Real Presence. The play purports to narrate the events of a miracle that took place in 1461 (though similar legends are found as early as 1290),[21] and underscores the central importance of the Blessed Sacrament to the whole of the Catholic faith. Belief in the Real Presence, that the Host (the sacramental bread, from the Latin *hostia* meaning 'victim') is truly the same victim that was sacrificed on the 'altar of the cross', is central to Redemption theology and necessitates undergoing the sacrament of Penance – a second sacramental feature of the play – as a prerequisite for partaking worthily of Communion.[22] The play itself tells of how a group of Jews connive to purchase the consecrated Host from a Christian merchant with a view to subjecting it to a series of abuses that parallel the events of the Crucifixion.[23] Their actions do not, as they expect, disprove the doctrine of the Real Presence, but instead confirm its truth.

After acquiring the Host from the Christian merchant, whose sale of the Host echoes Judas' betrayal (l. 315), the Jews begin to make trial of the Host by inflicting five wounds on it, which symbolize the five wounds Christ received at the Crucifixion:

> [Jason] Yff þat thys be he that on Caluery was mad red,
> Onto my mynd, I shall kenne yow a conceyt good:
> Surely with owr daggars we shall ses on thys bredde,
> And so with clowtys we shall know yf he haue eny blood. (ll. 449–52)
> [… Jasdon] And with owr strokys we shall fray hym as he was on þe
> rood. (l. 455)[24]

The final wound, corresponding to the spear wound (John 19: 34), triggers a miracle. Jonathas, the chief Jew, cries: 'Yt bledyth as yt were woode, iwys!' (l. 483). The miracle of the bleeding Host is found elsewhere in medieval literature,[25] and recalls the biblical episode in which Thomas, who was absent when Christ first appeared to his disciples after the Resurrection, refuses to believe that Christ had risen, saying: 'Except I shall see in his hands the print of the nails, and put my finger into the place of the nails and put my hand into his side, I will not believe' (John 20: 25). Although the bleeding Host indicates faithlessness, the unbeliever is granted a true vision of the Eucharist in order to secure his belief, and, consequently, his salvation. Christ's rebuke to Thomas, however, underlines the importance of faith: 'Because thou hast seen me, Thomas, thou hast believed: blessed are they that have not seen, and have believed' (John 20: 28).This message permeates and forms the didactic crux of the Croxton play.

The Jews, fearful and horrified at the miraculous bleeding Host, decide to deal with the problem by boiling it in a 'cawdron full of oyle' (ll. 486) for 'thre howrys' (ll. 488), representing the three days from Crucifixion to Resurrection. However, when Jonathas tries to throw the Host into the cauldron, it clings to his hand. At this point, what seems to be a second version of the Crucifixion takes place: the Jews decide to 'faste bynd hyme [the Host] to a poste' (l. 507). They achieve this with 'an hamer and nailys thre' (l. 508), the number of nails used to nail Christ to the cross and a well-known feature of medieval iconography.[26] After nailing the Blessed Sacrament to a post, they try to pull Jonathas' hand away, but succeed only in wrenching his arm off. The Host (with Jonathas' hand attached) is then taken down, wrapped 'in a clothe' (l. 659) – corresponding to the deposition and burial of Christ – and thrown into the cawdron (l. 660). Whereas the flesh boils off the bones in the hand, the Host remains untouched and continues to bleed (ll. 705–6). Jonathas then suggests throwing it into the oven to staunch the bleeding. There, thus, seem to be two versions of the Harrowing of Hell (Christ's descent to Hell to free the imprisoned souls from torment) in the play:[27] the boiling oil and the oven.[28]

The oven bursts and a vision of Christ with bleeding wounds emerges, apparently the injuries caused by the Jews' actions, and rebukes them for their unkindness, ingratitude and lack of faith:

Why blaspheme yow me? Why do ye thus?
Why put yow me to a newe tormentry,
And I dyed for yow on the crosse?
[…] I shew yow the streytnesse of my greuaunce,
And all to meue yow to my mercy. (ll. 731–40)

Notably, Christ appears to the Jews not as the adult who was crucified on Calvary, but as a wounded child, as Jonathas later describes to the bishop:

The holy Sacrament, þe whyche we haue done tormentry,
And ther we haue putt hym to a newe Passyon,
A chyld apperyng with wondys blody. (ll. 802–4)

The connection between the Crucifixion, the sacrifice of the Mass and the Incarnation is evident in the vision of the sacrificed infant Jesus, a common miracle seen during the elevation of the Eucharist in the Middle Ages.[29] The appearance of Christ as 'a chyld […] with wondys blody' recalls both the Christ-child in the lyrics prophesying His own Crucifixion, and the Image of Pity in Isaiah. There are, however, other traditions at work. The miraculous vision of the child seems here to have been merged with the anti-Semitic tradition in which Jews were held responsible for the murdering of a Christian child in a gruesome re-enactment of the Crucifixion, as in the stories of Saint Hugh of Lincoln, Saint William of Norwich and Chaucer's 'Prioress' Tale'.[30] The tradition of the Jews seeking to replay that original crime appears to be a legacy of Matthew's Gospel where the Jews accept full responsibility for Christ's death, calling down eternal guilt upon their nation: 'His blood be upon us and our children' (Matthew 27: 25).

The nature of the violent action in the Croxton play has been much disputed by critics. David Bevington, for instance, comments that '[t]he central action of the play […] is an extended symbolic re-enactment of Christ's passion'.[31] Sister Nicholas Maltman contradicts this view:

> the action shown is the passion of Christ; it is not a symbolic re-enactment of the Crucifixion except in so far as all drama is symbolic representation. This is what the doctrine of the true presence and the play is about.[32]

Maltman emphasizes that the action is a replaying of Christ's sufferings rather than a symbolic representation and so draws attention to the theological connection between the Host and the Crucifixion. Thus, she also objects that the violence is not a parody:

> This central part of the play is in no way a parody of the Crucifixion. It is, in fact, a re-enactment of the Crucifixion. What is done to the Host, although certainly crude and grotesque, is no other than a re-enactment of the torment done to Christ on Calvary.[33]

Both Bevington's and Maltman's readings reduce the action of the play to a single 're-enactment' of the Crucifixion. The central problem of the play, however, is not so much the excessive violence, or whether the re-enactment is symbolic or not, but rather that the play seems to offer multiple versions of the Crucifixion. At the level of the play's narrative, the stolen Host has already been consecrated, and thus sacrificed, by the priest (an act that is also parodied by the Jews, ll. 399–404). Any subsequent violent action, therefore, must be a travesty of the Crucifixion. Indeed, the banns of the play suggest that the Jews are not re-enacting the Crucifixion, but rather are

> Put[ting] hym [Christ] to a new passyoun;
> With daggers gouen hym many a greuios wound;
> Nayled hym to a pyller, with pynsons plukked hym doune. (l. 38–40)

The banns further claim that

> thay [the Jews] putt hym to a new turmentry:
> In a hoote ouyn speryd hym fast. (ll. 45–6)

The torments inflicted on the Host are twice identified as 'new'; this explains why they do not correspond to those of the Crucifixion: the first series of tortures is the 'new passyoun', which self-consciously reflects the Crucifixion narrative (though even here there seem to be two versions: the five stab wounds and the nailing to the pillar); and the second comprises the 'new turmentry', which involves placing the Host in an oven. The play thus exhibits several different layers which offer numerous perspectives of the Crucifixion: not just by replicating the events of the Gospel narratives, but by presenting the Crucifixion in terms of other iconographic images (the five wounds, the three nails) and traditions (the child-host miracle and child murder), as well as inventing 'new' torments. Such repetition draws attention to the necessity of the frequent celebration of the Eucharist – the grace obtained by the Crucifixion is continually reaped through the sacrifice/sacrament of the Eucharist – and the paradox of an event that seems to be endlessly repeated, but is always the same sacrifice.[34]

There is, however, a second problem with the play's representation of tormenting the Eucharist. Theologically, the Host cannot bleed as a consequence of being subjected to such tortures, as Aquinas explains:

> all that belongs to Christ, as He is in Himself, can be attributed to Him both in His proper species, and as He exists in the sacrament; such as to live, to die, to grieve, to be animate or inanimate, and the like; while all that belongs to Him in relation to outward bodies, can be attributed to Him as He exists in His proper species, but not as He is in this sacrament; such as to be mocked, to be spat upon, to be crucified, to be scourged, and the rest. Hence some have composed this verse:
>
> Our Lord can grieve beneath the sacramental veils,
> But cannot feel the piercing of the thorns and nails.[35]

The wounds inflicted by the Jews in the play may seem to be the result of physical actions, but can only be symbolic (Christ in the Eucharist cannot be physically harmed) and a consequence of their sinfulness and faithlessness. Such an awareness of every person's individual contribution to the Crucifixion is everywhere evident in medieval literature and iconography.[36] In one example from the *Gesta Romanorum* (The Deeds of the Romans), Mary appears to a sinner – whose sinful life has rent the body of Christ – to show him the consequences of his crime:

> 'I ame marie, the modre of Iesu Criste'.
> 'Why come ye hidere?'
> 'For to shew thee my sone. Lo!' she saide, 'here is my sone, lying in my lappe, with his hede all to-broke, and his Eyen drawen oute of his body, and layde on his breste, his armes broken a-two, his legges and his fete also.' […] Than seide oure ladie, 'for so the thou art that man, that thus hathe made my sone.' […] 'with thy grete othes thou haste thus rente him, and with thy synfull leuyng'.[37]

This description of Christ's injuries is at odds with the wounds suffered in the Crucifixion. Indeed, John's Gospel explicitly mentions that Christ was pierced in the side with a spear instead of having His legs broken and that this is an important requirement for the fulfilment of the Old Testament prophecies:

> But after they were come to Jesus, when they saw that he was already dead, they did not break his legs. But one of the soldiers with a spear opened his side, and immediately there came out blood and water. […] For these things were done, that the scripture might be fulfilled: You shall not break a bone of him. And again another scripture saith: They shall look on him whom they pierced. (John 19: 32–7)

In the *Gesta Romanorum*, however, Christ's head, arms and legs are broken, and His eyes have been drawn out. These excessive, non-biblical wounds are inflicted by the unrepentant sinner, who continues to torture Christ with his crimes. Rather than being a representation of the Crucifixion per se, both the Croxton play and the *Gesta Romanorum* seem to offer a poignant dramatic and literary realization of a verse from Saint Paul's Letter to the Hebrews, which speaks of the apostates who 'are fallen away […] crucifying again to themselves the Son of God, and making him a mockery' (Hebrews 6: 6).

The variety of ways that the Crucifixion is depicted in medieval lyric and drama not only attests to a complex devotional response to the event, but also indicates a profound interest in exploring and explaining its different aspects. The expansion of scriptural sources and the attempt to explain theological truths, however, can result in a tension between popular representation of religious beliefs, and the theology itself. Medieval literary texts, however, are not intending to be doctrinally comprehensive, even though they are religiously sophisticated and presuppose an equally sophisticated level of understanding in their audiences. Instead, the various ways of portraying aspects of the torments of the cross – the anticipation of His suffering as an infant, His Passion, and mankind's post-Crucifixion contribution to His agonies – are expressive of the power of the Crucifixion over the medieval imagination.

Notes

1. *The Holy Bible*, Douai Rheims translation (London: Baronius Press, 2005), I Corinthians 15: 3. All further biblical references are to this edition and are given parenthetically in the text.

2. See Aquinas: 'this sacrament is not only a sacrament, but also a sacrifice. For, it has the nature of the sacrifice inasmuch as in this sacrament Christ is represented, whereby Christ *offered Himself as a victim to God* (Eph. V. 2), and it has the nature of a sacrament inasmuch as invisible grace is bestowed in this sacrament under a visible species.' Thomas Aquinas, *Summa Theologica* (5 vols), trans. Fathers of the English Dominican Province (Notre Dame, IN: Ave Maria Press, 1981 [1911]), Q. 79, A. 7, pp. 2478–9. See also Joseph Pohle, 'Sacrifice of the Mass', *The Catholic Encyclopedia*, Vol. 10 (New York: Robert Appleton Company, 1911), pp. 6–24.

3. Herbert Thurston, 'Devotion to the Passion of Christ', in *The Catholic Encyclopedia*, Vol. 11 (New York: Robert Appleton Company, 1911), pp. 527–8, 529.

4. Thurston, 'Devotion to the Passion of Christ', p. 529.

5. Eamon Duffy, *The Stripping of the Altars: Traditional Religion in England c. 1400–c.1580* (New Haven and London: Yale University Press, 1992), p. 108 (see also Plates 47 and 85).

6. *Religious Lyrics of the Fourteenth Century*, ed. Carleton Brown (Oxford: Clarendon Press, 1957 [1924]), p. 17 (Phillipps MS. 836), and p. 88 (Commonplace Book of John Grimstone).

7. See 'Mans Leman on the Rood' (Trinity Coll. Camb. MS. 323), *English Lyrics of the Thirteenth Century*, ed. Carleton Brown (Oxford: Clarendon Press, 1962 [1932]), p. 61.

8. 'When I think on Jesus' Death' (MS. Harley 2253), in *English Lyrics of the Thirteenth Century*, pp. 150–2.

9. See, for instance, 'Think, Man, of my Hard Stundes' (MS. Royal 12.E.i) (p. 2), 'Look to Me on the Cross' (New Coll. Oxf. 88) (p. 3) and 'Homo vide quid pro te patior' (Commonplace Book of John Grimstone) (p. 88), in *Religious Lyrics of the Fourteenth Century*.

10. 'A Dialogue between Our Lady and Jesus on the Cross' (MS. Digby 86), *English Lyrics of the Thirteenth Century*, pp. 87–8.
11. See David Bevington, 'The Passion Play', in *Medieval Drama* (Boston, MA: Houghton Mifflin Company, 1975), p. 477.
12. 'Dialogue between the B.V. and her Child' (Commonplace Book of John Grimstone), *Religious Lyrics of the Fourteenth Century*, pp. 70–5.
13. Bevington, 'The Passion Play', p. 477.
14. Cf. Matthew 27: 12, 14; Mark 14: 61; Mark 15: 5; Luke 23: 9.
15. 'The Crucifixion' (York), in David Bevington, *Medieval Drama* (Boston, MA: Houghton Mifflin Company, 1975), pp. 569–80.
16. Aquinas, *Summa Theologica*, Vol. IV, Q. 47, A. 3. p. 2274.
17. 'Conspiracy', *Towneley Plays*, eds. Martin Stevens and A. C. Cawley, EETS Vol. 1 (2 vols) (London, New York and Toronto: Oxford University Press, 1994), pp. 227–51. All further references to the Towneley plays are to this edition.
18. 'Scourging', *Towneley Plays*, pp. 270–87.
19. Cf. Matthew 26: 8–11; and Mark 14: 3–9.
20. 'The Hanging of Judas', *Towneley Plays*, pp. 432–5.
21. David Bevington, 'Introduction' to *The Play of the Sacrament* (Croxton), in *Medieval Drama* (Boston, MA: Houghton Mifflin Company, 1975), p. 754.
22. See Duffy, *The Stripping of the Altars*, p. 91.
23. The trope of testing God is a biblical one. See Deuteronomy 6:16, and Matthew 4: 7.
24. *The Play of the Sacrament* (Croxton), in *Non-cycle Plays and Fragments* ed. Norman Davis EETS (London, New York and Toronto: Oxford University Press, 1970), pp. 58–89. All further references are to this edition and are given parenthetically in the text.
25. For other examples, see Jacobus de Voraigne, 'Of S. Gregory the Pope', in *The Golden Legend, or Lives of the Saints as Englished by William Caxton*, Vol. 3 (London: J. M. Dent, 1900), pp. 60–70 (p. 69); and *Magna Vita Sancti Hugonis (The Life of Saint Hugh of Lincoln)*, 2 vols, ed. Decima L. Douie and David Hugh Farmer (Oxford: Clarendon Press, 1985), Vol. 2, V. iii, p. 86 and V. iv, p. 94.
26. For the question of the tradition of the number of nails used in the Crucifixion, see Herbert Thurston, 'Holy Nails', in *The Catholic Encyclopedia*, Vol. 10 (New York: Robert Appleton Company, 1911), p. 672.
27. See *The Gospel of Nicodemus,* or *Acts of Pilate*, in *The Apocryphal New Testament*, trans. J. K. Elliott (Oxford: Clarendon Press, 1993), pp. 164–204.
28. Cf. Duffy, *The Stripping of the Altars*, p. 106.
29. See Aquinas: 'what appears miraculously in this sacrament is sometimes seen as a small particle of flesh, or at times as a small child. [...] Nor is there any deception there, as occurs in the feasts of magicians, because

such species is divinely formed in the eye in order to represent some truth, namely for the purpose of showing that Christ's body is truly under this sacrament.' Aquinas, *Summa Theologica*, Vol. 5, p. 2455. See also Leah Sinanoglou, 'The Christ child as sacrifice: a medieval tradition and the Corpus Christi plays', *Speculum*, 48.3 (1973), 491–509 (p. 491).

30. See Sinanoglou, 'Christ child as sacrifice', p. 493.
31. Bevington, 'Introduction' to *The Play of the Sacrament*, p. 754.
32. Sister Nicholas Maltman, 'Meaning and art in the Croxton *Play of the Sacrament*', *ELH*, 41.2 (Summer, 1974), 149–64 (p. 62).
33. Maltman, 'Meaning and art', pp. 157–8.
34. 'Christ himself, immolated on the altar of the Cross, became present on the altar of the parish church, body, soul, and divinity, and his blood flowed once again, to nourish and renew Church and world.' Duffy, *The Stripping of the Altars*, p. 91.
35. Aquinas, *Summa Theologica*, Vol. 5, Q. 81, A. 4, p. 2497.
36. See also Geoffrey Chaucer, 'The Pardoner's Tale' in *The Riverside Chaucer*, 3rd Edition, ed. Larry D. Benson (Oxford: Oxford University Press, 1988), ll. 472–6.
37. 'LXXXVIII Of the Death-bed of a Profane Swearer', *The Gesta Romanorum*, ed. Sir Frederic Madden (London: EETS, Trübner and Co., 1879), p. 410.

11

Encountering *Piers Plowman*

Catherine Batt

Piers Plowman is a dream-vision poem, part theological allegory about the quest for truth and part social satire. It recounts the experience of the poet-narrator, Will, who receives a series of dream visions when he falls asleep in the Malvern Hills. The narrator's 'merveillous swevene' [wonderful dream] (B Prologue.11) opens up further levels of, and perspectives on, experience and reflection on the question of salvation in a social context.[1]

Textual history of the poem

From over fifty surviving manuscripts of the poem, nineteenth-century scholarship identified three distinct versions, named the A, B and C texts according to their order of composition (which was established from internal references to historical events). The A-text is dated to the 1360s, the B-text to the late 1370s, and the C-text to c. 1388–90.[2] The A-text runs to some 2500 lines, and recounts three dreams in the course of its eleven sections, called *passus* (Latin for 'step'); the B-text, which is three times the length of A, is organized into twenty *passus* and eight dreams; and the C-text presents eight dreams in twenty-two *passus*. The B-text thus represents just one version of Langland's continually recreated text, but is the most commonly used text. Little is known of the author, William Langland, whose name, which also punningly identifies the narrator with the human will, emerges in the narrator's self-identification (B.15.152). A brief account of Will's career in the C-text has been taken as a semi-autobiographical representation of its creator as a London-based jobbing administrator in lower clerical orders.[3] Robert Adams's recent research on the Rokeles, a family with which a note on the Trinity College Dublin MS 212 copy of the C-text associates Langland, suggests that the poet's family was both well connected and well-to-do.[4]

A. V. C. Schmidt's scholarly parallel-text edition of all three versions (and also of the Z-text, based on A) makes it straightforward to appreciate their similarities and differences;[5] however, as Ralph Hanna warns, a modern edition can also gloss over major differences between manuscript witnesses to the 'same' version, quite apart from the complexities and challenges that scribal textual and editorial interventions pose to the reconstruction of what a single author wrote.[6] Langland's rewriting projects are chronologically and materially interwoven with, rather than consistently anterior to, the further work of his readers. The complex extant manuscript testimony shows readers-turned-writers, as well as the author (none of whose own manuscripts of the poem survive), engaged in changing and modifying these versions, every manuscript reinforcing the poem's status as (in Steven Justice's words) an 'insistently provisional enterprise'.[7] *Piers Plowman*'s fraught textual history is an altogether medieval witness to its provisionality, and also testimony to its popularity and broad dissemination, its capacity to provoke its readers into debate and active participation. A modern reader of necessity trades a full understanding of the historical cultural trajectories of Langland's poem(s) for a conveniently 'stable' text.[8]

Beginnings

The B-text's opening lines deserve full attention because, even before the dream-frame of the poem as a whole is announced, they anticipate not only the swirling range of the speaker's experience in the body of the poem (from the real to the marvellous, from the judgemental to the bewildered, from active to passive), but also the problems and pleasures of interpreting that experience and making poetry from it – and of using poetry to understand the world:

> In a somer seson, whan softe was the sonne,
> I shoop [dressed] me into shroudes [clothes] as I a sheep were,
> In habite as an heremite unholy of werkes,
> Wente wide in this world wondres to here.
> Ac [but] on a May morwenynge on Malverne Hilles
> Me bifel a ferly [wonder], of Fairye [a place of enchantment] me thoghte.

These opening lines demand that the audience engage their senses, as well as their literary sensibilities. The alliterative long line that the poet uses dictates the alliteration of two stressed syllables in the first half-line (or 'verse') and one in the second, with a break (a caesura) in the middle of the line. The line depends on this alliterative stress and on rhythm, as against the 'notional predictability' that a regular metrical syllable count, such as Shakespeare's iambic pentameter, affords.[9] The alliterative line is at once rigorous and open to experimental variation, and from the start, the poet fully exploits its possibilities.[10] The supplementary 's' of 'sonne' in line 1, for example, compounds the sibilant susurration evocative of warm springtime, and delightedly announces the poem's beginning by showing off the poet's craft. In its excess, it makes for an arresting poetic aural equivalent of the visual exuberance that a brightly illuminated initial would provide on the manuscript page. But what kind of poem is this?

For the medieval listener or reader, attuned to the literary cues and clues in the tumble of tropes crowding these initial verses, that first line would invoke the *reverdi* ('making green again'), a celebration of springtime – and of love – found in French and English medieval lyric. Chaucer draws, more expansively, on the same topos, in the opening lines of the 'General Prologue' to the *Canterbury Tales* (begun c. 1387). In his poem, Chaucer slyly undercuts audience expectation of a love story by announcing that the season prompts a longing for pilgrimage.[11] Langland here anticipates Chaucer's playfulness, as the narrator comically describes himself as looking like a sheep, bundled up in his clothes. Yet, is the self-deprecating woolly narrator primarily expressing humility, indicating a lack of means, or even confessing to a certain fecklessness? A 'sheep' can metonymically signify a shepherd, as well as the animal he looks after, and so metaphorically, the narrator could be in need of guidance, or himself a would-be protector. A commonplace of the medieval Church has priests watching over the souls of those in their care, on the model of Christ the Good Shepherd (John 10: 1–18),[12] but an early fourteenth-century preacher's handbook also uses this simile to stress individual spiritual self-regulation and responsibility. At the Last Judgement, it warns, 'no one will be able to hide [...] but everyone will render an account of his deeds, as a shepherd of his smallest sheep'.[13]

In line 3, the caesura makes possible a further double interpretation, in that the second half-line could describe both the speaker and the hermit. That the hermit is 'unholy' rather than saintly, and up to no good, would be a characterization typical of estates satire, the established literary mode that holds up to scrutiny and ridicule the various social orders and their moral shortcomings, and which Chaucer will so deftly invoke in his own sophisticated take on perceptions and perspectives in his account of the Canterbury pilgrims with whom he shares his journey. But Langland's words can equally have a confessional, even penitential, cast, describing a narrator who, from the start, cuts an unreliable figure; in his woollen garments, he looks like a hermit, but he is far from acting like someone with a religious vocation. The next line, rather than sharpening the focus, opens up a world of possibility, as the narrator expresses a promiscuous curiosity and appetite for 'hearing about wonders'. A 'wonder' can signify a 'manifestation of divine power', a miracle, a heinous crime, a puzzle or a phenomenon against nature.[14] The wished-for marvel, which the term 'Fairye' would seem to identify with the supernatural world of, say, a medieval romance, nonetheless has a specific geographical location, the Malvern Hills that straddle Worcestershire, Herefordshire and Gloucestershire, and from which one can survey huge stretches of the surrounding countryside. For anyone familiar with this landscape, the hills make a fine setting for imagining the poet-dreamer's panoramic perspective of the busy 'fair feeld ful of folk' (Prologue.17) that he will see in his dream wilderness, although it is for the reader to puzzle out how the earthly reality of the Malverns could inform revelation. Even before the poem's dream-world unfolds, then, its half-a-dozen opening lines have signalled generic markers that confuse rather than reassure.[15] The poem seems preoccupied all at once with confession and penance, satire, nature, romance adventure, realism, geographical detail, and uncertainty about narratorial identity. The narrating voice may strike one as humble or bigoted, as authoritative or self-exposing and vulnerable. In this ambiguous context, the literary allusions are less about plotting co-ordinates for working out meaning, than about engaging the reader to think about how those co-ordinates are set in the first place.

Dream vision and narrative

Piers Plowman is part of a distinguished literary and philosophical tradition of dream interpretation texts and dream-lore. Macrobius' fifth-century *Commentary* on Cicero's *Dream of Scipio*, highly influential on medieval thinking about how to categorize dreams, distinguishes five principal types, ranging from authoritative revelations of transcendent truths to false dreams that result simply from physical distress of some kind. The categorization provides a rich opportunity for thinking about the interrelation of the earthbound and the intellectual/divine in the middle ground of what Macrobius identifies as the *somnium*, an ambiguous dream in which truths are revealed through fictions, and in whose space, Steven Kruger notes, 'body and idea meet to work out their mutual roles'.[16] Even those episodes that conform to Macrobius's category of *oraculum*, in which an authority figure (such as Lady Holy Church) provides advice, focus on the response of the dreamer, whose material and earthbound experience remains integral to his understanding of abstracts.

Langland's allegorical dream-world has precedent in mainland European vernacular poems, such as the French Cistercian monk Guillaume de Deguileville's c. 1331 *Pèlerinage de vie humaine* (Pilgrimage of Human Life), in which a spiritual life is allegorically imagined as a visionary pilgrimage to the heavenly city of Jerusalem, with Dame Grace Dieu (Grace of God) as a guide, and as protector against personified sins and worldly vicissitudes.[17] Dream worlds ostensibly structure *Piers Plowman* and its negotiation of social experience, revelation, political experiment, and social and internal debate. However, there is also play with expectation as, across the B-text's eight visions (and two 'dreams-within-dreams', Passus 10, 16), 'dream' can leach into 'lived experience', as when the personification of Need upbraids the dreamer in his waking life (B.20.1–50), and vice versa, as the poem poses continually the question of how revelation relates to the practicalities of living. The first seven Passus, collectively known as the 'Visio', frame the dreamer's search for salvation with a pressing concern for the proper organization of society in general, and an exploration of the language available for individual self-knowledge. The dreamer's first vision, in the Prologue, locates sharply observed realist historical social detail, in tune with his wry division of humans into 'winners' and 'wasters' (Prologue.20–2), in a figurative space; the crowd of bustling humanity is poised between (as they are later explained) a Tower of Truth and the stronghold of the Devil (B.1.12–62). The Prologue ends with a fable about power and responsibility evidently based on the young kingship of Richard II (Prologue.146–208), the meaning of which the dreamer nonetheless explicitly refuses to declare (ll. 209–10), which directs attention less to speculation about historical interpretations, than to the nature and forms of political allegory *per se*.

In Passus 1, Lady Holy Church descends from the Tower of Truth to instruct the dreamer, but her eloquence is more than he can understand, and it is his bewilderment at her rich and beautiful allusive account of truth and love that leads to his demand to learn instead by their contrary, 'False', which results in the vision of Lady Mede ('Reward'), whose progress through legal and royal courts exposes their corruption, but whom the King overcomes, by working with Conscience and Reason, within the rule of law. The dreamer's central preoccupation is clear from his words to the Lady who personifies Holy Church in Passus 1: '[T]el me […] How I may save my soule' (1.84). The very form of the request acknowledges individual agency even as it assumes that the institution appealed to can prescribe a programme of spiritual action, but Lady Holy Church's response, which is to trust in 'Truth' (1.85), raises questions of perception, action, methodology, faith and understanding that dreamer and poet will take a lifetime to explore. Central to the dreamer's anxiety is the recognition that individual spiritual salvation has a social context; but how can one save one's soul in a fallen world where spiritual vision is imperfect, where the agents of the institutions that should provide for material and spiritual needs are corrupt? This emotionally and philosophically moving poem asks questions at once deeply religious, sceptical, and socially and politically aware. It is a poem of contrasts and confusions, as the dreamer struggles with doubt and belief, and with the problems and practicalities of social organization and order; he yearns for 'kynde knowinge' (1.138), an intuitive, experiential understanding of the divine, in the context of a deep concern for the common good.[18]

Will's second dream, which begins in Passus 5, focuses again on the mass of humanity, and their inner lives, as Reason preaches to the crowd, and the Seven Sins publicly confess. A search for 'St Truth' prompts the appearance of Piers Plowman, the honest labourer who radically recasts spiritual endeavour as physical work when he asks that everyone help him plough his half-acre of land. Although the enterprise meets with limited success and culminates in confusing warnings of impending apocalypse, Truth sends Piers a pardon, which, far from initiating closure, precipitates a change of direction for both poem and dreamer when Piers, reacting angrily to a priest's objections to the pardon, tears it up and vows to change his way of life.

Passus 8–20 constitute the second movement of the poem, known as the 'Vita', in which the often irascible and argumentative narrator embarks on a search for the active principle of 'Do-well'. Biblical figures and allegorical characters – some representing Will's inner faculties (such as Wit), some manifestations of external forms of knowledge (for example, Dame Study) and some veering between both (like Imaginatif) – appear in the course of this journey, which is at once internal, spatial, satirical, philosophical, rhetorical, spiritual and historical. The dreamer encounters hypocritical clerics, puzzles over the best course of spiritual action and the benefits or otherwise of learning, meets Fortune (in whose service he grows old), and is given a vision of the world by 'Kynde' ('Nature'; also, God as creative principle) (Passus 11). The character of Imaginatif (Passus 12), a projection of the poet's own poetic faculty, as well as a mode of recollection, brings together the poem's arguments up until that point, and reminds the reader that the poem is always in the process of self-examination. The subsequent visions see the dreamer determine to search for Charity (Passus 15). The narrative builds, through the reappearance of Piers tending the Tree of Charity and encounters with biblical characters Abraham/Faith and Moses/Hope, to the witness of the full expression of love on earth in Christ's sacrifice on the cross, the means by which Mercy fulfils and transcends the Justice of the Old Law. But this access of joy gives way to more confusion and bewilderment. In the final two Passus, Pride and Hypocrisy undermine the institution of Holy Church, and the poem ends, not with harmony, but with Conscience setting out on a pilgrimage to seek Piers; his crying aloud for grace wakes the dreamer for the last time.

Concerns of the poem

A central inquiry of the poem is the extent to which spiritual values can translate into social practice. Christian doctrine assures the sinner that s/he is the recipient of God's grace and mercy, but how can one exercise mercy in the human world without producing gross injustice? Moreover, what is the nature of God's mercy? Does it extend to all humanity? What is the relationship between community and individual? In what ways does language shape selfhood, especially penitential language, the language of religious knowledge and self-examination that would have been familiar to everyone from confession and was actively promoted by the Church from at least 1215 (the date of the Fourth Lateran Council) onwards?[19] What are the poetic forms suitable to the exploration, if not the resolution, of pressing social and spiritual problems? Langland recognizes the urgency and intractability of these issues, especially the evils of poverty and corruption, and the potential spiritual dangers of institutionalized religion. The satirical and reformist aspects of his work evidently prompt a 'tradition' of poems of social critique, one so politically of its moment as to risk being difficult to access today.[20] *Piers Plowman* gives no neat and ready answers to the social questions it raises. However, the sympathetic account of how women in poverty suffer (C.9.70–85), for example, and the alarm at the idleness of the able-bodied (B.6) belong to the poem's continuing meditation on the imperative to see poverty as an urgent ethical issue for all of society.[21]

Evidently the poem is more than its bare narrative; it excavates meaning from returning to and reimagining themes and ideas, rather than from 'what happens'.[22] Its extraordinary texture arises in part from how the author draws on deep learning in medieval languages (and in the diverse registers of each of those languages – Latin, English, French, Anglo-Norman), on philosophy, theology and rhetoric, and also on sharp observation, to think through a range of related issues simultaneously. It also, endearingly – if, for the modern reader, confusedly and confusingly – shows how its own limitations make necessary a continual re-focusing of attention. Love, for example, emerges as the most powerful force in the poem, and among Langland's most moving and pellucid lines is the simple advice offered by Kynde (Nature) late in the poem to a dreamer anxious to know what 'craft' will best serve him: 'Lerne to love [...] and leef all other [leave all else]' (B.20.207–8). The dreamer's immediate anxiety about how he will support himself (B.20.209), however, demonstrates the continuing difficulty of intuiting what is good and of implementing theoretical knowledge.

On first meeting Holy Church, the dreamer struggles to distinguish between heavenly and earthly things and values; he is clearly not ready for Lady Holy Church's bewilderingly beautiful account of Christ's Incarnation as the supreme expression of love which, lime tree leaf-light yet too heavy for heaven, is both natural and transcendent of natural laws (B.1.153–8). Similarly, Piers' description of pilgrimage as an internal spiritual journey to find Truth in a 'chayne of charity' in one's own heart (B.5.607) is off-putting rather than inspirational for some of his would-be pilgrims. It is not simply that the dreamer has to overcome a stubborn earthbound perspective, but that such truths are embedded in an allusive and inclusive mode of imagination and debate that is itself part of the inquiry. Lady Holy Church uses (to medieval ears) familiar metaphors when, for example, she describes love as a 'triacle' (B.1.148), a heavenly healing remedy.[23] But her speech encompasses salvation history by way (*inter alia*) of political analogy, and social and moral satire; spiritual truth is not to be extrapolated from, but is part of, the urgent moral inquiry about life on earth. This makes for a kaleidoscopic poem, the language of which demands a simultaneous multi-faceted approach and awareness. Indeed, Imaginatif's scolding of the dreamer for wasting his time – 'thou medlest thee with makynge' [you busy yourself with writing] (B.12.116–17) – is only one instance of a questioning of the status and authority of the poem itself.

Allegory and personification

In thinking about how to make sense of the world, Langland clearly shows the influence of *The Consolation of Philosophy*, a standard text for the Western European Middle Ages, which the philosopher Boethius (c. 480–524) wrote when imprisoned by the Emperor Theodoric on treason charges. In *The Consolation*, the Boethius figure, bewildered and distressed at what has happened to him, encounters the personification of Philosophy who, by re-familiarizing him with the terms of philosophical discourse, shows him how to face the world's reversals, as he grapples with his own situation and with larger questions about the human condition, free will and destiny. As Emily Steiner notes, there are echoes of Boethius's relationship with Lady Philosophy in the dreamer's encounter with Lady Holy Church in Passus 1.[24] At the same time, the *Consolation* illuminates something about the difficulty of Langland's allegory. Boethius expresses frustration at the unfairness of the world, at why the evil thrive while bad things happen to good people, and at why a capricious and amoral Fortune apparently governs human affairs. If God knows what is to happen, asks Boethius, where does that leave human free will? Lady Philosophy responds with a reminder that the human intellect can never encompass God, nor see the universe as God sees it, but that how and what we understand depends also on our capacity to understand:

> [...] people think that the totality of their knowledge depends on the nature and capacity to be known of the objects of knowledge. But this is all wrong. Everything that is known is comprehended not according to its own nature, but according to the ability to know of those who do the knowing.[25]

Allegory (etymologically, 'speaking other'), as sustained metaphor, represents the unknown by means of the known, and *Piers Plowman* exposes both the joys and the limitations of allegorical procedures as a fallen mode of knowing and explication.

Scriptural commentary traditionally recommends a 'fourfold' exposition of a biblical passage, whereby the literal meaning is supplemented by other readings: the allegorical (that anticipates Christ); the topological (that supplies a general moral); and the anagogical, or mystical, that relates to the soul's afterlife. Langland's own poem, rather than asking to be spiritually 'decoded' in this way, instead constitutes itself out of its working, that is, through the means that the dreamer has to understanding, such as allegorical models.[26] This makes for a supple, rather than fixed, allegorical mode, and Langland achieves some of his most potent effects by recourse to vivid realism, locating his figurative subjects in the literal, as when the drunken Glutton's smelly vomit materially realizes the sin's excesses (B.V.350–6). As Jill Mann observes, personifications are often presented as 'quasi-human' as a tactic to show how abstracts 'represent real [...] agents in the world'.[27] Moreover, allegorical referents are protean; for example, the wronged but pragmatic, worldly and easily bought-off Peace in B.3's trial scene is hardly the same character as B.18's Peace, Daughter of God. Meaning is, accordingly, fugitive, not for lack of control, but in an honest acknowledgement of the processes of human engagement and understanding.

Mede the Maid bursts onto the scene in a blaze of scarlet clothing and dazzling gems, to be married to Falsehood, in response to the dreamer's request to recognize the 'false' (B.1. 4). The concept of 'meed' ('reward') is susceptible to plural interpretation, including 'bribery', 'corruption', a 'fee', 'reparation', 'due wages', 'recompense', 'kingly largesse' and 'heavenly reward'. In the course of Mede's frustrated marriages, first to Falsehood and then to Conscience, and her eventual exile from the court, Passus 2–4 offer a satire on how corruption blights the due process of law, but also, as Emily Steiner has analysed, a sophisticated meditation on the operation of desire and reward in society.[28] The question also extends to how God's mercy and the spiritual reward of heaven correlate with earthly paradigms of fairness and justice. Mede's personification as seductress, moreover, exemplifies how the vehicle of the exposition animates and troubles its ostensible subject, as Elizabeth Kirk notes: 'introducing gender into ostensibly ungendered problems produces destabilizing effects where Langland's epistemological strategy requires them'.[29] Marriage, the construction of gender, and attitudes to female authority all shape moral questions in particular ways, and can displace and defer their problems and their solutions. Laurie Finke's analysis of allegory (and, more broadly, language) as a problematic means of representing does well to observe that, rather than being able to identify the perfect correspondence between actuality and representation, it continually generates more signs, more ways of saying, in an explication that in itself becomes an act of faith, 'an epistemological exploration of the mysteries of the Incarnation'.[30]

Piers Plowman and synthesis

Piers enters the poem in response to the crowd's search for Truth as a literal place, and appears immediately attractive in his claim to employ actively the very form of knowledge that the dreamer seeks. He announces that he 'know(s) (Truth) as kindely [naturally]' as a scholar knows his books (B.5.538). At once identified as an active principle and as a mode of access to the divine, his first word − a mild oath, '[By Saint] Peter!' (B.5.537) − links him with the keeper of heaven's gate. He sets about reforming the world, and would seem to promise the translation of theory into practice. If his summoning of Hunger to force his co-workers to labour is not a fully successful social experiment, he nonetheless registers a desired synthesis of understanding and of communal action in the poem. In this character, the dreamer concentrates his desire for cohesion, for the mediation between earthly and heavenly, and for privileged experience. In keeping with the self-reflexive tone of the poem, Piers' interventions mark the process of spiritual search, rather than its conclusion. It is fitting, then, that when Truth sends Piers a pardon, and a priest points out that it contains no more than the terms of strict justice, rather than universal forgiveness − it states that those who do well will be rewarded and the evil-doers damned (B.7.111−12) − Piers' tearing of the document is both dismaying and necessary, as it precipitates the next stage of the poem, the dreamer's inner spiritual search. The tearing of the pardon signals that the question of the relationship between justice and mercy in human as in divine terms remains unresolved, and also requires a revised engagement on poetic terms, a further testing of method and approach.

If the pardon scene demonstrates the need for revision, on moral, perceptual and poetic levels, Passus 18's dream, in all its moving power, is a profound and triumphant poetic expression of faith. Medieval liturgy, the dreamer's experience and historical time all come together in the event of the Crucifixion that completes and transcends time and space, and resolves all contradictions in Christ's ultimate sacrifice. Piers is identified as Christ's human nature, as Christ will joust against Death in 'Piers armes' (B.18.23). Christ suffers as man, but His action has cosmic significance:

The lord of life and of light tho leide hise eighen [eyes] togideres.
The day for drede withdrough and derk bicam the sonne. (B.18.59−60)

Christ's abjection is the necessary prelude to his descent into Hell to reclaim, by law, the souls that the devil has taken for his own since the disobedience and fall of Adam and Eve. The arguments between Peace, Righteousness, Mercy and Truth over the rights of the case and the testimony of Book, the clear-eyed Bible who acts as witness and as prophet, preface Christ's Harrowing of Hell, and His declaration that, as Lord of life, He acts against the Devil, the 'doctor of deeth' (B.18.365), out of perfect love and a deep kinship with 'my brethren', humanity: 'blood may noght se blood blede, but hym rewe [without feeling pity]' (B.18.396). The dreamer is caught up in the happy celebration of Christ's success, and rouses his family to celebrate in their turn the joy of Christ's Resurrection.

The vision of Passus 18 is not sustained, however. The synthesis of literal and figurative, historical and spiritual unravels, and the work of the poem is necessarily unfinished, because the questions remain of individual responsibility, of how to prevent the corruption of earthly institutions, and how to resolve the problems posed by human sin.[31] But Conscience's final determination to seek out Piers, and his cry for Grace (B.20), affirms both the poem's values and its aesthetic.

Modern Langland

Harriet Monroe, writing in 1915, suggests that while the 'urbane Chaucer' ignores 'the burden-bearing poor', Langland, the 'modern socialist, anarchist, anti-militarist', with his 'rougher' style and his social conscience, may be the medieval poet 'to bridge the centuries and clasp hands with the poets of the future'.[32] A century on from Monroe's idealized vision of Langland as an inspirational, unproblematic and ideologically driven poet, Langland seems to have few modern imitators, with the exceptions of John Wheatcroft's poetic drama, 'A Fourteenth-Century Poet's Vision of Christ' (1977), based on the B-text Passus 18, or, more allusively, W. H. Auden's adaptation of Langland's alliterative line for his ambitious and complex post-war poem, *The Age of Anxiety* (1947).[33] Modern Chaucer-inspired poetry, meanwhile, seems to be in the ascendancy. Patience Agbabi's *Telling Tales* (2014) wittily and spiritedly reinvents the *Canterbury Tales*' pilgrims aboard a Routemaster bus, a richly multicultural band of storytellers, each with a distinctive contemporary voice and register, while Lavinia Greenlaw's *A Double Sorrow* (2014) sensitively reimagines Chaucer's most famous lovers, Troilus and Criseyde, and the poetry that created them.

By contrast, Ian Sansom's 2014 work for radio, '*Piers the Plowman* Revisited', meta-textually considers the problems that the modern poet encounters in understanding and reworking Langland, rather than supplying the listener with his new version (which, the end of the programme indicates, is finished and performed after all, but not broadcast).[34] Sansom's allusive, *non-finito* treatment, which charts the adventures of its hapless, comically overwhelmed poet-persona, is nevertheless an appropriate homage to a poem that is more about negotiating difficult questions (about poetry as much as about belief) than suggesting their easy solution. A Langland transported to modern London would be intrigued by the continuing financial crisis and by social responses to it, by phenomena such as the Occupy movement that seek redress for the poor, by those who feel entitled to amass wealth and by the machinations of the political classes. He would be perplexed at a humanity apparently at war even with the environment that has until now sustained it. He would be both anxious and passionate about the constraints under which people labour, and about the possibility of justice. Above all, he would be concerned about how to translate those anxieties, passions and concerns into poetry, and how that poetry could affect and effect religious and political thought and change. In these respects, Langland is a poet for the twenty-first century, the very condition of which demonstrates why the questions he poses, about what constitutes integrity and truth, about individual responsibility, and about how one engages, politically, morally and socially, are still worth asking.

Notes

1. William Langland, 'The Vision of Piers Plowman': A critical edition of the B-Text based on Trinity College Cambridge MS B.15.17, ed. A. V. C. Schmidt (London: Dent Everyman, 1995), Prologue, ll. 1–6. All further references to the B text are to this edition and are given parenthetically (Passus and line number) in the text.
2. Ralph Hanna, 'The versions and revisions of Piers Plowman', in Companion, ed. Cole and Galloway, pp. 33–49.
3. 'Piers Plowman': A New Annotated Edition of the C-Text, ed. Derek Pearsall (Exeter: University of Exeter Press), p. 112, 5. 35–52.
4. Robert Adams, 'The Rokeles: an index for a "Langland" family history', in Companion, ed. Cole and Galloway, pp. 85–96. See also his Langland and the Rokele Family: The Gentry Background to 'Piers Plowman' (Dublin: Four Courts Press, 2013).
5. William Langland, 'Piers Plowman': A Parallel-Text Edition of the A, B, C and Z Versions, 2 vols, ed. A. V. C. Schmidt (London: Longman, and Kalamazoo: Medieval Institute, 1995–2008).
6. Hanna, 'Versions and revisions', pp. 38–42.
7. Steven Justice, 'The genres of Piers Plowman', in Medieval English Poetry, ed. and intro. Stephanie Trigg pp. 99–118 (p. 113).
8. Stephen Kelly's essay, 'Piers Plowman', in A Companion to Medieval English Literature and Culture c.1350 – c.1500, ed. Peter Brown (Oxford:

Blackwell, 2007), pp. 537–53, brings out especially well the problems its many versions pose, as also 'the necessity of [the poem's] difficulty' (pp. 540–6).

9. The phrase is from David A. Lawton, 'Alliterative style', in *A Companion to 'Piers Plowman'*, ed. John A. Alford (Berkeley, CA: University of California Press, 1988), pp. 223–50 (p. 224).

10. For a helpful account of the context for Langland's alliterative line, see Ralph Hanna, 'Alliterative poetry', in *The Cambridge History of Medieval English Literature*, ed. David Wallace (Cambridge: Cambridge University Press, 1999), pp. 488–512. See also Macklin Smith, 'Langland's alliterative line(s)', *Yearbook of Langland Studies*, 23 (2009), 163–216; and 'Langland's Unruly Caesura', *Yearbook of Langland Studies*, 22 (2008), 57–101.

11. Geoffrey Chaucer, 'General Prologue' to *The Canterbury Tales*, in *The Riverside Chaucer*, ed. Larry D. Benson, 3rd edn (Oxford: Oxford University Press, 2008), pp. 23–36 (ll. 1–18).

12. Adam of Exeter's thirteenth-century 'Commentary on the *Pater Noster*' warns prelates not to be 'bad shepherds' in preferring worldly goods to spiritual duty: *'Cher Alme': Texts of Anglo-Norman Piety*, ed. Tony Hunt, trans. Jane Bliss, intro. Henrietta Leyser (Tempe, AZ: Arizona Center for Medieval and Renaissance Studies, 2010), pp. 71–125 (p. 101).

13. *'Fasciculus Morum': A Fourteenth-Century Preacher's Handbook*, ed. and trans. Siegfried Wenzel (University Park, PA: Pennsylvania State University Press, 1989), p. 107.

14. *Middle English Dictionary*: http://quod.lib.umich.edu, 'wonder (n.)'.

15. James Simpson discusses how Langland breaks the expected contract between teller and audience, a characteristic of Middle English alliterative poetry, in *'Piers Plowman': An Introduction to the B-Text* (Harlow: Longman, 1991), pp. 7–8. See also Ralph Hanna on the narrator's ambiguous initial self-presentation: 'William Langland', in *The Cambridge Companion to Medieval English Literature 1100-1500*, ed. Larry Scanlon (Cambridge: Cambridge University Press, 2009), pp. 125–38 (p. 128). There is a growing and ever more sophisticated body of work on Langland's poem, especially on his theological thought and expression and historical contexts. See, for example, David Aers' provocative account of grace and human agency in *Salvation and Sin: Augustine, Langland, and Fourteenth-Century Theology* (Notre Dame, IN: University of Notre Dame Press, 2009); Kathryn Kerby-Fulton, *Books under Suspicion: Censorship and Tolerance of Revelatory Writing in Late-Medieval England* (Notre Dame, IN: University of Notre Dame Press, 2006). There are some excellent guides for new readers. Simpson's *Introduction* is a sound general account of the poem and its principal theological, social and literary concerns; Anna Baldwin, *A Guidebook to 'Piers Plowman'* (Basingstoke: Palgrave Macmillan, 2007), is in a similar vein. *The Cambridge Companion to 'Piers Plowman'*, ed. Andrew Cole and Andrew Galloway (Cambridge: Cambridge University Press, 2014), offers a well-organized synthesis of recent developments in Langland

research. See also *William Langland's 'Piers Plowman': A Book of Essays*, ed. Kathleen M. Hewett-Smith (London: Routledge, 2001). Emily Steiner, *Reading 'Piers Plowman'* (Cambridge: Cambridge University Press, 2013), is a rewarding study that illuminates the poem with a lucid exposition of Langland's cultural and religious contexts.

16. Steven F. Kruger, *Dreaming in the Middle Ages* (Cambridge: Cambridge University Press, 1994), p. 34.
17. Béatrice Stumpf has edited the poem at: http://www.atilf.fr/dmf/VieHumaine.
18. On the latter, see Anne Middleton's insightful 'The Idea of Public Poetry in the Reign of Richard II', *Speculum*, 52 (1978), 94–114.
19. Leonard E. Boyle, 'The fourth Lateran council and manuals of popular theology', in *The Popular Literature of Medieval England*, ed. Thomas J. Heffernan (Knoxville, TN: University of Tennessee Press, 1985), pp. 30–60.
20. Helen Barr, *The 'Piers Plowman' Tradition* (London: Dent, 1993).
21. See Anne M. Scott, *'Piers Plowman' and the Poor* (Dublin: Four Courts Press, 2005).
22. See Anne Middleton, 'Narration and the invention of experience: episodic form in *Piers Plowman*', in *The Wisdom of Poetry: Essays in Early English Literature in Honor of Morton W. Bloomfield*, ed. Larry D. Benson and Siegfried Wenzel (Kalamazoo, MI: Medieval Institute Publications, 1982), pp. 91–122.
23. See Rosanne Gasse, 'The practice of medicine in *Piers Plowman*', *Chaucer Review*, 39 (2004), 177–97.
24. Steiner, *Reading 'Piers Plowman'*, pp. 21–5.
25. Boethius, *The Consolation of Philosophy*, trans. V. E. Watts (Harmondsworth: Penguin, 1969), Bk 5, Prosa IV, p. 157.
26. See Nicolette Zeeman, 'Medieval religious allegory: French and English', in *The Cambridge Companion to Allegory*, ed. Rita Copeland and Peter T. Struck (Cambridge: Cambridge University Press, 2010), pp. 148–61.
27. Jill Mann, 'Allegory in *Piers Plowman*', in *Companion*, ed. Cole and Galloway, pp. 65–82 (pp. 79–81).
28. Steiner, *Reading 'Piers Plowman'*, pp. 38–45.
29. Elizabeth D. Kirk, '"What is this womman?" Langland on Women and Gender', in William Langland, *Piers Plowman*, ed. E. Robertson and S. A. Shepherd (New York: Norton, 2006), pp. 616–26 (p. 625).
30. Laurie A. Finke, 'Truth's treasure: allegory and meaning in *Piers Plowman*', in *Medieval Texts and Contemporary Readers*, ed. Laurie A. Finke and Martin B. Shichtman (Ithaca, NY: Cornell University Press, 1987), pp. 51–68 (p. 67).
31. See Helen Barr, 'Major episodes and moments in *Piers Plowman* B', in *Companion*, ed. Cole and Galloway, pp. 15–32 (pp. 29–32).
32. Harriet Monroe, 'Chaucer and Langland', *Poetry*, 6.6 (1915), 297–302 (p. 301); see Steve Ellis, *Chaucer at Large: The Poet in the Modern Imagination* (Minneapolis, MN: University of Minnesota Press, 2000), p. 152.

33. W. H. Auden, *The Age of Anxiety*, ed. and intro. Alan Jacobs (Princeton, NJ: Princeton University Press, 2011); John Wheatcroft, *A Voice from the Hump* (Cranbury, NJ: A. S. Barnes, 1977).
34. Patience Agbabi, *Telling Tales* (Edinburgh: Canongate, 2014); Lavinia Greenlaw, *A Double Sorrow: Troilus and Criseyde* (London: Faber and Faber, 2014); Ian Sansom, '*Piers the Plowman* Revisited', First broadcast 18 August, 2014, Radio 4.

12

Work in Progress: Spiritual Authorship and the Middle English Mystics

Roger Ellis

The Middle English mystics are five spiritual writers from the fourteenth and fifteenth centuries:[1] the hermit Richard Rolle (c. 1300–1349); the anchoress Julian of Norwich (c. 1343–c. 1416); Walter Hilton, an Augustinian canon (c. 1343–1396); an anonymous Carthusian, writing in the 1380s; and an illiterate laywoman, Margery Kempe (c. 1373–c. 1438). Rolle and Hilton wrote works in Latin as well as English; the others wrote only in English. Their works fall into two broad classes, though each presupposes the other: works of spiritual direction, often addressed to particular (sometimes named) individuals; and records of spiritual experiences. The most important of the former are Hilton's *Scale of Perfection*, in English, and *The Cloude of Vnknowyng,* by the anonymous Carthusian; of the latter, Julian's revelations on the Passion of Christ – surviving in short and long versions (ST, LT) – and Margery's spiritual autobiography, the first of its kind in English. These writers and their readers (now as then) are beneficiaries of programmes of spiritual instruction for religious and lay people that were started in the thirteenth century and developed exponentially thereafter up to, and including, the Reformation. The present essay, a literary introduction to their writings, principally considers the ambiguous and provisional nature of the authority they claim for themselves and their work, an issue complicated by the religious model of authorship which underpins their literary practice[2] and brought most clearly into focus in their readiness to rework their materials, characteristically by adding to them, so as to suggest that their literary project is always work in progress.

The medieval idea of the author

Before the advent of print culture – and even after – literary production was often similarly understood by both religious and secular
authors as work in progress. Unfinished or unrevised works regularly
circulated (examples of the former include Chaucer's *Canterbury Tales*
and *Legend of Good Women*; of the latter, his *Boece*).[3] Alternatively,
authors revised their own works (Langland's *Piers Plowman* survives in
at least three major versions); completed unfinished works (Jean de
Meun added a massive 16,000 lines to the 4000 written by Guillaume
de Lorris as his *Roman de la rose*); or even adapted them (as when
Wycliffite writers inserted heterodox materials into the Psalter of
Richard Rolle).[4] The medieval author, therefore, became a convenient fiction for later scribes to build upon, and the study of medieval
texts necessarily involves what Zumthor called 'mouvance':[5] that is,
every surviving copy of a text is, in some sense, a new text, which
readers would be unlikely to encounter in any other form.

At the same time, English writers in the late fourteenth century
were well aware of developments in France and Italy, where writers
like Dante, Petrarch and Boccaccio were identifying themselves as vernacular 'authors' and seeking total control over the publication, in their
name, of their own works. Thus, in three separate places in his work,
Chaucer lists his writings; he also writes a poem to a scrivener, excoriating him for miscopying the text of his *Troilus*. In short, he demands
to be recognized, and treated, as an author. For writers of mystical, as
of all religious, texts, however, there was usually no place for such self-
publicizing appetite. This can be seen in the way in which the mystics
refer to themselves in their works. Margery Kempe refers to herself
throughout her *Book* as 'the creature'. Julian starts LT in the third person, referring to herself only as 'a simple creature unletterde [ignorant
of Latin]' (LT 2/1);[6] indeed, she owes her name to the church where
she was an enclosed anchoress. The *Cloude* author identifies himself only
as a 'wreche' (107/39).[7] But their works all bear witness to extremely
strong and distinct authorial identities; one consequence of this was that
numerous anonymous works were credited to Rolle after his death.[8]

The *Cloude* author

Paradoxically, the anonymous *Cloude* author comes closest to assuming Chaucer's mantle of vernacular author. In possibly his last surviving work, Þe *Book of Priuy Counseling*, he refers his reader, for
elucidation of a difficult point, to his other works:

> I touche no vertewe here in specyal, for [...] þou hast hem touchid [...]
> in oþer diuerse places of myn owne writyng. For þis same werk [...] is
> [...] þe frute departid fro þe tre þat I speke of in þi lityl *Pistle of Preier.*
> Þis is *þe Cloude of Vnknowyng;* þis is þat priue loue put in purete of spirit;
> þis is þe Arke of þe Testament. Þis is *Denis Deuinite*, his wisdom and his
> drewry, his liʒty derknes and his vnknowyn kunnynges. (87/40–88/3;
> italics mine)

This quotation identifies three other surviving works by the author
(if *The Arke of the Testament* is a fourth, it is now lost): *Preier* and
Cloude, both original works, and *Denis Deuinite,* a translation of
the *Mystical Theology* of Pseudo-Dionysius.[9] Apparently these other
works reinforce the message of *Priuy Counseling.* The passage suggests, almost irresistibly, the *Cloude* author's interest in the status
of his own works by grouping them and identifying them as the
work of a single author. He identifies *Preier* as a 'lityl Pistle'. He
fails to note that *The Cloude* is an altogether more substantial work.
The Cloude calls itself a 'book' and a 'treatise' (1/10, 70/9), as if
acknowledging its authoritative status (75 chapters, prologues, a
table of contents).[10] *Priuy Counseling* supports this understanding. It
speaks three times of other men's 'books', which, in context, seems
to mean authoritative writings on the spiritual life. All the same,
when he lists his works in *Priuy Counseling* and identifies *Preier* as
an epistle, the author does not distinguish between his major and
minor writings.

He also talks about his work in the prologue to *Denis Deuinite:*

> þis writyng [...] is þe Inglische of a book þat Seynte Denys wrote [...]
> in Latyn [...] *Mistica Theologia.* Of þe whiche book, forþi þat it is mad
> minde in þe 70 chapter of a book wretin before ([...] *þe Cloude of
> Vnknowyng*) how þat Denis sentence wol cleerli afferme al þat is wretyn
> in þat same book: þerfore, in translacioun of it, I haue [...] folowed þe
> nakid lettre of þe text, [and...] þe sentence of þe Abbot of Seinte Victore.
> (119/1–10)

So *The Cloude* predates *Denis Deuinite,* and we have the beginnings of
a chronology for the *Cloude* author's works: *Cloude, Denis Deuinite,
Priuy Counseling. Denis Deuinite* was produced, as noted, in response
to a throw-away line in *Cloude* Chapter 70:

> Seynte Denis seyde: 'þe moste goodly knowyng of God is þat þe whiche
> is knowyn by vnknowyng'. And trewly, whoso wil loke Denis bokes, he
> schal fynde þat his wordes wilen cleerly aferme al þat I haue seyd or
> schal seye, fro þe biginnyng of þis tretis to þe ende. (70/5–9)

This quotation needs unpacking. Often, the author does not name
his sources, so blurring the boundaries between his work and theirs,
and claiming for his words an authority that he appears to deny them.
Moreover, he quotes them only in English: Pseudo-Dionysius here;[11]
Saints Gregory and Augustine in the work's penultimate paragraph.
This is true even of quotations from his major source, the Latin
(Vulgate) Bible.[12] This apparent privileging of the vernacular over the
Latin of the Vulgate has formal links with the Bible translations being
produced by the Wycliffites, who by the early 1380s were provoking a
vigorous reaction from the religious establishments of the day.[13]

But the *Cloude* author's radicalism is very different from that of the
Wycliffites, as we can see from the final words of Chapter 70:

> somtyme men þou3t it meeknes to sey nou3t of þeire owne hedes, bot
> 3if þei afermid it by Scripture and doctours wordes: and now it is turnid
> into corioustee and schewyng of kunnyng. To þee it nediþ not, and þer-
> fore I do it nou3t. (70/10–14)

Previously, it seems, modesty led writers to distinguish their own
words from those of their authorities, so that a reader could access an
original text unencumbered by their additions: hence, for example,
Rolle's Psalter distinguishes his words from those of earlier commen-
tators and the words of the Vulgate by means of different scripts.[14]
According to the *Cloude* author, academics of his own time are
similarly highlighting their scriptural and patristic sources, but only
so as to demonstrate their superior knowledge. So the *Cloude* author's
choice of the vernacular, far from being – as it is with Chaucer – part
of a campaign to claim the status of author, is a barely coded attack on
the exercise of an intelligence devoted to the satisfaction of curiosity
and the pursuit of self-promotion.

Two important consequences follow from this understanding of
authorial function. Whatever formal completeness a work possesses
exists only in relation to the traditions in which it originates – in the
case of *The Cloude*, the apophatic spirituality embodied in Pseudo-
Dionysius and mediated through Sarracenus and Gallus; the patristic
traditions of Augustine and Gregory; and above all, the Bible. Second,
questions of authorship presuppose consideration of the audience
of the text. But which audience? *Denis Deuinite* does not name its
first reader(s). All the other texts are addressed to a 'goostly freende
in God' (7/21, 29, 75/1, 101/1; cf. 74/28), as is another work almost
certainly by the *Cloude* author, the epistle *Of Discrecioun of Stirings*
(Discernment of Spiritual Impulses) (109/1). This address could be a

convenient fiction. But other details at the start of *The Cloude* suggest an actual (male) reader, aged 24 (11/31), whose journey through the different stages of the spiritual life, as these were conventionally understood in the Middle Ages, has brought him to the point of embracing the solitary life (7/29–8/15). Probably *Priuy Counseling* is addressed to this same individual, since it has to face a problem which *The Cloude* had attempted, but failed, to resolve. Both at the start and at the end of *The Cloude*, the author had attempted to restrict its circulation to readers seriously engaged in pursuing contemplative practice: not necessarily professed solitaries, but certainly not those 'corious lettred [...] men' (2/5), whom Chapter 70 so roundly criticized. If so, the opening of *Priuy Counseling* suggests the attempt was a failure:

> Goostly freende in God [...] I speke at þis tyme in specyal to þiself, and not to alle þoo þat þis writyng scholen here in general. For ȝif I schuld write vnto alle, þan I must write þing þat were acordyng to alle generaly. (75/1–5)

By implication, *The Cloude* had had to include material not strictly relevant to its first reader. So *Priuy Counseling* promises its first reader a much more in-depth treatment of matters only cursorily handled in *The Cloude*. In the end, however, it cannot deliver on its promise either, and we find ourselves much where we started in the Prologue to *The Cloude*. The reader is being offered a simple test to prove his calling: if 'þis mater' (95/20) gives a pleasure which ends with the reading, he is not called to be a contemplative. It seems, then, that he has still not internalized the author's teachings (cf. 98/40–99/4). The author can only offer, as a conclusion, the hope that he will eventually take to heart the work's lessons.

Preier and *Stirings* are produced in response to questions by a 'goostly freende' (possibly the first reader of the other works). In *Stirings*, this friend has written requesting spiritual counsel, and the author summarizes the requests before answering them:

> þou askest of me, as I haue parceyued bi þi lettre, two þinges: [...] my conseite of þee and þi steringes, and [...] my counsel in þis caas, and in alle soche oþer whan þei comen. (110/3–4)

The questioner is a young person (112/12) who wants to embrace a solitary life and abandon the practices of communal living ('speking', 'comoun dietyng', 'dwelling in companye', 109/2–4) which he is finding increasingly difficult to bear. But he urgently needs advice,

since, he tells the author, he knows about the 'periles' of solitary life
(109/11). The relation of the author to his first reader is rather different from what we get in the other works. For instance, the author
knows the first reader of *The Cloude* well enough to send him, unso-
licited, what he clearly sees as a major work. Here, by contrast, the
first reader seems an unknown quantity: the author does not yet know
his reader's 'inward disposicioun and [...] abelnes' (110/8) for the
things he has asked about. If in the major works he second-guesses a
readership beyond the initial one, here he is forced to anticipate the
capacities and needs of his first reader. He makes telling use of this
ignorance, though, by observing that his reader may understand his
own motives scarcely better than the writer: 'And parauenture þou
knowest not ȝit þin owne inward disposicioun þiself so fully as þou
schalt do herafter' (110/15–16). If, therefore, the young man rejects
the offered advice, he risks proving the author's point. The advice
being given is, of course, open to other readers to make use of, but
the author has no interest in anticipating their responses, and keeps
his eye firmly on the task in hand.

His relationship with the young man has a further interest: it presupposes a network of religious relationships to which he can readily
appeal. Not just books this time, but actual people. The writer knows
of a 'goostly broþer of þine and of myne' recently in the young man's
neighbourhood, who shared the young man's spiritual impulses, was
'touchid' with them, and learned only 'after longe comounyng wiþ
me [...] when he had proued [...] his steringes' that he had been copying a deeply holy hermit in the same area (113/7–10). So the author
offers the young man two role models (besides himself, of course,
though he is not directly offering himself as a model): the holy hermit
and the copy-cat. In so doing, he acknowledges that his reader must
actually complete the work: or rather, that the true *auctor*, God, must
complete it in him. That is, both reader and writer must jointly defer
to the ultimate source of all human authority, God.

Richard Rolle, Walter Hilton and Margery Kempe

Various models underpin the *Cloude* author's practices: sermons, traditions of academic disputation and the English epistles of Richard
Rolle.[15] Of these last, only Rolle's *Form of Living* directly addresses
a named reader, Margaret Kirkby, shortly before her enclosure as an
anchoress, but colophons in one MS to copies of the other epistles (the *Commandments*, *Ego Dormio*) similarly identify her as the
unnamed recipient. The relationship of Rolle with his first reader,

however, is a much more shadowy affair than was the *Cloude* author's with his: whatever his personal feelings for her, Rolle uses her to reach a wider readership to whom he can recommend himself, by implication, as a spiritual role model. He treats a climactic spiritual experience in his own life almost as a proof-text,[16] and recycles it effortlessly and (it seems to this reader) unstoppably. Repetition here gives very little sense of unfinished business, of work still in progress.[17]

With Hilton's *Scale of Perfection* the situation is rather different. Though we know only that the first reader is, like Margaret Kirkby, a newly professed anchoress at the start of what will become Book I, she acquires a more significant role at the end:

> yif it [the work] conforteth thee nought, or ellis thou takest it not redeli, studie not to longe theraboute, but lei hit beside thee til another tyme and gyve thee to praier or to othir occupacioun. Take it as it wole come and not al at onys. Also thise wordes [...] take hem not to streiteli, but theras thee thenketh bi good avysement that I speke to schorteli, outhir for lackyng of Ynglische or wantyng of resoun, I preye thee mende it there nede is oonli. Also thise wordis [...] longen not alle to oon man whiche hath actif liif but to thee or to another whiche hath the staat of liyf contemplatif. (I. 92/2620–7)[18]

Like the *Cloude* author, Hilton recognizes his work may have been taken up by readers for whom it was not originally intended – in this case, the laity. Unlike the *Cloude* author, Hilton does not try to stop them from reading the book; however, he warns them to skip, or adapt, material specifically addressing the situation of an enclosed female religious.[19] Like *The Cloude*, too, whose author advises his first reader to take time over its reading (1/24–5), Hilton recommends the anchoress not to attempt the work at a single sitting. In one respect, though, he goes further than the *Cloude* author, encouraging the reader not to take his words too literally, and even to amend his text when it is terse, or poorly expressed. (Though acknowledging that his reader may surpass him in the spiritual life, the *Cloude* author does not license any comparable editorial function by his reader, and he expects his words to be taken straight.) Hilton's offered freedom probably allows only for stylistic modifications to his text (the replacement of unfamiliar by more familiar words).[20] But it recognizes that the reader may herself complete the work. Hilton's authorship is always, therefore, work in progress.

What would become *Scale* I was a major achievement, and when he completed it, Hilton may not have anticipated revisiting it. But he made a few minor alterations to the text,[21] and, in response to a reader's request, a major one:

> for as muche as thou coveitest greteli [...] to heere more of an image the whiche y haue before tymes in partie discried to thee, therfore [...] y schal opene to thee lityl more of this image. (II. 1/1–8)

Referring back to *Scale* I, this request, recorded at the start of what will become *Scale* II, generates a work related to its predecessor much as *Priuy Counseling* does to its predecessor *The Cloude*. *Scale* II may not have anticipated a need for further revisions. However, it ends: 'the goostli thinges that I spak of befor [...] I do but touche hem [...] for a soule that is [...] stired [...] to use of this wirkynge, mai seen more in an hour of siche goostli mater than myght be writen in a great book' (II. 46/3591–4). Hilton, at least by implication, calls his book 'great', and it is. But this ending points to the limits of even the greatest book (and its author) compared with the actual experiences to which it is directing its humblest reader.

Like the *Scale,* Margery Kempe's *Book* comes as two books, the second very much shorter than the first, which is called variously a little book and a short treatise. As with the *Scale,* only the first book was originally planned. Book I frames itself at beginning and end with a story about the miraculous circumstances of its copying, so as to suggest that the book detailing God's gracious dealings with Margery over the course of a long life is being presented as a single unit. According to this story, God commands Margery to make the book, but she finds no-one to do so for her except an Englishman who has been living in Germany. His handwriting is 'neiþyr good Englysch ne Dewch [German], ne þe lettyr [...] not schapyn ne formyd as oþer letters ben' (4/3–4, 14–16):[22] consequently, when he dies, no-one can read the book, and it requires another instance of divine intervention four years later to enable a second scribe to make a good copy. The second scribe admits to further difficulties with his materials:

> Thys boke is not wretyn in ordyr, euery thyng aftyr oþer as it wer done, but lych as þe mater cam to þe creatur in mend whan it schuld be wretyn, for it was so long er it was wretyn þat sche had forgetyn þe tyme and þe ordyr whan thyngys befellyn. (5/12–16)

Hence, he notes that what is presently Chapter 21 should be read between Chapters 16 and 17 (38/4–5). Having copied Book I, he judges it 'expedient' (221/5) to bring it up to date: hence the much shorter Book II, completed in 1438. This Book does not so much develop the materials of Book I as repeat them. The contrast with Hilton's *Scale* II could hardly be greater.

Margery's *Book* is a fascinating mix of genres – (auto)biography, for which at the time literary models barely existed, and hagiography, normally undertaken only after the death of the protagonist, sometimes with a view to securing his/her canonization. The latter genre could accommodate either a thematic approach to its subject,[23] or a simpler chronological one. At the end of Book II, Margery is still, though an old woman of 65, very much alive: it ends with some of the prayers she recited, over the years, in her parish church. In the *Book*, then, art imitates life: it is repetitious, inconsistent and incomplete. Her story does not need an end. Nothing short of death can end the story of God's gracious dealings with her.

A contrast immediately suggests itself with Hilton's first reader, who may achieve in one hour, as we saw, a grace surpassing what s/he will have discovered in the whole of the *Scale*. So a single hour – indeed, what the *Cloude* author calls the smallest conceivable unit of time, an 'athomus', will suffice (10/6 and n.) – can symbolize and enact a spiritual drama and suggest the completeness which, for all sorts of reasons, a work of religious writing cannot deliver. Just such a moment characterizes the drama of Margery's conversion to the spiritual life:

> On a nygth, as þis creatur lay in hir bedde wyth hir husbond, sche herd a sownd of melodye so swet [...] as sche had ben in Paradyse [...] This melody [...] caused þis creatur whan sche herd ony [...] melodye aftyrward for to haue [...] habundawnt teerys of hy deuocyon. (11/12–21)

Margery's *Book* is always moving between the 'no time' of divine visitation, accessible only to the visionary, and a detailed account of its human circumstances, available to the readers and needed to provide a context for the visionary's spiritual gifts. The writing of visionary literature does not strictly need to acknowledge this latter timescale: it can present itself simply as a prayer or a meditation, like the ecstatic fourteenth-century *Talkyng of þe Loue of God* – though this text also has its eye on possible readers, as its prologue bears witness.[24]

Julian of Norwich

Of the story of Margery's illustrious predecessor, the visionary Julian of Norwich, we know almost as little as of the *Cloude* author. That there was a story, off the page, we can see from Margery's *Book*, which reports how God directed Margery to visit Julian for advice and encouragement, possibly around 1413 (42/8–43/20). The advice she reports herself as receiving is embarrassingly anodyne, so if Margery has not rewritten the encounter, Julian has pulled her spiritual punches. That Julian is a spiritual heavyweight, though, is immediately apparent from her text, our main witness to her life. From this we learn the genesis of the revelations, which are mostly meditations on, or visions of, the Passion, and very little more about their human context.[25] They were received over two days in May 1373 (not quite the 'athomus' of the *Cloude* author, but closer to it than the 40-odd years of Margery's visions). Important in their own right, when written down, as a contribution to literature about the Passion, they generated a commentary by Julian quite extraordinary for its scale and profundity. Both the revelations and commentary are present and well developed in the first Short Text version of the work (ST). Previously ST was dated to a time shortly after the reception of the revelations. More recently, a date as late as 1388 has been proposed – in the aftermath, therefore, of the first condemnation of the Wycliffites in 1382[26] – which gives a better sense of the achievement of the work.

Twenty or more years later (LT 51/73 for this detail), in an example of authorial second thoughts rivalling Hilton's, Julian produced a hugely extended second Long Text (LT) version. LT owes to ST its overarching shape and most of its details, which, if we reflect that 20 years had elapsed between ST and LT, gives a clear sense of the authority accorded to the former. LT does not refer to ST, as, say, *Priuy Counseling* does to *The Cloude*, or *Scale* II to *Scale* I. Notwithstanding the many modifications to ST in LT, though, Julian appears to have seen the latter as a supplement to it and as itself open to supplementation: as the final chapter of LT states, 'this boke is begonne by Goddes gifte and his grace, but it is not yet performed, as to my sight' (LT 86/1–2). A precise instance of the practice of supplementation occurs in this final chapter, which functions almost as a coda to the work. In response to a long-held desire (over at least fifteen years, LT 86/12) to understand the meaning of the revelations, Julian received enlightenment in a new revelation:

> I was answered in gostly understonding, seyeng thus: What, woldest thou wit thy lordes mening in this thing? Wit it wele, love was his mening. Who shewed it the? Love. What shewid he the? Love. Wherfore shewed he it the? For love. Holde the therin, thou shalt wit more in the same. But thou shalt never wit therin other withouten ende. (LT 86/13–16)

If Julian remains faithful to her original vision, she will receive more understanding about it, but never anything other than what, explicitly or implicitly, was first communicated through it. The comforting nature of this message is of a piece with the many similar words received by Julian in the course of the original revelations. How she received the message ('in gostly understonding') also approximates to the taxonomy she created for her revelations near the start of ST ('bodilye sight [...] worde formede in mine understandinge, [...] gastelye sight', ST 7/2–3, LT 9/24–5), which, as a distinctive take on current understandings of the question, seeks perhaps to forestall criticism from (mostly male) religious authorities that, as a woman, she is presuming to teach *them*.[27] Equally important is the opening phrase: 'I was answered'. This reminds us that, however the divine message comes to her, as words or vision, Julian is initially a passive recipient. Generally she can identify the speaker, if the message includes a first-person reference. But when, as here, she cannot identify the speaker, her inability to do so itself becomes part of the drama. We have a good example of this near the end of the climactic eighth revelation of the Passion, when she is invited by 'a profer in [her] resone, as if it hadde beene frendelye' (ST 10/53–4), to look away from the crucifix and up to God in heaven: a 'profer' which she has to disavow, even though she never identifies its source. Revelation, then, always plays out against the visionary's struggle both to understand it and to remain faithful to her understanding.

Another revelation, the hugely important Chapter 51 of LT, containing the 'wonderful example of a lorde that hath a servant' (LT 51/1–2), was received at the same time as the others, but did not make it into ST because Julian could not understand aspects of it at the time, and needed divine direction, nearly twenty years later: 'take hede to alle the propertes and the condetions that were shewed in the example, though the thinke [...] it [...] misty and indefferent to thy sight' (LT 51/74–6). A third proved similarly difficult to understand, but was written up in ST, and thence, considerably enlarged, in LT, because Julian's very difficulties of understanding are, again, a vital part of its meaning.[28] This revelation presents a vision of the physical abuse Christ suffered at the hands of his torturers, and includes much more detail than she can relate (ST 8/4). But, even as she receives it, she cannot see the vision clearly and she asks for 'mare [more] bodelye light to hafe sene more clerelye'. Instead, she is told 'in [... her] resone': 'if God walde shewe me mare he shulde, botte me neded na light botte him' (ST 8/6–8). This voice is not God's, but she cannot or will not tell us whose it is. So the revelation presents two kinds of obscurity, one literal, the other spiritual, each a metaphor for the other.

ST seems to have no doubts about the vision, only about its interpretation. (Julian's failure to understand her visions is a regular feature
of visionary writing.) LT takes a very different view: 'my spirites were
in great traveyle in the beholding [...] for I was sometime in a feer
whether it was a shewing [revelation] or none' (LT 10/25–7). Julian
has been unable to reconcile the bloodied face of the vision with the
'blessed face' of the divine Christ (LT 10/34). This doubt generates an
extended meditation on the value of partial understanding ('seking is
as good as beholding', LT 10/62–3), and two further revelations. In
the first, Julian finds herself at the bottom of the sea, and comes to
understand that even there, in that place of obscurity, God is present, if
we only had the eyes to see properly. In the second, at different times,
she learns that the physical disfigurement of Christ in the revelation
is indeed a metaphor of her (and our) spiritual 'foulhede and [...]
wretchednes' (10/47–8). One last detail of this revelation shows how
far we have come from ST. As another way of explaining its details,
Julian cross-refers it to another vision of the Passion, the eighth, and
even identifies the relevant chapter, the sixteenth (LT 10/53). This
exercise of editorial function (most probably her own) shows how
clearly Julian saw LT as a whole book, hers no less than God's. In this
understanding, she may even have surpassed the *Cloude* author and
Walter Hilton.

This essay has examined the major writings of the Middle English
mystics in the context of their literary production and its potential
conflict with the complex spirituality of their texts. In so doing, it has
sought to address a central feature of their writings: their conviction
that literary processes, like life itself, are always dynamically evolving,
always the product of an ongoing dialogue between author, reader
and God.

Notes

1. For criticism of the term, see Nicholas Watson, 'The Middle English
   mystics', in *The Cambridge History of Medieval English Literature,* ed. David
   Wallace (Cambridge: Cambridge University Press, 1999), pp. 539–40.
2. Major accounts of medieval views of authorship are A. J. Minnis,
   Medieval Views of Authorship, 2nd edn. (Aldershot: Scolar Press, 1988) and
   Rita Copeland, *Rhetoric, Hermeneutics and Translation in the Middle Ages*
   (Cambridge: Cambridge University Press, 1991).
3. On the *Boece* as an unrevised translation, see Tim William Machan,
   Techniques of Translation: Chaucer's Boece (Norman: Pilgrim Books, 1985),
   p. 121.

4. See Anne Hudson, ed. *Two Revisions of Rolle's English Psalter Commentary and the Related Canticles*, 3 vols, EETS OS 340–1, 343 (Oxford: Oxford University Press, 2012–13).

5. Paul Zumthor, *Essai de poétique médiévale* (Paris : Editions du Seuil, 1972).

6. *The Writings of Julian of Norwich*, ed. Nicholas Watson and Jacqueline Jenkins (University Park, PA: The Pennsylvania State University Press, 2006). All further references are to this edition and are given in the body of the text by chapter (LT)/section (ST) and line number.

7. Quotations from the *Cloude* author's works, cited in the body of the text by page and line number, are from *The Cloud of Unknowing and Related Treatises*, ed. Phyllis Hodgson, Analecta Cartusiana 3 (Salzburg: Institut für Anglistik und Amerikanistik, 1982).

8. Rolle's quasi-canonical status is partly a reflection of the numerous Latin works he produced, partly an accident of chronology.

9. See *Pseudo-Dionysius The Complete Works*, trans. Colm Luibheid, assisted by Paul Rorem (London: SPCK, 1987); and Denys Turner, *The Darkness of God: Negativity in Christian Mysticism* (Cambridge: Cambridge University Press, 1995).

10. Wolters argues, oddly, that the chapter headings 'are not part of the original text'. *The Cloud of Unknowing and Other Works*, trans. Clifton Wolters (Harmondsworth: Penguin, 1978), p. 29.

11. He uses the Latin translation of John Sarracenus, supplemented by the commentary of Thomas Gallus (the 'abbote of Seinte Victore').

12. Admittedly, his other writings offer a translation of texts from the Vulgate only after quoting them in Latin.

13. The work of the Wycliffites provides a vital backdrop to the writings of the mystics. On their Bible translations see, for example, David Lawton, 'Englishing the Bible 1066-1549', *The Cambridge History of Medieval English Literature,* pp. 470ff., and 'The Bible', *The Oxford History of Literary Translation in English,* Vol. 1, *To 1550*, ed. Roger Ellis (Oxford: Oxford University Press, 2008), pp. 220–8.

14. Similar practices in the fifteenth century probably witness to anxiety rather than modesty on the part of their authors. For comment on developments in fifteenth-century vernacular religious writing, see Nicholas Watson, 'Censorship and Cultural Change in Late Medieval England: Vernacular Theology, the Oxford Translation Debate, and Arundel's Constitutions of 1409', *Speculum* 70 (1995), 822–64, and *After Arundel: Religious Writing in Fifteenth-Century England*, ed. Vincent Gillespie and Kantik Ghosh (Turnhout: Brepols, 2011).

15. See *English Writings of Richard Rolle Hermit of Hampole*, ed. Hope Emily Allen (Oxford: Clarendon Press, 1931); for a good modern translation, *Richard Rolle, the English Writings*, trans. Rosamund S. Allen (New York and Mahwah: Paulist Press, 1988).

16. This key episode is recorded in *Incendium Amoris* Chapter 15. See *Incendium Amoris of Richard Rolle of Hampole*, ed. Margaret Deanesly

(Manchester: Manchester University Press, 1915), p. 187; for a modern translation see Rolle, *The Fire of Love,* trans. Clifton Wolters (Harmondsworth: Penguin, 1972), pp. 91–5.

17. For a major study, which takes a very different view, see Nicholas Watson, *Richard Rolle and the Invention of Authority* (Cambridge: Cambridge University Press, 1991).

18. *Walter Hilton: The Scale of Perfection,* ed. Thomas H. Bestul (Kalamazoo, MI: TEAMS, 2000), citing quotations by Book, chapter, and line number. A modern translation, with excellent commentary, is *Walter Hilton: The Scale of Perfection,* trans. John P. H. Clark and Rosemary Dorward (New York and Mahwah: Paulist Press, 1991).

19. Such adaptation to lay readers of texts originally written for the professed religious, common in the later Middle Ages, provides a vivid instance of textual *mouvance.* See Vincent Gillespie, 'Religious Writing', *The Oxford History of Literary Translation,* Vol. I, *To 1550,* pp. 264–6.

20. This instance of *mouvance* is explicitly acknowledged in late fourteenth- and fifteenth-century works: for example, Chaucer (*Troilus II* Proem), Capgrave (prologue to the *Life of St Katharine*) and Caxton (prologue to the *Eneydos*).

21. See Marion Glasscoe, *English Medieval Mystics: Games of Faith* (London and New York: Longman, 1993), pp. 132–3.

22. Quotation, by page and line number, is from *The Book of Margery Kempe,* ed. Sandford Brown Meech and Hope Emily Allen, EETS OS 212 (Oxford: Oxford University Press, 1940). See also *The Book of Margery Kempe,* ed. Barry Windeatt (Harlow: Longman, 2000) and *Writing Religious Women; Female Spiritual and Textual Practices in Late Medieval England,* ed. Denis Renevey and Christiania Whitehead (Cardiff: University of Wales Press, 2000).

23. This happens in the first Book of the *Life of St Mary of Oignies* by Jacques de Vitry, a major role model for Margery.

24. *A Talkyng of Þe Loue of God,* ed. Sister Dr. M. Salvina Westra (The Hague: Martinus Nijhoff, 1950), pp. 2–3.

25. See Roger Ellis, 'Revelation and the Life of Faith: the Vision of Julian of Norwich', *Christian* 6 (1980), 61–5.

26. See Nicholas Watson, 'The Composition of Julian of Norwich's *Revelation of Love*', *Speculum* 68 (1993), 637–83.

27. See Rosalynn Voaden, *God's Words, Women's Voices: The Discernment of Spirits in the Writing of Late-Medieval Woman Visionaries* (Woodbridge: York Medieval Press, 1999).

28. See Ellis, 'Revelation and the Life of Faith', p. 69.

tales. Nonetheless, all four of these women are purely textual beings, or even, we might say, textual events. As Carolyn Dinshaw and David Wallace have put it, 'we know everything we do of these lives through texts; […] the lived lives themselves are constituted by bits and pieces of texts'.[6] H. Marshall Leicester may have been one of the first, but certainly not the last Chaucerian to state what should be the obvious: 'there is no Wife of Bath'.[7] Similarly, of course, there is no Prioress or Second Nun. They are the product of their male author's imagination and his clever and careful manipulation of 'bits and pieces' of other prominent and valorized male-authored texts.

But what does this mean for historical women like Julian and Margery, who are also made of texts? Lynn Staley writes of Margery and Julian: 'They inherited a tradition whereby the female text – whether that text was written word or life of a holy woman – was mediated and thus verified by a male author or scribe'.[8] In this respect, then, both Julian's and Margery's books might be seen as no different from the prologues and tales of the Wife of Bath and the Prioress. It is the investment of a male writer that allows us to have these women's texts and these textual women. Like Alice and Eglantine, then, Julian and Margery might well be seen as male-authored texts modelled on, influenced by and constituted of other male-authored texts. As Dinshaw and Wallace suggest, Margery's 'scribe […] may have fashioned her narrative to fit into the tradition of written lives of other holy devouts. Julian of Norwich, as an anchoress, used the rules of anchoritic life in order to constitute herself'.[9]

Are we prepared, then, to go so far as to say, following Leicester, that there is no Julian of Norwich and Margery Kempe, since we can access them only through what might, in these respects, be considered the male-authored writings that are their texts? Or is this precisely where the stakes change with the gender of the author? And what exactly is at stake? Before we can answer these questions, it will be helpful to consider how voices, figuratively or otherwise, emerge from these writings, and what these voices say when they are made essentially from texts.

The Wife of Bath and the Prioress

Voice, of course, is located in the body. One way that Chaucer prepares us to 'hear' the voices of his pilgrims is through his 'General Prologue' descriptions of the bodies from which those voices will speak. One thing is clear about the Wife and the Prioress: their bodies are large and well dressed. The Prioress 'was nat undergrowe' (I [A]

156),[10] and the narrator takes six lines to describe her 'fetys' 'cloke' (I [A] 157) and her assortment of impressive ecclesiastical bling (I [A] 158–62). The Wife has 'hipes large' (I [A] 472), 'an hat/As brood as is a bokeler or a targe' (I [A] 470–1), red stockings (I [A] 456), new shoes (I [A] 457) and 'spores sharpe' (I [A] 473). The heads whose mouths give voice are also distinctive. With her shapely nose, grey eyes, broad forehead and small, soft, red mouth (I [A] 151–5), Madame Eglantine, the Prioress, is as pretty as a courtly heroine. While Alice, the Wife of Bath, lacks aristocratic loveliness, she is still striking: '[b]oold was hir face, and fair, and reed of hewe' (I [A] 458), although she is 'somdel deef' (I [A] 456) and '[g]at-tothed' (I [A] 468). Even before we get to their prologues and tales, we can almost (and it is always 'almost' with the notoriously ambiguous Chaucer) predict the tenor and timbre of their voices.

The Wife, with her bold, red face and its gap-toothed mouth – a sign of being highly sexed – can be as brash and bawdy and body-bound as one would expect from Chaucer's description of her. In her long prologue, she is frank about turning the marriage bed into a market place (III [D] 407–22) and equally frank about what goes on there as she admits to faking it to get her own way: 'For wynnyng wolde I al his lust endure,/ And make me a feyned appetit;/ For yet in bacon hadde I nevere delit' (III [D] 416–18). But there is more to her than that. Like Chaucer's highly complex Criseyde, the Wife has a voice with many, often contradictory tonalities. With Alison of Bath, there is plenty that is brassy. However, there is also plenty that is self-evaluative, introspective, even rueful. Thinking of her lost youth, she is poignantly wistful as well as resilient: 'I have had my world as in my tyme./ [...] The flour is goon; ther is namoore to telle; [...] But yet to be right myrie wol I fonde' (III [D] 473–9). She acknowledges the pain of being beaten and then rationalizes her way to asserting her love for her abuser because he is sexy and plays hard to get (III [D] 503–24):[11] 'I trowe I loved hym best, for that he/ Was of his love daungerous to me' (III [D] 513–14). Finally, after the seemingly fairy-tale ending of her story – 'And thus they lyve unto hir lyves ende/In parfit joye' (III [D] 1257–8), she switches in mid-line back to the bold, bantering Alice of her prologue: 'and Jhesu Crist us sende/Housbondes meeke, yonge, and fresh abedde/ [...] And olde and angry nygardes of dispence,/God sende hem soone verray pesti-lence' (III [D] 1258–64).[12] Chaucer has even given the Wife what we now call 'a senior moment' when she loses her train of thought: 'But now, sire, lat me se what I shal seyn./A ha! By God, I have my tale ageyn' (III [D] 585–6). Assuming that real medieval people were as inconsistent as we are, it is little wonder that generations of Chaucer readers have responded as though there really were a Wife of Bath.

From the Prioress's soft little red mouth, we could justifiably expect a courtly, gentle and refined voice. Madame Eglantine's prologue to her tale does not disappoint. Interestingly, we need only take one glance at the page to see how elegant the voice will be. The iambic pentameter couplets pervasive in most of the tales have given way to the more complex, stately and difficult seven-line rime royal stanza, a form Chaucer invented and one befitting the courtly Prioress. Her tale's prologue, which is a paeon to Christ and Mary, has a sweetness, a daintiness, almost a breathlessness in its awed apostrophes: 'O Lord, oure Lord, thy name how merveilous' (VII 453); 'O mooder Mayde, O mayde Mooder Free!' (VII 467). If her prologue begins with the tender oral imagery of suckling children, oral imagery recurs in her particular formulation of the modesty topos at the end: 'as a child of twelf month oold, or lesse,/ That kan unnethes any word expresse,/ Right so fare I' (VII 484–6). It is jarring, then, a mere two lines later, when she launches into her venomous excoriation of the Jews. Sweetness a-plenty surrounds her representation of the 'litel clergeon' (VII 502), but that makes the virulence of her tale's treatment of the Jews all the more remarkable. The finicky Prioress, with her impeccable table manners, has the Jews throw the boy's body '[w]here as thise Jewes purgen hire entraille' (VII 573). What's more, all the Jews who even knew about the boy's murder are summarily delivered a shameful death: 'Therfore with wilde hors [the provost] dide hem drawe,/ And after that he heng hem by the lawe' (VII 633–4). The dainty Prioress who cries over dead mice tells a tale whose body count is arguably the highest in *The Canterbury Tales*. No matter how small, soft and red, this baby's mouth is mean.[13] If Chaucer's two fictional women narrators demonstrate a remarkable tonal range rooted in their large, well-clad female bodies, what happens when the texts' voices come from women who once breathed?

Julian of Norwich and Margery Kempe

Given their different purposes and emphases, Julian's and Margery's texts do not provide the same detailed physical representations of themselves or their bodies as does Chaucer's 'General Prologue'. Yet, while Margery never tells us what she looks like, she is certainly aware of the significance of clothes. Even after she had her first vision, she was still vain. In addition to fashionable cloaks, 'sche weryd gold pypys on hir heuyd & hir hodys with the typettys were daggyd' (p. 9).

In this way, as Sheila Delany has noted, Margery resembles the Wife of Bath – and, we might add, the Prioress.[14] Later, at Christ's behest, she wears white clothes that stir controversy about a woman who is neither virgin nor nun. But although we do not know what Margery and Julian look like, their texts are still very much rooted in the body, the site, after all, of the mystical encounters that are the reasons we have their texts at all.[15] The way in which each woman registers her own mystical experiences somatically determines the voice(s) that speak from her text.

As is not uncommon for medieval women mystics, Julian and Margery receive their first visions at times of physical crisis. Julian is quite specific about the onslaught of her illness in a way that provides what little biographical information we have about her: 'This revelation was made to a simple creature unlettyrde leving in deadly flesh the yer of our Lord a thousand and thre hundered and lxiii, the xiii daie of May' (p. 4).[16] And she continues: 'And when I was xxxth yere old and a halfe, God sent me a bodily sicknes, in the which I ley iii daies and iii nightes' (p. 6). She thinks she is dying: 'by then was my bodie dead from the miedes downward as to my feeling' (p. 6),[17] and later, 'the over part of my bodie began to die so farforth that unneth I had anie feeling' (p. 7). And then suddenly, 'all my paine was taken from me' (p. 7), and there commences a series of sixteen extraordinary showings/revelations that occur over the course of the ensuing day and the contemplation of which becomes Julian's life's work. After this initial representation of her illness, Julian's own body becomes more or less absent from her text. But physicality remains centrally important because the startlingly corporeal representations of the Passion become the centerpieces, one might even say, altarpieces, of her showings, which are so visual that they are, as Denise N. Baker has noted, actually 'painterly'.[18]

Margery's life as a mystic similarly begins in a sick bed, or, more specifically, in childbed, as her first vision of Christ ends an eight-and-a-half-month siege of violent psychological instability following the very difficult birth of her first child.[19] It is unclear whether her sickness involves post-partum psychosis or whether, as she attests, it stems from her abrupt silencing by her short-tempered confessor, when, in fear of death and damnation, she is about to tell the sin she has never voiced (and never does reveal). The effects are powerful: 'this creatur went owt of hir mende & was wondyrlye vexed' (p. 7) by visions of flaming devils threatening to swallow her up. She mutilates herself: 'sche bot hir owen hand so violently that it was seen al hir lyf aftyr' (p. 8). And she gouges her skin with her nails so badly that she is put in restraints. In this terrifying plight, Christ comes to her 'in lyknesse of a man, most semly, most bewtyuows, & most amiable […] clad in a mantyl of purpyl sylke, syttyng up-on hir beddys syde' (p. 8). All he needs to do is ask her why she has forsaken him when he never forsook her for her to be 'stabelyd in hir wyttys & in hir reson' (p. 8). This may be her first vision, but it is far from her last.

If, for both Julian and Margery, their lives as mystics begin in beset bodies, the presence of the body and its relation to the voice(s) of their texts develop in remarkable ways throughout their writings. Julian's concerns with the body and embodiment focus on Christ and his humanity; she renders them vividly in her visions of the Passion. To take but one example: Julian offers a detailed portrait of Christ as he is on the point of dying. It is like seeing a finely detailed Flemish altarpiece come to life:

> I saw the swete face as it were drye and blodeles with pale dyeng, and deede, pale langhuryng, and than turned more deede in to blew and after in browne blew as the flessch turned more depe dede. (p. 26)

Here is the slow dying of a very human, very physical body. The copious amount of blood Christ shed in Revelation IV, Chapter 12 (p. 22) slowly drains and dries, as his nostrils become pinched, as his body becomes blackened, and as there blew 'a dry, sharp wynd, wonder colde as to my syght' (p. 27). The wind speeds the drying and dying, two words that Julian repeats so often they form an incantation. Throughout, Christ and his dying body are, over and over, called 'swete'. And thus the sweet sadness and tenderness of the authorial voice become almost a soundtrack for the odd and plangent beauty of the scene, which culminates for Julian in a climax of pain: 'I [said] in my reson: "But of alle peyne that leed to salvacion, thys is the most, to se the lover to suffer." How might ony peyne be more then to see hym that is alle my lyfe, alle my blysse, and all my joy suffer?' (p. 29). Although voiced by her 'reson', here is quiet ecstacy in Julian's embrace of her dying lover.[20]

There is nothing quiet about the ecstasies of Margery Kempe. Laurie Finke writes of Julian and Margery: 'in personality, the two women could not be more different'.[21] Margery's mystical experiences are voiced deeply, loudly and dramatically in and through her body, which emits a distinctive repertoire of non-verbal sounds. During one tempestuous episode in St Stephen's Church in Norwich, she runs the gamut of them: 'she cryed, sche roryd, sche wept, sche fel down to the grownd' (p. 147).[22] Sometimes, she turns leaden grey and sweats profusely (p. 140). These somatic displays go on for at least ten years and become a defining feature of her text. Needless to say, her weepings and roarings provoke a mixed response from those around her. On her way to Jerusalem, for example, 'many men merveyled & wonderyd of the gret grace that God wrowt in hys creatur' (p. 61). But her companions on the long journey are not impressed: 'thei wer most displesyd for sche wepyd so mech [...] & therfor schamfully they reprevyd hir' (p. 61). Because of the way her body sounds, they assault that body: 'They cuttyd hir gown so schort that it come but lytil be-nethyn hir kne', and they dress her up in white sackcloth to make her look like a fool (p. 62). But Margery embraces this pain not only because it is sent from Christ as a sign of his love and thus of her specialness, but also because, by suffering the persecution, she can show her love through her own body and its *imitatio Christi*.[23] Her body's non-verbal language in turn legitimizes her verbal language – her voice. Still, both get her into significant trouble. Because of her wailings and propensity toward wiseacre words to powerful men, Margery is hauled up on charges of heresy more than once, as happens at York. When the Archbishop of York asks her, '"Why wepist thu so, woman?" She, answering, seyde, "Syr, ye xal welyn sum day that ye had wept as sor as I"' (p. 125). When he says to her, '"I her seyn thu art a ryth wikked woman." And sche seyd a-geyn, "Ser, so I her seyn that ye arn a wikkyd man"' (p. 125). Throughout her *Book*, Margery can manifest a forthrightness, directness and acid sense of humour in the midst of high emotionalism.

The texts of Julian and Margery might not manifest the wide and sometimes surprising range of voices that we get in the texts of Alice and Eglantine, though this is not to say they lack a variety of intonations. Perhaps the voices of these historical women derive from the intervention and shaping of male scribes, as Lynn Staley suggests,[24] or perhaps they come from the women themselves as they told their lives to scribes (or, maybe, in the case of Julian, as she wrote her *Showings* herself). Both Julian and Margery had before them a weighty task, perhaps the weightiest that could confront a medieval woman writer: to justify the ways of God (and woman) to man.

In particular, this task involved radically transforming the role of the mother and of the mother's body in order to express the ways their mystical visions had brought them to a higher understanding of God. For Julian, on the one hand, this movement involves the formulation of her justifiably famous figuration of Jesus as Mother: what Caroline Walker Bynum calls 'one of the greatest reformulations in the history of theology'.[25] The tenderness and sweetness of Julian's own voice permeate this reformulation, which extends over many chapters in the last portions of her work. Thus, for example:

> The moder may geve her chylde sucke hyr mylke, but oure precious Moder Jhesu, he may fede us with hym selfe and doth ful curtesly and full tendyrly with the blessyd sacrament…The moder may ley hyr chylde tenderly to hyr brest, but oure tender Mother Jhesu, he may homely lede us in to hys blessyd brest by his swet opyn syde. (p. 94)

Given the suffusion of maternal love and tenderness that character-izes Julian's text, it is no wonder that, after twenty years of contem-plating in her anchor-hold the visions that visited her but once, she approaches one of the most radical theological conclusions she could reach: a denial if not of sin, then at least of the possibility of damna-tion. As Laurie Finke writes, 'She simply cannot imagine a wrathful God because she cannot imagine a wrathful mother'.[26]

For Margery, on the other hand, this movement involves a trans-formation that is not theologically, but rather personally and individu-ally radical: an eschewal of her own body's roles as wife and mother. Knowing, as she does, that most women honoured with *bona fide* mystical visions are, if not virgins, at least celibate, she seeks such a mar-riage from her husband John, at first to little effect (even though she has taken to wearing a hair shirt, they continue to conceive children) – that is, until the fateful Friday of that Midsummer's Eve. By the cross at a crossroads, in a scene worthy of the Wife of Bath, Margery strikes a deal with John that is basically brokered in a side conversation with Christ: they will live chastely if she will eat with him on Fridays and pay his debts before she goes to Jerusalem (pp. 23–5): '[t]han seyd hir husband a-yen to hir, "As fre mot yowr body ben to God as it hath ben to me"' (p. 25). Then they say their prayers and 'etyn & dronkyn to-gedyr in gret glandnes of spyryt' (p. 25). Her own marriage and motherhood are unmade at this symbolic crossroads as she is remade into a bride of Christ. Unlike Julian who withdraws to the anchor-hold to contemplate the meaning of the visions that her lover/Mother Jesus sent her on her *dies mirabilis*, Margery will now leave the cross-roads and take to the pilgrimage trails as she experiences her ongoing trysts with her heavenly groom.

Who gets to speak, and how? Gender and ventriloquism

To circle back to the questions in my subtitle, and the question of how the stakes change according to the author's gender, I am going to invoke ventriloquism as a useful trope for ending an essay on the connection between voices and bodies. Etymologically, ventriloquism is 'belly speech,' that is, speech coming from a part of the body usually not used for talking in order to voice a being other than oneself.[27] As such, ventriloquism is an apt trope for addressing the kind of speaking that occurs when Chaucer, Julian and Margery write their texts because it allows us to consider how, in late medieval England, voicing the Other/another might mean something different, and have different stakes, depending on gender.

In his Wife of Bath and Prioress, Chaucer has created two compelling and complex female characters capable of luring us straight into the trap of the mimetic fallacy. But these are not real women. They are characters created by a male author from various other male-authored texts, including, significantly, one that the Wife and Prioress share in their literary DNA: La Vieille in Jean de Meun's continuation of *Le Roman de la Rose*. That a wife and a nun are both birthed from a bawd should give us pause. What is Chaucer suggesting about these female characters? It would not be hard to see a misogynistic power play here. But what is peculiar in Chaucer's voicing of first-person female narrators is how distinctly unsettling to his own identity the process seems to be. There's a reason Alice and Eglantine are super-sized.

As soon as the Prioress finishes her tale, the Host significantly calls Chaucer the narrator forward to tell his. He no longer seems to be the gregarious guy we met in the 'General Prologue', but rather a strangely reclusive figure, riding at the back, staring at the ground. After noting that he and Chaucer are both big-bellied (the better to 'belly speak'?), Harry adds about Chaucer: 'This were a popet in an arme t'enbrace/For any womman, smal and fair of face./He semeth elvyssh by his contenaunce' (VII 701–4). Ventriloquizing big women has had the effect, it seems, of reducing Chaucer to a dummy. While 'popet' means 'doll,' and not our Modern English 'puppet', Chaucer still becomes a little toy that a woman can voice. What's more, he is not only a little doll, but a little doll controlled by a little woman. He shrinks before our eyes. Of course, since Chaucer the narrator seems 'elvyssh' (VII 704), his pixie grin may mean he is just spoofing about being diminished by voicing big women. Whatever he has in mind, he's not telling. But this image is. His representation of his fictional surrogate suggests the possibility, however debatable, that the medieval court poet occupies something of the feminized position of the 'Woman' in his society.[28] His masculinity is somehow at stake.

In late medieval English culture, it seems that the women most legitimized to voice their texts are mystics. If this is the case, then, inevitably, their text will attempt to ventriloquize God. As a result, comparing Julian's and Margery's stakes with Chaucer's stakes as he voices his fictional female narrators may seem like the proverbial apples and oranges match-up. Chaucer's women are, after all, his own creations. Julian and Margery are God's. And yet, when we read *The Book of Margery Kempe*, it is hard to escape the sense that, all possible scribal intervention aside, Margery ventriloquizes a version of Christ/God who manages to say exactly what she wants and needs. For example, Margery may have negotiated a chaste earthly marriage, but the result is that she now has Christ claiming her as his bedmate: 'Therfore most I nedys to be homly wyth the & lyn in thi bed wyth the [...] & therfor thu mayst boldly take me in the armys of thi sowle & kyssen my mowth, myn hed, & my fete as sweetly as thow wylt' (p. 90). One can see a scribe hastening to insert 'of thi sowle' after 'in the armys'! The Christ whom Margery ventriloquizes may say what she wants when she wants it, because, in her *Book,* her whole life is at stake. Christ's words legitimize the identity as mystic of an illiterate wife and (fourteen times) mother. In this new calling, despite its significant challenges, she feels honoured, exalted and loved.

The Christ whom Julian ventriloquizes shares with her the voice of quiet and sweet tenderness that marks her *Showings*. As she speaks Him, His words, with their simple diction and unadorned cadences, can assume an incantatory, almost spell-binding quality. Through her ventriloquism, then, Julian can evoke for her reader the ways in which her mystical experience involves profound moments of quiet contemplation. Throughout Chapters 31 and 32, there reverberate variations of the phrase for which, across the centuries, Julian has become most famous: 'Alle maner a thing shalle be wele' (p. 44, but 44–6 passim). In Chapter 26, we are swept into the incremental repetition of 'I it am, I it am. I it am that is highest. I it am that thou lovyst. I it am that thou servyst. I it am that thou longeth. I it am that thou desyreth' (p. 39). Here, as elsewhere in her text, Julian leads us to contemplate the physicality and presence of the Word as an object of meditation. Her Christ speaks in the comforting repetitions of the mother helping her child enter a dream in which love as the ultimate meaning awaits (pp. 124–5). Julian's stake in her *Showings* is to give this love its voice.

The Christ whom Julian voices asks her to imagine that all of creation is a hazelnut that He places in her hand: 'It is all that is made' (p. 9). In her anchor-hold, she grew through confinement. Margery, on the other hand, needed to see for herself 'all that is made', accompanied by a Christ who liked to talk as much as she did. Chaucer, a man of the medieval world and its texts, made texts from voicing women who had their own distinctive connection to the world around them: one a cloistered Prioress somehow out on pilgrimage; another, a much married woman who seems to have escaped motherhood in order to travel as widely as Margery Kempe. These four women, in one way or another, take love as their theme. All of them seem very conscious of what it means to speak.

Interestingly, the two pairs of women know each other. The Wife and the Prioress are traveling in the same pilgrimage company, although, alas, we do not see them interact (as we do in the 'quytyngs' and exchanges among some of the male pilgrims). Julian and Margery actually did meet each other and spend several days together, during which Julian affirmed for Margery the legitimacy of her visions in an extended discourse, recorded in *The Book,* in which Margery seems to be ventriloquizing Julian: 'Holy wryt seyth that the sowle of a rytful man is the sete of God, & so I trust, syster, that ye ben' (p. 43). I am sure that Julian assured her that all would be well so that Margery could launch forward on her pilgrimage and this new phase of her life.

But I wonder what the Wife and Prioress might have said to each other, or if they would have thought to assure each other that 'alle shal be welle'. We can only imagine. As the old saying goes, I would love to have been a fly on the wall.

Notes

1. Nicholas Watson, 'Julian of Norwich', in *The Cambridge Companion to Medieval Women's Writing*, ed. Carolyn Dinshaw and David Wallace (Cambridge: Cambridge University Press, 2003), p. 210. Laurie A. Finke, *Women's Writing in English: Medieval England* (London: Longman, 1999), p. 176.
2. Lynn Staley, 'The Trope of the Scribe and the Question of Literary Authority in the Works of Julian of Norwich and Margery Kempe', *Speculum*, 66.4 (Oct. 1991), 834–5.
3. *The Book of Margery Kempe*, ed. Hope Emily Allen and Sanford Meech, EETS (London: Oxford University Press, 1961). All further references are to this edition and will be cited by page number in the body of the text. I have transliterated the thorn and yogh as 'v' and 'u'.
4. For the sake of focus and coherence, I have chosen not to discuss the Paston Letters or the Second Nun here.
5. See Lynn Staley's 'The Trope of the Scribe' for a comprehensive discussion of the question of authority in the texts of Julian and Margery.
6. Dinshaw and Wallace, *Cambridge Companion to Medieval Women's Writing*, pp. 7–8.
7. H. Marshall Leicester, 'Of a fire in the dark: Public and private feminism, *The Wife of Bath's Tale*', *Women's Studies*, 11 (1984), 175. See also Elaine

Tuttle Hansen's discussion on Leicester's article in *Chaucer and the Fictions of Gender* (Berkeley, CA: University of California Press, 1992), pp. 48–51.

8. Staley, 'The trope of the scribe,' p. 827.

9. Dinshaw and Wallace, *Cambridge Companion to Medieval Women Writers,* p. 8.

10. *The Canterbury Tales*, in *The Riverside Chaucer*, ed. Larry D. Benson (Boston, MA: Houghton Mifflin, 1987). All further references are to this edition and will be cited by fragment and line number(s) within the text.

11. On the Wife of Bath as victim of domestic violence, see Elaine Tuttle Hansen, '"Of his love daungerous to me": Liberation, Subversion, and Domestic Violence in the Wife of Bath's Prologue and Tale', in *Geoffrey Chaucer: The Wife of Bath*, ed. Peter G. Beidler (Boston, MA: Bedford Books, 1996), pp. 273–89.

12. For two different treatments of the Wife's tonal change at the end of her *Tale*, see Elaine Tuttle Hansen, *Chaucer and the Fictions of Gender*, pp. 38–9, and Elizabeth Scala, 'Desire in the *Canterbury Tales*: Sovereignty and Mastery Between the Wife and Clerk,' *Studies in the Age of Chaucer*, ed. David Matthews, Vol. 31, 2009, pp. 90–1.

13. For an interesting discussion of the relation of the mouth and the body in the Prioress's texts, see R. A. Shoaf, *Chaucer's Body: The Anxiety of Circulation in the 'Canterbury Tales'* (Gainesville, FL: University Press of Florida, 2001), pp. 22–5.

14. Sheila Delany, *Writing Woman: Women Writers and Women in Literature Medieval to Modern* (New York: Schocken Books, 1983), p. 81.

15. For a comprehensive discussion of medieval medical ideas about women and women's mystical experience, see Elizabeth Robertson, 'Medieval Medical Views of Women and Female Spirituality in the *Ancrene Wisse* and Julian of Norwich's *Showings*', in *Feminist Approaches to the Body in Medieval Literature*, ed. Linda Lomperis and Sarah Stanbury (Philadelphia, PA: University of Pennsylvania Press, 1993), especially pp. 143–9.

16. *The Showings of Julian of Norwich*, ed. Denise N. Baker (New York: W.W. Norton, 2005). All further references are to this edition, are taken from the Long Text (unless otherwise specified) and will be cited by page number within the body of the text. For useful overviews of the scene and composition of Julian's text, see Baker's introduction to this edition, pp. ix–xxi, as well as Finke, *Women's Writing in English,* pp. 166–7.

17. On Julian's paralysis 'unsex[ing]' her, see Wendy Harding, 'The Body into Text: *The Book of Margery Kempe*' in *Feminist Approaches to the Body in Medieval Literature*, p. 180.

18. Baker, 'Introduction' to *The Showings*, p. xii.

19. For useful overviews of the scene and composition of Margery's text, see Finke, *Women's Writing in English*, pp. 176–87, and Lynn Staley's introduction to *The Book of Margery Kempe*, trans. and ed. Lynn Staley (New York: W.W. Norton, 2001), pp. vii–xix.

20. For an extended treatment of Julian's relationship to Christ's humanity and sensuality as well as to her own female physicality, see Elizabeth Robertson, 'Medieval Medical Views of Women,' pp. 153–60.

21. Finke, *Women's Writing in English*, p. 176.
22. See Carolyn Dinshaw's commentary on this scene in her essay, 'Margery Kempe', in *Medieval Women's Writings*, p. 225.
23. See Caroline Walker Bynum, *Holy Feast and Holy Fast: The Religious Significance of Food to Medieval Women* (Berkeley, CA: University of California Press, 1987), pp. 254–9.
24. See Lynn Staley, 'The trope of the scribe'.
25. Caroline Walker Bynum, *Jesus As Mother: Studies in the Spirituality of the High Middle Ages* (Berkeley, CA: University of California Press, 1982), p. 136.
26. Finke, *Women's Writing in English*, p. 173.
27. For an extended discussion of medieval attitudes about ventriloquism, see Mary Hayes, *Divine Ventriloquism in Medieval English Literature: Power, Anxiety, and Subversion* (New York: Palgrave Macmillan, 2011), and especially her discussion of 'belly speech' (pp. 139–68). While Hayes does not address medieval women mystics and their acts of ventriloquism or Chaucer himself as a ventriloquist, she explores the ways in which ventriloquism proceeds for some of the Canterbury pilgrims, including the clergeon in the 'Prioress's Tale'.
28. See Elaine Tuttle Hansen's extensive discussion of this issue in *Chaucer and the Fictions of Gender,* and especially her chapter, 'The Wife of Bath and the Mark of Adam'.

14

History, Frescoes and Reading the Middle Ages: A Final Note

Martin Coyle

It was 21 December 2003 when *The Daily Telegraph* announced that the Doom Fresco in Holy Trinity Church, Coventry, depicting the Last Judgement, was ready to be revealed after seventeen years of restoration work. That work involved removing varnish put over the Fresco by a local restorer in 1831 which had been intended to preserve the painting but instead had turned it black. Prior to this, the Doom Fresco had been covered over by Protestant reformers sometime in the 1560s. Along with many others, the Fresco had proved unacceptable to the reformers given its strong visual representation of Christ at the Last Judgement and its overt connection to Catholicism. Remarkably, the Fresco had survived the attempt to hide it as well as the unintended blackening of the 1831 restoration work and today is a fine example of its kind. The Fresco is usually dated somewhere around 1430.

The survival of the Fresco is not without its significance. The attempt to cover over the work and the attempt to preserve it had both had the opposite effect from that intended, as if to suggest that history lies outside human control. Both actions – covering and varnishing – had made the Fresco invisible until 2003, when the Middle Ages were, as it were, made visible again, or at least one sign of their passing. The restoration of the Fresco also suggests that the past is made up of layers that can be scraped away, though as they are stripped away so other pasts, or at least other past moments, are lost. Such an argument, that remains like the Fresco simultaneously recover and undo images of the past, in turn raises a series of questions about the boundaries of history (where do the Middle Ages end and the Modern Period begin?), and questions about texts: are all texts (not just pictures and paintings) palimpsests, or multi-layered records mingling past and present? If so, how should we read them? How can we know the best way to read medieval literature, if there is, indeed, a best way?

Recently, a number of critics have emphasized the extent to which we always read in the present: that Shakespeare, for example, is not simply our contemporary, as Jan Kott once had it,[1] but that we should interpret texts in relation to current affairs. More subtly, the argument of presentism is built on the troubling perception that, as Jean Howards argues:

> There is no transcendent space from which one can perceive the past 'objectively'. Our view is always informed by our present position: the objects we view available only in the slipperiness of their textualization [...] all historical knowledge is produced from a partial and a positioned vantage point.[2]

In this argument, the objective past must always remain elusive, or at least the absolute past must do so. The past we discuss is evidently different from what happened daily to people and different from their view of what was happening in their lives, but that does not necessarily invalidate our discussion. Rather, what it means is that our view is provisional, tentative, more than a guess, but necessarily cautious.

Of course, when reading criticism such as the essays in the present volume one might miss that sense of caution, but every critical act begins with an invisible 'this is my very best tentative view, however assertive it might appear'. Read this way, critical essays which seem to be offering definitive answers become arguments or propositions to be tested. Two examples may help. At the end of *The Oxford Handbook of Medieval English Literature* there is a very fine historical essay by Greg Walker setting out his argument that the ending of the Middle Ages can be best dated to 1547 when the Chantries Act dissolved 'those chapels founded to provide prayers and masses for individual donors', and with them closed off the idea of purgatory while transferring their wealth to the state.[3] The essay wonderfully sets out its case, covering both political and religious events, and no student can read the essay without learning a great deal. If one effect of the essay is to close off the Middle Ages in terms of period boundary, its other effects are to open up the past and its meanings so that, for example, we might hesitate in our all-too-modern fashion to turn Chaucer into a proto-novelist or humanist, just as we might also hesitate to think of the Middle Ages in block terms as one long period from 600 to 1500. Chaucer no more represents the whole of the Middle Ages than his pilgrims represent the entire way people lived or thought. Walker allows us to see a different world where our discussion of realism or character needs refining to take account of the traces of history, of how Chaucer or any writer is surrounded by and immersed in a web of historical events, including, as presentism suggests, our awareness of those events.

A second example is an essay by David Matthews, which offers a cultural reading of the term 'Middle Ages' and the cognate terms 'Dark Ages' and 'Medieval'.[4] Like Walker, Matthews combines scholarly investigation with critical acumen, showing how in the 1800s the term 'Middle Ages' gradually took hold after its invention in the Renaissance. We invent period terms, it seems, in order to label difference but also to elevate our own period. The term 'Dark Ages' was useful to the Protestant reformers in order to characterize the preceding period as one dominated by Catholicism and its rituals of faith. The prejudice of the term remains today, but a moment's thought will soon reveal the shortcomings of the words. Think, for example, of the magnificence of medieval cathedrals and their stained glass in comparison to the architecture of today with its emphasis on space without meaning. The 'Dark Ages' left behind frescoes; our own period leaves behind an unmade bed masquerading as art.

Matthews' work exposes the extent to which preconceptions about the Middle Ages are the work of previous ages but also the extent to which such preconceptions are hard to remove. One reason why they are hard to shift, as the introduction to the present volume notes, is that Middle English is different from modern English and needs to be expounded:

Whan that Aprill with his shoures soote
The droghte of March hath perced to the roote,
And bathed every veyne in swich licour
Of which vertu engendred is the flour;
Whan Zephirus eek with his sweete breeth
Inspired hath in every holt and heath
The tendre croppes, and the yonge sonne
Hath in the Ram his halve cours yronne,
And smale foweles maken melodye,
That slepen al the nyght with open ye
(So priketh hem nature in hir corages);
Thanne longen folk to goon on pilgrimages,
And palmeres for to seken straunge strondes,
To ferne halwes, kowthe in sondry londes;
And specially from every shires ende
Of Engelond to Caunterbury they wende,

The hooly blisful martir for to seke,
That hem hath holpen whan that they were seeke.[5]

These lines from Chaucer's 'General Prologue' are only a small sample but each line signals its distance from us, a distance that, paradoxically, is also a huge critical gain. When we read contemporary literature we are almost at the service of the text. By contrast, the Chaucerian lines allow us to approach them as text rather than as content, to move away from our own presentism to a more nuanced position. The opening lines, we might feel, simply set the scene for the descriptions that follow, but this omits to see the lines' emphasis on calendar and longing. April is not just April but a time when people's thoughts are stirring, as is their need to make pilgrimage, to visit a holy place that meets their sense of duty and faith.

Critics have filled out our understanding not only of the social and historical significances of the various orders of characters Chaucer gives us, but also of the extent to which he creates a rich human interplay between them.[6] All of this normalizes the figures for us, but by noting the actual text, we will see that these figures sound different from those of today. The voices, though lost, carry across the centuries and each word still has a power; these are not individual figures but 'folk' who together make a company; they are banded together by their shared desire and longing which is collective rather than individual. The opening of the 'General Prologue' to *The Canterbury Tales* suggests that pilgrimage is a natural impulse and part of a yearly cycle as the weather begins to soften after the bleak winter. There is, in Chaucer's lines, something more than narrative and character, something all but vanished in the language but which later periods looking back came to see – how human actions are framed in and by other orders, natural and religious, even as language is ordered by its sounds and syntax.

There are no dates or times in Chaucer's lines, only the month of April. Nevertheless, the language remains specific to its period and texts are the best evidence we have of what it might have been like to be alive in 1400, or before, or after. Presentism does not mean that we should not read with some humility or imagination; it is only a reminder that we can import the present into the past and so lose the few remaining signs of something different. Presentism, too, is a reminder that we can easily misread: the Coventry Doom Fresco may be no more than an accident of history or of technology – a different covering may have stripped it to nothing even as the altars were stripped. In other words, its significance may be that history is no more than a set of accidentals, but even if this is the case, we should not ignore the fact that the Fresco is about history – not the history we take from books or events but Christian history, or rather the end of earthly history. The 'Doom' is the scene of the Last Judgement, Doomsday, the end of the world, the Second Coming, the moment when God decides who will be saved and who damned eternally.

Our presentism doubtless struggles with notions of finality: we cannot imagine a world without us, or without tomorrow or yesterday. The Doom Fresco does imagine these last things, but also expects them to happen without warning. This seems to have been the shared belief of the Catholic Middle Ages, but alongside that we need to set Chaucer's lines in which life is sustained in a rich pattern of nature and social order, where folks in their stories ask us to think about sin, guilt, penance and forgiveness but also the rich comedy of life and its foibles. When we read literature of the Middle Ages, we need, then, to be alert to something like its several levels of meaning in which religious ideas no doubt have a central place but are alongside and sometimes covered by other ideas no less medieval. Chaucer only seems modern because we respond to the part of his writings that speaks more directly to our presentism, a presentism that is largely secular. The Coventry Doom now restored can, however, show us a different way to think of the past: the gathering of 'folk' always already has pre-echoes of the Last Judgement: the pilgrimage to Canterbury which starts at a tavern is not so much a pub outing as a rehearsal for the last pilgrimage that all will make even in the midst of life.

Notes

1. See Jan Kott, *Shakespeare Our Contemporary* (London: Methuen, 1964).
2. Jean Howard, 'The new historicism in renaissance studies', *ELR* 16 (1986), 13–43 (pp. 22–3).
3. Greg Walker, 'When did "the medieval" end? Retrospection, foresight and the end(s) of the English middle ages', *The Oxford Handbook of Medieval English Literature,* ed. Elaine Treharne and Greg Walker (Oxford: Oxford University Press, 2010), pp. 725–38 (p. 733).
4. David Matthews, 'From mediaeval to mediaevalism: A new semantic history', *RES* 62 (2011), 695–715.
5. Geoffrey Chaucer, *The Canterbury Tales* in *The Riverside Chaucer*, ed. Larry D. Benson (Oxford: Oxford University Press, 1987), 'General Prologue', ll. 1–18.
6. See Jill Mann, *Chaucer and Medieval Estates Satire: The Literature of Social Classes and the General Prologue to the Canterbury Tales* (Cambridge: Cambridge University Press, 1973).

Further Reading

Medieval history and literature

Aers, David (ed.), *Medieval Literature: Criticism, History, Ideology* (Brighton: Harvester, 1986).

Allen, Valerie, *On Farting: Language and Laughter in the Middle Ages* (Basingstoke: Palgrave Macmillan, 2007).

Aston, T. H. (ed.), *Landlords Peasants and Politics in Medieval England* (Cambridge: Cambridge University Press, 1987).

Aston, T. H., P. R. Coss, Christopher Dyer and Joan Thirsk (eds), *Social Relations and Ideas: Essays in Honour of R. H. Hilton* (Cambridge: Cambridge University Press, 2009).

Baugh, A. C., and Thomas Cable, *A History of the English Language* (London: Routledge, 2002).

Brown, Peter (ed.), *A Companion to Medieval English Literature and Culture c. 1350-c. 1500* (Oxford: Wiley–Blackwell, 2007).

Burrow, J., *Medieval Writers and their Work: Middle English Literature 1100-1500* (Oxford: Oxford University Press, 2008).

Burrow, J. A., *Ricardian Poetry: Chaucer, Gower, Langland and the 'Gawain' Poet* (London: Routledge, 1971).

Cannon, Christopher, *Middle English Literature: A Cultural History* (Cambridge: Polity Press, 2008).

Carruthers, Leo (ed.), *Heroes and Heroines in Medieval English Literature* (Cambridge and Rochester, New York: D. S. Brewer, 1994).

Coleman, Janet, *English Literature in History 1350-1400* (London: Hutchinson, 1981).

Coss, Peter, and Maurice Keen (eds), *Heraldry, Pageantry and Social Display in Medieval England* (Cambridge and Rochester, New York: Boydell and Brewer, 2012).

Davenport, Tony, *Medieval Narrative: An Introduction* (Oxford: Oxford University Press, 2004).

Duffy, Eamon, *The Stripping of the Altars* (New Haven, CT and London: Yale University Press, 1992).

Goldberg, P. J. P., *Medieval England: A Social History 1250-1550* (London: Bloomsbury Academic, 2004).

Hilton, Rodney, *Peasants, Knights and Heretics: Studies in Medieval English Social History* (Cambridge: Cambridge University Press, 1976).

Hines, John, *Voices in the Past: English Literature and Archaeology* (Cambridge and Rochester, New York: D. S. Brewer, 2004).

Holmes, George (ed.), *The Oxford History of Medieval Europe* (Oxford: Oxford University Press, 2001).

Horrox, Rosemary, and W. Mark Ormrod (eds), *A Social History of England, 1200-1500* (Cambridge: Cambridge University Press, 2006).

Hsy, Jonathan, *Trading Tongues: Merchants, Multilingualism, and Medieval Literature* (Columbus, OH: Ohio State University Press, 2013).

Humphrey, Chris, and W. M. Ormrod (eds), *Time in the Medieval World* (York: York Medieval Press, 2001).

Johnson, David F., and Elaine Traharne (eds), *Readings in Medieval Texts: Interpreting Old and Middle English Literature* (Oxford: Oxford University Press, 2005).

Keen, Maurice, *English Society in the Later Middle Ages: 1348-1500* (Harmondsworth: Penguin, 1990).

King, Pamela, *Medieval Literature, 1300-1500* (Edinburgh: Edinburgh University Press, 2011).

Lacy, Norris J. (ed.), *A History of Arthurian Scholarship* (Cambridge and Rochester, New York: D. S. Brewer, 2006).

Radulescu, Raluca, and Alison Truelove (eds), *Gentry Culture in Late Medieval England* (Manchester: Manchester University Press, 2005).

Rudd, Gillian, *Greenery: Ecocritical Readings of Late Medieval English Texts* (Manchester: Manchester University Press, 2007).

Scanlon, Larry (ed.), *The Cambridge Companion to Medieval English Literature, 1100-1500* (Cambridge: Cambridge University Press, 2009).

Southern, R.W., *The Making of the Middle Ages* (London: Arrow Books, 1959).

Sutton, John William, *Death and Violence in Old and Middle English Literature* (Lewiston, NY: Mellen, 2007).

Tavormina, M. Teresa, and R. F. Yeager (eds), *The Endless Knot: Essays on Old and Middle English in Honour of Marie Boroff* (Cambridge and Rochester, New York: D. S. Brewer, 1995).

Tracey, Larissa, *Castration and Culture in the Middle Ages* (Cambridge and Rochester, New York: D. S. Brewer, 2013).

Traherne, Elaine, and Greg Walker (eds), *The Oxford Handbook of Medieval Literature in English* (Oxford: Oxford University Press, 2010).

Tuchman, Barbara W., *A Distant Mirror: The Calamitous Fourteenth Century* (London: Macmillan, 1979).

Wallace, David (ed.), *The Cambridge History of Medieval English Literature* (Cambridge: Cambridge University Press, 2002).

Chaucer's dream poems (*The Book of the Duchess*, *The House of Fame*, *The Parlement of Foulys* and *The Legend of good women*)

Bennett, J. A. W., *Chaucer's Book of Fame: An Exposition of 'The House of Fame'* (Oxford: Clarendon Press, 1968).

Bernstein, Antje, *Rhetoric in the Middle Ages: Geoffrey Chaucer's 'The Parliament of Fowls'* (Norderstedt: Grin Verlag, 2006).

Collette, Carolyn P., *The Legend of Good Women: Context and Reception* (Cambridge and Rochester, New York: D. S. Brewer, 2006).

Condren, Edward I., *Chaucer from Prentice to Poet: Metaphors of Love in Dream Visions and Troilus and Criseyde* (Gainesville, FL: University Press of Florida, 2008).

Crocker, Holly, *Chaucer's Visions of Manhood* (Basingstoke: Palgrave Macmillan, 2008).

Delany, Sheila, *The Naked Text: Chaucer's Legend of Good Women* (Berkeley, CA: University of California Press, 1994).

Delany, Sheila, *Chaucer's House of Fame, the Poetics of Skeptical Fideism* (Chicago, IL and London: Chicago University Press, 1972).

Holley, Linda Tarte, *Reason and Imagination in Chaucer, the Perle-poet, and the Cloud-author: Seeing from the Centre* (Basingstoke: Palgrave Macmillan, 2011).

Hume, Cathy, *Chaucer and the Cultures of Love and Marriage* (Cambridge and Rochester, New York: D. S. Brewer, 2012).

Kiser, Lisa J., *Telling Classical Tales: Chaucer and the 'Legend of Good Women'* (Ithaca, NY and London: Cornell University Press, 1983).

Koonce, B. G., *Chaucer and the Tradition of Fame: Symbolism in the 'House of Fame'* (Princeton, NJ: Princeton University Press, 1966).

Kruger, Steven F., *Dreaming in the Middle Ages* (Cambridge: Cambridge University Press, 2005).

Phillips, Helen, and Nick Havely (eds), *Chaucer's Dream Poems* (Longman Annotated Texts) (Harlow: Longman–Pearson, 1997).

Quinn, William A. (ed.), *Chaucer's Dream Visions and Shorter Poems* (London: Routledge, 1999).

Quinn, William A., Chaucer's *Rehersynges: The Performability of the 'Legend of Good Women'* (Washington, DC: Catholic University of America Press, 1994).

Rowe, Donald W., *Through Nature to Eternity: Chaucer's 'Legend of Good Women'* (Lincoln, NE: University of Nebraska Press, 1988).

Spearing, A. C., *Medieval Dream-Poetry* (Cambridge: Cambridge University Press, 1976).

Windeatt, Barry, *Chaucer's Dream Poetry: Sources and Analogues* (Cambridge and Rochester, New York: D. S. Brewer, 1970).

Winney, James, *Chaucer's Dream Poems* (London: Chatto and Windus, 1973).

Chaucer, *The Canterbury Tales*

Allen, Valerie, *The Age of Chaucer* (Cambridge: Cambridge University Press, 2004).

Allen, Valerie, and Ares Axiotis (eds), *Chaucer: New Casebooks* (London: Macmillan, 1997).

Blamires, Alcuin, *Chaucer, Ethics and Gender* (Oxford: Oxford University Press, 2006).

Blamires, Alcuin, *The Canterbury Tales* (London: Macmillan, 1987).

Boitani, Piero, and Jill Mann (eds), *The Cambridge Chaucer Companion* (Cambridge: Cambridge University Press, 1986).

Cooper, Helen, *Oxford Guides to Chaucer: The Canterbury Tales* (Oxford: Clarendon Press, 1989).

Cooper, Helen, *The Structure of the Canterbury Tales* (London: Duckworth, 1983).

Correale, Robert M. (ed.), *Sources and Analogues of the Canterbury Tales*, 2 vols (Cambridge and Rochester, New York: D. S. Brewer, 2001–5).

Crane, Susan, *Gender and Romance in Chaucer's Canterbury Tales* (Princeton, NJ: Princeton University Press, 1994).

Ellis, Roger, *Patterns of Religious Narrative in the Canterbury Tales* (London: Croom Helm, 1986).

Fisher, Sheila, *Chaucer's Poetic Alchemy: A Study of Value and Its Transformation in The Canterbury Tales* (New York and London: Garland, 1988).

Grey, Douglas (ed.), *The Oxford Companion to Chaucer* (Oxford: Oxford University Press, 2003).

Hines, John, *The Fabliau in English* (London and New York: Longman, 1993).

Hodges, Laura F., *Chaucer and Array: Patterns of Costume and Fabric Rhetoric in The Canterbury Tales, Troilus and Criseyde and Other Works* (Cambridge and Rochester, New York: D. S. Brewer, 2014).

Kendrick, Laura, *Chaucerian Play: Comedy and Control in the Canterbury Tales* (Berkeley, CA: University of California Press, 1988).

Knight, Stephen, *Geoffrey Chaucer* (Oxford: Blackwell, 1986).

Knight, Stephen, *Rymyng Craftily: Meaning in Chaucer's Poetry* (Sydney: Angus and Robertson, 1972).

Knight, Stephen, *The Poetry of the Canterbury Tales* (Sydney: Angus and Robertson, 1973).

Kolve, V. A., *Chaucer and the Imaginary Narrative* (Stanford, CA: Stanford University Press, 1982).

Mann, Jill, *Chaucer and Medieval Estates Satire: The Literature of Social Classes and the General Prologue to the 'Canterbury Tales'* (Cambridge: Cambridge University Press, 1973).

Mann, Jill, *Geoffrey Chaucer* (Hemel Hampstead, Herts: Harvester Wheatsheaf, 1991).

Neuse, Richard, *Chaucer's Dante: Allegory and Epic Theatre in The Canterbury Tales* (Berkeley, CA: University of California Press, 1991).

Phillips, Helen (ed.), *Chaucer and Religion* (Cambridge and Rochester, New York: D. S. Brewer, 2010).

Phillips, Helen, *An Introduction to the Canterbury Tales: Fiction, Reading, Context* (Basingstoke: Palgrave Macmillan, 2000).

Rudd, Gillian, *The Complete Critical Guide to Geoffrey Chaucer* (London: Routledge, 2001).

Saunders, Corinne J. (ed.), *Chaucer* (Oxford: Blackwell, 2001).

Chaucer, *Troilus and Criseyde*

Barney, Stephen A., *Studies in 'Troilus': Chaucer's Text, Meter and Diction* (Mediaeval Texts and Studies) (East Lansing, MI: Colleagues Press, 1993).

Benson, C. David (ed.), *Critical Essays on Chaucer's 'Troilus and Criseyde' and His Major Early Poems* (Toronto: University of Toronto Press, 1995).

Bishop, Ian, *Chaucer's Troilus and Criseyde: A Critical Study* (Essex: TBS, 1981).

Frantzen, Allen J., *'Troilus and Criseyde': The Poem and the Frame* (Woodbridge, CT: Twayne Publishers Inc., 1993).

Gordon, Ida L., *Double Sorrow of Troilus: Study of Ambiguities in 'Troilus and Criseyde'* (Oxford: Oxford University Press, 1970).

Hodges, Laura F., *Chaucer and Array: Pattern of Costume and Fabric Rhetoric in the Canterbury Tales, Troilus and Criseyde and Other Works* (Cambridge and Rochester, New York: D. S. Brewer, 2014).

McAlpine, Monica E., *Genre of 'Troilus and Criseyde'* (Ithaca, NY and London: Cornell University Press, 1978).

Nuttal, Jenni, *Troilus and Criseyde: A Reader's Guide* (Cambridge: Cambridge University Press, 2012).

Pugh, Tison, and Angela Jane Weisl (eds), *Chaucer's Troilus and Criseyde and the Shorter Poems* (Approaches to Teaching World Literature) (New York: Modern Language Association of America, 2006).

Pugh, Tison, and Marcia Smith Marzec (eds), *Men and Masculinities in Chaucer's Troilus and Criseyde* (Cambridge and Rochester, New York: D. S. Brewer, 2008).

Quinn, William A., *Olde Clerkis Speche: Chaucer's Troilus and Criseyde and the Implications of Authorial Recital* (Washington, DC: Catholic University of America Press, 2013).

Salu, Mary (ed.), *Essays on Troilus and Criseyde (Chaucer Studies)* (Cambridge and Rochester, New York: D. S. Brewer, 1991).

Wetherbee, Winthrop, *Chaucer and the Poets: Essay on 'Troilus and Criseyde'* (Ithaca, NY and London: Cornell University Press, 1984).

Windeatt, Barry, *Oxford Guides to Chaucer: Troilus and Criseyde* (Oxford: Clarendon Press, 1995).

Langland, *Piers Plowman*

Aers, David, *Piers Plowman and Christian Allegory* (London: Edward Arnold, 1975).

Alford, John A. (ed.), *A Companion to 'Piers Plowman'* (Berkeley, CA: University of California Press, 1988).

Alford, John A., *Piers Plowman: A Glossary of Legal Diction* (Cambridge and Rochester, New York: D. S. Brewer, 1988).

Baldwin, Anna P., *A Guidebook to Piers Plowman* (Basingstoke: Palgrave Macmillan, 2007).

Baldwin, Anna P., *The Theme of Government in Piers Plowman* (Cambridge and Rochester, New York: D. S. Brewer, 1987).

Barr, Helen, *Signes and Sothe: Language in the Piers Plowman Tradition* (Cambridge and Rochester, New York: D. S. Brewer, 1994).

Cole, Andrew and Andrew Galloway (eds), *Cambridge Companion to Piers Plowman* (Cambridge: Cambridge University Press, 2014).

Davilin, Mary Clemente, *A Game of Heuene: Word Play and the Meaning of 'Piers Plowman'* (Cambridge and Rochester, New York: D. S. Brewer, 1989).

Du Boulay, F. R. H., *The England of Piers Plowman: William Langland and his Vision of the Fourteenth Century* (Cambridge and Rochester, New York: D. S. Brewer, 1991).

Griffiths, Lavinia, *Personification in Piers Plowman* (Cambridge and Rochester, New York: D. S. Brewer, 1985).

Harwood, Britton J., *Piers Plowman and the Problem of Belief* (Buffalo and Toronto: University of Toronto Press, 1992).

Rudd, Gillian, *Managing Language in Piers Plowman* (Cambridge and Rochester, New York: D. S. Brewer, 1994).

Salter, Elizabeth, *Piers Plowman: An Introduction* (Oxford: Blackwell, 1962).

Scase, Wendy, *Piers Plowman and the New Anticlericalism* (Cambridge: Cambridge University Press, 2007).

Schmidt, A. V. C., *The Clerkly Maker: Langland's Poetic Art* (Cambridge and Rochester, New York: D. S. Brewer, 1987).

Simpson, James, *Piers Plowman: An Introduction* (Exeter Medieval Texts and Studies), eds Vincent Gillespie, Marion Glasscoe and Michael Swanton (Liverpool: Liverpool University Press, 2nd rev. edn. 2007 [1990]).

Steiner, Emily, *Reading Piers Plowman* (Cambridge: Cambridge University Press, 2013).

Stokes, Myra, *Justice and Mercy in Piers Plowman* (London: Croom Helm, 1984).

Zeeman, Nicolette, *Piers Plowman and the Medieval Discourse of Desire* (Cambridge: Cambridge University Press, 2009).

Sir Gawain and the Green Knight

Anderson, J. J., *Language and Imagination in the Gawain Poems* (Manchester: Manchester University Press, 2005).

Barron, W. R. J., *Trawthe and Treason: The Sin of Sir Gawain Reconsidered* (Manchester: Manchester University Press, 1980).

Baswell, Christopher, and William Sharpe (eds), *The Passing of Arthur: New Essays in Arthurian Tradition* (New York and London: Garland, 1988).

Benson, Larry D., *Art and Tradition in 'Sir Gawain and the Green Knight'* (New Brunswick, NT: Rutgers University Press, 1965).

Blanch, Robert J., *The Gawain Poems: A Reference Guide 1978-1993* (Albany, NY: Whitson, 2000).

Blanch, Robert J. (ed.), *Sir Gawain and Pearl: Critical Essays* (Bloomington, IN and London: Indiana University Press, 1966).

Blanch, Robert J., and Julian N. Wasserman, *From Pearl to Gawain: Forme to Fynisment* (Gainesville, FL: University Press of Florida, 1995).

Borroff, Marie, *'Sir Gawain and the Green Knight': A Stylistic and Metrical Study* (New Haven, CT and London: Yale University Press, 1963).

Borroff, Marie, *Traditions and Renewals: Chaucer, the Gawain-Poet and Beyond* (New Haven, CT and London: Yale University Press, 2003).

Brewer, Derek, and Jonathan Gibson (eds), *A Companion to the Gawain-Poet* (Cambridge and Rochester, New York: Boydell and Brewer, 1997).

Brewer, Elizabeth (ed.), *Sir Gawain and the Green Knight: Sources and Analogues* (Cambridge and Rochester, New York: D. S. Brewer, 1992).

Burrow, J. A., *A Reading of Sir Gawain and the Green Knight* (London: Routledge and Kegan Paul, 1965).

Burrow, J. A., *The Gawain Poet* (Horndon: Northcote House, 2001).

Davenport, W. A., *The Art of the Gawain-Poet* (London: Athlone Press, 1978).

Fox, Denton (ed.), *Twentieth Century Interpretations of 'Sir Gawain and the Green Knight'* (Englewood Cliffs, NT: Prentice-Hall, 1968).

Hill, Ordelle G., *Looking Westward: Poetry, Landscape and Politics in Sir Gawain and the Green Knight* (Newark, DE: University of Delaware Press, 2009).

Ingledew, Francis, *Sir Gawain and the Green Knight and the Order of the Garter* (Notre Dame, IN: Notre Dame Press, 2006).

Krueger, Roberta L. (ed.), *The Cambridge Companion to Medieval Romance* (Cambridge: Cambridge University Press, 2000).

Morgna, Gerald, *Sir Gawain and the Green Knight and the Idea of Righteousness* (Sallins, Co. Kildare: Irish Academic Press, 1992).

Nicholls, Jonathan, *The Matter of Courtesy: A Study of Medieval Courtesy Books and the Gawain Poet* (Cambridge and Rochester, New York: D. S. Brewer, 1985).

Putter, Ad, *An Introduction to the Gawain Poet* (London and New York: Longman, 1996).

Putter, Ad, *Sir Gawain and the Green Knight and the French Arthurian Romance* (Oxford: Clarendon Press, 1995).

Shoaf, R. Allen, *The Poem as Green Girdle: Commercium in Sir Gawain and the Green Knight* (Gainesville, FL: University Press of Florida, 1984).

Spearing, A. C., *The Gawain Poet: A Critical Study* (Cambridge: Cambridge University Press, 1970).

Stainsby, Meg, *Sir Gawain and the Green Knight: An Annotated Bibliography, 1978-1989* (New York and London: Garland, 1992).

Stanbury, Sarah, *Seeing the 'Gawain'-Poet: Description and the Act of Perception* (Philadelphia, PA: University of Pennsylvania Press, 1991).

Tavormina, M. Teresa, and R. F. Jeager (eds), *The Endless Knot: Essays on Old and Middle English in Honour of Marie Borroff* (Cambridge and Rochester, New York: D. S. Brewer, 1995).

Thompson, Raymond H., and Keith Busby (eds), *Gawain: A Casebook* (London: Routledge, 2005).

Wilson, Edward, *The Gawain-Poet* (Leiden: Brill, 1976).

Malory, *Le Morte Darthur* and the Arthurian tradition

Archibald, Elizabeth, and Ad. Putter (eds), *The Cambridge Companion to the Arthurian Legend* (Cambridge: Cambridge University Press, 2009).

Archibald, Elizabeth, and A. S. G. Edwards (eds), *A Companion to Malory* (Cambridge and Rochester, New York: D. S. Brewer, 1996).

Aronstein, Susan, *An Introduction to British Arthurian Narrative* (Gainesville, FL: University Press of Florida, 2012).

Ashton, Gail, *Medieval English Romance in Context* (London and New York: Continuum, 2010).

Baswell, Christopher, and William Sharpe (eds), *The Passing of Arthur: New Essays in Arthurian Traditions* (London and New York: Garland, 1988).

Batt, Catherine, *Malory's Morte Darthur: Remaking Arthurian Tradition* (Basingstoke: Palgrave Macmillan, 2002).

Cartlidge, Neil, *Heroes and Anti-Heroes in Medieval Romance* (Cambridge and Rochester, New York: D. S. Brewer, 2012).

Cartlidge, Neil (ed.), *Boundaries in Medieval Romance* (Cambridge and Rochester, New York: D. S. Brewer, 2008).

Clark, David, and Kate McClune (eds), *Arthurian Literature XXVIII: Blood, Sex, Malory: Essays on the Morte Darthur: 28* (Cambridge and Rochester, New York: D. S. Brewer, 2011).

Fenster, Thelma S. (ed.), *Arthurian Women: A Casebook* (New York: Garland, 1996).

Fellows, Jennifer, Roaslind Field, Gillian Rogers, and Judith Weiss (eds), *Romance Reading on the Book: Essays on Medieval Narrative Presented to Maldwyn Mills* (Cardiff: University of Wales Press, 1996).

Field, P. J. C., *Romance and Chronicle: A Study of Malory's Prose Style* (Bloomington, IN and London: Indiana University Press, 1971).

Fries, Maureen, and Jeanie Watson (eds), *Approaches to Teaching the Arthurian Tradition* (New York: Modern Language Association of America, 2006).

Fulton, Helen (ed.), *A Companion to Arthurian Literature* (Oxford: Wiley-Blackwell, 2012).

Ingham, Patricia Clare, *Sovereign Fantasies: Arthurian Romance and the Making of Britain* (Philadelphia, PA: University of Pennsylvania Press, 2001).

Knight, Stephen, *Arthurian Literature and Society* (London: Macmillan, 1983).

Knight, Stephen, *Merlin: Knowledge and Power through the Ages* (Ithaca, NY and London: Cornell University Press, 2009).

Kruger, Roberta L. (ed.), *The Cambridge Companion to Medieval Romance* (Cambridge: Cambridge University Press, 2000).

Lacy, Norris J. (ed.), *Text and Intertext in Medieval Arthurian Literature* (London and New York: Garland, 1996).

Lupack, Alan (ed.), *The Oxford Guide to Arthurian Literature and Legend* (Oxford: Oxford University Press, 2007).

Meale, Carol M. (ed.), *Readings in Medieval English Romance* (Cambridge and Rochester, New York: D. S. Brewer, 1994).

Mehl, Dieter, *The Middle English Romances of the Fourteenth and Fifteenth Centuries* (London: Routledge and Kegan Paul, 1968).

238 — Further Reading

Mills, Maldwyn, Jennifer Fellows, and Carol Meale (eds), *Romance in Medieval England* (Cambridge and Rochester, New York: D. S. Brewer, 1991).

Moll, Richard James, *Before Malory: Reading Arthur in Later Medieval England* (Toronto: University of Toronto Press, 2003).

Pearsall, Derek, *Arthurian Romance: A Short Introduction* (Oxford: Blackwell, 2003).

Purdie, Rhiannon, and Michael Cichon (eds), *Medieval Romance, Medieval Contexts* (Cambridge and Rochester, New York: D. S. Brewer, 2011).

Radulescu, Raluca L., *Romance and its Contexts in Fifteenth-Century England: Politics, Piety and Penitence* (Cambridge and Rochester, New York: D. S. Brewer, 2013).

Radulescu, Raluca L., *The Gentry Context for Malory's Morte Darthur* (Cambridge and Rochester, New York: D. S. Brewer, 2003).

Radulescu, Raluca L., and Cory James Rushton (eds), *A Companion to Medieval Popular Romance* (Cambridge and Rochester, New York: D. S. Brewer, 2011).

Radulescu, Raluca L., and K. S. Whetter (eds), *Re-viewing the Morte Darthur: Texts and Contexts, Characters and Themes* (Cambridge and Rochester, New York: D. S. Brewer, 2005).

Rider, Jeff, and Jamie Friedman (eds), *The Inner Life of Women in Medieval Romance Literature: Grief, Guilt and Hypocrisy* (Basingstoke: Palgrave Macmillan, 2011).

Saunders, Corinne, *Magic and the Supernatural in Medieval English Romance* (Cambridge and Rochester, New York: D. S. Brewer, 2010).

Saunders, Corinne (ed.), *Cultural Encounters in the Romance of Medieval England* (Cambridge and Rochester, New York: D. S. Brewer, 2005).

Schmolke-Hasselmann, Beate, *The Evolution of Arthurian Romance: The Verse Tradition from Crétien to Froissart*, trans. Margaret Middleton and Roger Middleton (Cambridge: Cambridge University Press, 2006).

Shichtman, Martin B., and James P. Carley (eds), *Culture and the King: The Social Implications of the Arthurian Legend. Essays in Honour of Valerie M. Lagorio* (Albany, NY: State University of New York Press, 1994).

Tolhurst, Fiona, and Bonnie Wheeler (eds), *On Arthurian Women: Essays in Memory of Maureen Fries* (Dallas: Scriptorum Press, 2001).

Wenthe, Michael, *Arthurian Chivalry and Knightly Outsiders in Medieval Literature* (Basingstoke: Palgrave Macmillan, 2014).

Wheeler, Bonnie (ed.), *Arthurian Studies in Honour of P. J. C. Field* (Cambridge and Rochester, New York: D. S. Brewer, 2004).

Wittig, Susan, *Stylistic and Narrative Structures in the Middle English Romances* (Austin, TX: University of Texas Press, 1978).

Medieval drama

Beadle, Richard, and Alan J. Fletcher (eds), *The Cambridge Companion to Medieval English Theatre* (Cambridge: Cambridge University Press, 2008).

Clopper, Lawrence M., *Drama, Play and Game: English Festive Culture in the Medieval and Early Modern Period* (Chicago, IL and London: University of Chicago Press, 2001).

Davenport, W.A., *Fifteenth-Century English Drama* (Cambridge and Rochester, New York: D. S. Brewer, 1982).

Davidson, Clifford, *Festivals and Plays in Late Medieval Britain* (Aldershot: Ashgate, 2007).

Denny, Neville (ass. ed.), *Medieval Drama* (Stratford-upon-Avon Studies 16) (London: Edward Arnold, 1973).

Dillon, Janette, *The Cambridge Introduction to Early English Theatre* (Cambridge: Cambridge University Press, 2006).

Gibson, Gale McMurray, *The Theatre of Devotion: East Anglia Drama and Society in the Late Middle Ages* (Chicago, IL and London: Chicago University Press, 1989).

Granger, Penny, *The N-Town Play: Drama and Liturgy in Medieval East Anglia* (Cambridge and Rochester, New York: D. S. Brewer, 2009).

Happe, Peter, *English Drama before Shakespeare* (London and New York: Longman, 1999).

Happe, Peter (ed.), *Medieval Drama: A Casebook* (London: Macmillan, 1984).

Harty, Kevin J. (ed.), *The Chester Mystery Cycle: A Casebook* (London: Garland, 1993).

King, Pam, *The York Cycle and the Worship of the City* (Cambridge and Rochester, New York: D. S. Brewer, 2006).

Kolve, V. A., *The Play Called Corpus Christi* (London: Arnold, 1966).

Nelson, Alan Holm, *The Medieval English Stage: Corpus Christi Pageants and Plays* (Chicago, IL and London: Chicago University Press, 1974).

Normington, Kate, *Medieval English Drama* (Cambridge: Polity Press, 2009).

Ogden, Dunbar H., *The Staging of Drama in the Medieval Church* (Newark, DE: University of Delaware Press, 2002).

Owens, Margaret E., *Stages of Dismemberment: The Fragmented Body in Late Medieval and Early Modern Drama* (Newark, DE: University of Delaware Press, 2005).

Record of Early English Drama Resources: http://www.reed.utoronto.ca/

Simon, Eckehard (ed.), *The Theatre of Medieval Europe: New Research in Early Drama* (Cambridge Studies in Medieval Literature) (Cambridge: Cambridge University Press, 2008).

Sponsler, Claire, *Drama and Resistance: Bodies, Goods, and Theatricality in late Medieval England* (Minneapolis, MN: University of Minnesota Press, 1997).

Taylor, Jerome, and Alan Holm Nelson (eds), *Medieval English Drama: Essays Critical and Contextual* (Chicago, IL and London: Chicago University Press, 1972).

Vince, Ronald W. (ed.), *A Companion to the Medieval Theatre* (New York and London: Greenwood Press, 1989).

Wickham, Glynne, *The Medieval Theatre* (Cambridge: Cambridge University Press, 1987).

Robin Hood

Bellamy, John G., *Robin Hood: An Historical Enquiry* (London: Croom Helm, 1985).

Carpenter, Kevin (ed.), *Robin Hood: The Many Faces of that Celebrated Outlaw* (Oldenburg: Bibliotheks- und Informationssystem der Universität Oldenburg, 1995).

Dobson, R. B., and John Taylor (eds), *Rymes of Robin Hood: An Introduction to the English Outlaw* (London: Heinemann, 1976).

Hahn, Thomas (ed.), *Robin Hood in Popular Culture: Violence, Transgression, and Justice* (Cambridge and Rochester, New York: Boydell and Brewer, 2000).

Holt, J. C., *Robin Hood* (London: Thames and Hudson, 1989).

Kaufman, Alexander L., *British Outlaws of Literature and History: Essays on Medieval and Early Modern Figures from Robin Hood to Twm Shon Catty* (Jefferson, NC: MacFarlane and Co., 2011).

Keen, Maurice, *The Outlaws of Medieval Legend* (London: Routledge, 2000).

Kevelson, Roberta, *Inlaws / Outlaws: A Semiotics of Systemic Interaction: 'Robin Hood' and the 'King's Law'* (Bloomington, IN and London: Indiana University Press, 1977).

Knight, Stephen, *Robin Hood: A Complete Study of the English Outlaw* (Oxford: Blackwell, 1994).

Knight, Stephen, *Robin Hood: A Mythic Biography* (Ithaca, NY and London: Cornell University Press, 2003).

Knight, Stephen (ed.), *Robin Hood: Anthology of Scholarship and Criticism* (Cambridge and Rochester, New York: D. S. Brewer, 1999).

Knight, Stephen (ed.), *Robin Hood: The Forresters Manuscript* (Cambridge and Rochester, New York: D. S. Brewer, 1998).

Phillips, Helen (ed.), *Bandit Territories: British Outlaws and Their Traditions* (Cardiff: University of Wales Press, 2008).

Phillips, Helen (ed.), *Robin Hood: Medieval and Post-Medieval* (Dublin, OH: Four Courts Press, 2005).

Pollard, A. J., *Imagining Robin Hood: The Late Medieval Stories in Historical Context* (London: Routledge, 2007).

Potter, Lois, and Joshua Calhoun (eds), *Images of Robin Hood: Medieval to Modern* (Newark, DE: University of Delaware Press, 2008).

Singman, Jeffrey L., *Robin Hood: The Shaping of the Legend* (Westport, CN: Greenwood Press, 1998).

Medieval men, women and gender

Aers, David, *Community, Gender and Individual Identity: English Writing 1360-1430* (London: Routledge, 1988).

Aers, David, and Lynn Staley, *The Powers of the Holy: Religion, Politics and Gender in Late Medieval English Culture* (Philadelphia, PA: University of Pennsylvania Press, 1996).

Bennett, Judith M., and Ruth Mazo Karras (eds), *The Oxford Handbook of Women and Gender in Medieval Europe* (Oxford: Oxford University Press, 2013).

Blamires, Alcuin, *The Case for Women in Medieval Culture* (Oxford: Clarendon Press, 1997).

Blamires, Alcuin (ed.), *Woman Defamed and Defended: An Anthology of Medieval Texts* (Oxford: Clarendon Press, 1992).

Bynum, Caroline Walker, *Fragmentation and Redemption: Essays on Gender and the Human Body in Medieval Religion* (New York: Zone Books Cambridge, Mass., 1991).

Bynum, Caroline Walker, *Holy Feast and Holy Fast: The Religious Significance of Food to Medieval Women* (Berkeley, CA: University of California Press, 1987).

Bynum, Caroline Walker, Stevan Harrell, and Paula Richman, *Gender and Religion: On the Complexity of Symbols* (Boston, MA: Beacon Press, 1986).

Bynum, Caroline Walker, and Catherine M. Mooney, *Gendered Voices: Medieval Saints and their Interpreters* (Philadelphia, PA: University of Pennsylvania Press, 1999).

Cullum, Patricia, and Katherine J. Lewis (eds), *Holiness and Masculinity in the Middle Ages* (Cardiff: University of Wales Press, 2005).

Cullum, Patricia, and Katherine J. Lewis (eds), *Religious Men and Masculine Identity in the Middle Ages* (Cambridge and Rochester, New York: Boydell and Brewer, 2013).

Dinshaw, Carolyn (ed.), *Cambridge Companion to Medieval Women's Writings* (Cambridge: Cambridge University Press, 2003).

Erler, Mary Carpenter, and Maryanne Kowaleski (eds), *Gendering the Master Narrative: Women and Power in the Middle Ages* (Ithaca, NY and London: Cornell University Press, 2003).

Evans, Ruth, and Lesley Johnson (eds), *Feminist Readings in Middle English Literature: The Wife of Bath and all her sect* (London: Routledge, 1994).

Fisher, Sheila, and Janet E. Halley (eds), *Seeking the Woman in Late Medieval and Renaissance Writings: Essays in Feminist Contextual Criticism* (Knoxville, TN: University of Tennessee Press, 1989).

Jordan, Erin L., *Women, Power and Patronage in the Middle Ages* (Basingstoke: Palgrave Macmillan, 2006).

Lees, Clare A., *Medieval Masculinities: Regarding Men in the Middle Ages* (Minneapolis, MN: University of Minnesota Press, 1994).

Lewis, Catherine, *Kingship and Masculinity in Late Medieval England* (London: Routledge, 2013).

Olson, Linda, and Kathryn Kerby-Fulton (eds), *Voices in Dialogue: Reading Women in the Middle Ages* (Notre Dame, IN: University of Notre Dame Press, 2005).

Robertson, Elizabeth, and Christine M. Rose (eds), *Representing Rape in Medieval and Early Modern Literature* (Basingstoke: Palgrave Macmillan, 2001).

Smith, Lesley, and Jane H. M. Taylor (eds), *Women, the Book, and the Godly: Selected Proceedings of the St Hilda's Conference* (Cambridge and Rochester, New York: D. S. Brewer, 1995).

Thibodeaux, Jennifer D. (ed.), *Negotiating Clerical Identities: Priests, Monks and Masculinity in the Middle Ages* (Basingstoke: Palgrave Macmillan, 2010).

Wogan-Browne, Jocelyn (ed.), Medieval *Women: Texts and Contexts in Late Medieval Britain, Essays for Felicity Riddy* (Turnhout: Brepols, 2000).

Medieval religious and mystical writings

Bartlett, Anne Clark, Thomas Bestul, Janet Goebel, and William F. Pollard (eds), *Vox Mystica: Essays on Medieval Mysticism in Honour of Professor Valerie M. Lagorio* (Cambridge and Rochester, New York: D. S. Brewer, 1995).

Beckwith, Sarah, *Christ's Body: Identity, Culture and Society in Late Medieval Writings* (London: Routledge, 1993).

Besserman, Lawrence (ed.), *Sacred and Secular in Medieval and Early Modern Cultures: New Essays* (Basingstoke: Palgrave Macmillan, 2006).

Bynum, Caroline Walker, *Jesus as Mother: Studies in the Spirituality of the High Middle Ages* (Berkeley, CA: University of California Press, 1982).

Bynum, Caroline Walker, and Paul H. Freedman (eds), *Last Things: Death and the Apocalypse in the Middle Ages* (Philadelphia, PA: University of Pennsylvania Press, 1999).

Dailey, Patricia, *Promised Bodies: Time Language and Corporeality in Medieval Women's Mystical Texts* (New York: Columbia University Press, 2013).

Dyas, Dee, *Images of Faith in English Literature, 700-1500: An Introduction* (London and New York: Longman, 1997).

Dyas, Dee, Valerie Edden, and Roger Ellis (eds), *Approaching Medieval English Anchoritic and Mystical Texts* (Christianity and Culture: Issues in Teaching/ Research) (Cambridge and Rochester, New York: D. S. Brewer, 2005).

Fanous, Samuel and Vincent Gillespie (eds), *The Cambridge Companion to Medieval English Mysticism* (Cambridge: Cambridge University Press, 2011).

Freeman, Elizabeth, *Narratives of a New Order: Cistercian Historical Writing in England, 1150-1220* (Turnhout: Brepols, 2002).

Ghosh, Kantik, and Vincent Gillespie (eds), *After Arundel: Religious Writing in Fifteenth Century England* (Turnhout: Brepols, 2012).

Gillespie, Vincent, *Looking in Holy Books: Essays on Late Medieval Religious Writings in England* (Turnhout: Brepols, 2012).

Glasscoe, Marion, *English Medieval Mystics: Games of Faith* (London and New York: Longman, 1993).

Glasscoe, Marion, *The Medieval Mystical Tradition in England* (Cambridge and Rochester, New York: D. S. Brewer, 1992).

Hilmo, Maidie, *Medieval Images, Icons and Illustrated English Literary Texts: From the Ruthwell Cross to the Ellesmere Chaucer* (Aldershot: Ashgate, 2004).

Jones, E. A. (ed.), *The Medieval Mystical Tradition in England: Papers Read at Charney Manor, July 2011* (Cambridge and Rochester, New York: D. S. Brewer, 2013).

Kratzmann, Gregory, and James Simpson (eds), *Middle English Religious and Ethical Literature* (Cambridge and Rochester, New York: D. S. Brewer, 1986).

Phillips, Helen (ed.), *Langland, the Mystics and the Medieval English Religious Tradition: Essays in Honour of S. S. Hussey* (Cambridge and Rochester, New York: D. S. Brewer, 1990).

Pollard, William F. and Robert Boenig (eds), *Mysticism and Spirituality in Medieval England* (Cambridge: D. S. Brewer, 1997).

Renevey, Denis, and Christiania Whitehead (eds), *Writing Religious Women: Female Spiritual and Textual Practices in Late Medieval England* (Cardiff: University of Wales Press, 2000).

Rice, Nicole R. (ed.), *Middle English Religious Writing in Practice: Texts, Readers and Transformations* (Turnhout: Brepols, 2013).

Robertson, Duncan, *Lectio Divina: The Medieval Experience of Reading* (Louisville, KY: Cistercian Publications, 2011).

Swanson, R. N. (trans.), *Catholic England: Faith, Religion and Observance Before the Reformation* (Manchester: Manchester University Press, 1993).

Wheeler, Bonnie (ed.), *Mindful Spirit in Late Medieval Literature: Essays in Honour of Elizabeth D. Kirk* (Basingstoke: Palgrave Macmillan, 2006).

Winston-Allen, Anne, *Convent Chronicles: Women writing about Women and Reform in the Late Middle Ages* (University Park, PA: Pennsylvania State University Press, 2004).

The end of the Middle Ages and the Reformation

Bernard, G. W., *The Late Medieval Church: Vitality and Vulnerability Before the Break with Rome* (New Haven, CT and London: Yale University Press, 2012).

Bush, M. L., *The Pilgrimage of Grace: A Study of the Rebel Armies of October 1536* (Manchester: Manchester University Press, 1996).

Duffy, Eamon, *Saints, Sacrilege and Sedition: Religion and Conflict in the Tudor Reformations* (London: Bloomsbury, 2012).

Duffy, Eamon, *The Stripping of the Altars* (New Haven, CT and London: Yale University Press, 1992).

Eisenstein, Elizabeth, *The Printing Press as an Agent of Change: Communications and Cultural Transformations in Early Modern Europe* (Cambridge: Cambridge University Press, 1979).

Erler, Mary C., *Reading and Writing during the Dissolution: Monks, Friars and Nuns 1530-1558* (Cambridge: Cambridge University Press, 2013).

Haigh, Christopher, *English Reformations: Religion, Politics and Society Under the Tudors* (Oxford: Oxford University Press, 1993).

Haigh, Christopher (ed.), *The English Reformation Revised* (Cambridge: Cambridge University Press, 1987).

Haigh, Christopher, *The Last Days of the Lancashire Monasteries and the Pilgrimage of Grace* (Manchester: Manchester University Press, 1969).

Hoyle, R. W., *The Pilgrimage of Grace and the Politics of the 1530s* (Oxford: Oxford University Press, 2001).

Huizinga, Johan H., *The Waning of the Middle Ages: A Study of the Forms of Life, Thought and Art in France and the Netherlands in the Fourteenth and Fifteenth Centuries*, trans. F. Hopman (London: Penguin, 1955).

Knowles, David, *Bare ruined choirs: The Dissolution of the English Monasteries* (Cambridge: Cambridge University Press, 1976).

Kreider, Alan, *English Chantries: The Road to Dissolution* (Cambridge, MA and London: Harvard University Press, 1979).

McGrath, Alister E., *The Intellectual Origins of the European Reformation* (Oxford: Blackwell, 1987).

McGrath, Alister E., *Reformation Thought: An Introduction* (Oxford: Blackwell, 1993).

Newcombe, D. G., *Henry VIII and the English Reformation* (London: Routledge, 1995).

Oberman, Heiko Augustinus, *The Dawn of the Reformation: Essays in Late Medieval and Early Reformation Thought* (Edinburgh: T&T Clark, 1986).

Ozment, Steven E., *The Age of Reform, 1250-1550: An Intellectual and Religious History of Late Medieval and Reformation Europe* (New Haven, CT and London: Yale University Press, 1980).

Pil, David Halton, *The English Reformation, 1529-58* (London: University of London Press, 1973).

Rex, Richard, *Henry VIII and the English Reformation* (Basingstoke: Palgrave Macmillan, 1993).

Rigby, S. H., *English Society in the Later Middle Ages: Class, Status and Gender* (Manchester: Manchester University Press, 1995).

Scarisbrick, J. J., *Henry VIII* (New Haven, CT and London: Yale University Press, 1997 [1968]).

Scarisbrick, J. J., *The Reformation and the English People* (Oxford: Blackwell, 1984).

Todd, John M., *Reformation* (London: Darton, Longman and Todd, 1972).

Todd, Margo (ed.), *Reformation to Revolution: Politics and Religion in Early Modern England* (London: Routledge, 1995).

Wallace, Peter G., *The Long European Reformation: Religion, Political Conflict, and the Search for Conformity, 1350-1750* (Basingstoke: Palgrave Macmillan, 2004).

Wilkie, William E., *The Cardinal Protectors of England: Rome and the Tudors before the Reformation* (Cambridge: Cambridge University Press, 1974).

Wood, Andy, *The Memory of the People: Custom and Popular Senses of the Past in Early Modern England* (Cambridge: Cambridge University Press, 2013).

Woodward, G. W. O., *The Dissolution of the Monasteries* (London: Blandford Press, 1966).

Youings, Joyce A., *The Dissolution of the Monasteries* (London: Allen and Unwin, 1971).

Index